British Railw

CW00501457

ELE
MULTIPLE UNITS

THIRTY-SEVENTH EDITION
2024

The Complete Guide to all
Electric Multiple Units which operate on
the national railway network

Robert Pritchard

ISBN 978 1915 984 12 8

© 2023. Platform 5 Publishing Ltd, 52 Broadfield Road, Sheffield, S8 0XJ,
England.

Printed in England by The Lavenham Press, Lavenham, Suffolk.

CONTENTS

PROVISION OF INFORMATION

This book has been compiled with care to be as accurate as possible, but some information is not easily available and the publisher cannot be held responsible for any errors or omissions. We would like to thank the companies and individuals who have been helpful in supplying information to us. The authors of this series of books are always pleased to receive notification of any inaccuracies that may be found, to enhance future editions. Please send comments to:

Robert Pritchard, Platform 5 Publishing Ltd, 52 Broadfield Road, Sheffield, S8 0XJ, England.

e-mail: robert.pritchard@platform5.com Tel: 0114 255 2625.

This book is updated to information received by 16 October 2023.

UPDATES

This book is updated to the Stock Changes given in **Today's Railways UK 261** (November 2023). The Platform 5 railway magazine **"Today's Railways UK"** publishes Stock Changes every month to update this book. The magazine also contains news and rolling stock information on the railways of Great Britain and is published on the second Monday of every month. For further details of **Today's Railways UK**, please contact Platform 5 Publishing Ltd or visit our website **www.platform5.com**.

Front cover photograph: New Merseyrail EMU 777049 arrives at Aintree with the 15.49 Ormskirk–Liverpool Central on 20 April 2023.   **Alex Ayre**

BRITAIN'S RAILWAY SYSTEM

The structure of Britain's railway system has changed significantly during recent years, following the ongoing Covid-19 pandemic and subsequent drop in passenger numbers. Although passengers have since been returning in numbers, that drop in passengers in 2020 meant that franchises were no longer profitable and the Government was forced to step in and provide financial support to operators. Initially in March 2020 the Transport Secretary suspended rail franchising and operators transitioned to "Emergency Measures Agreements". These EMAs suspended the normal financial agreements, instead transferring all revenue and cost risk to the Government. Operators in England all accepted these new arrangements and continued to operate trains (initially with reduced service frequencies) for a small management fee. Similar arrangements were put in place by the Scottish and Welsh Governments for ScotRail, Caledonian Sleeper and Transport for Wales.

The EMAs initially lasted for six months from which time longer "Emergency Recovery Management Agreements" (ERMAs) were put in place. These were similar management contracts which continued to see operators run services for a management fee. Since then operators have been transitioning to new National Rail Contracts (NRCs). During an NRC operators are paid a fixed management fee of around 1.5% for operating services and additional small performance fees if agreed targets are achieved.

In the longer term a new body called Great British Railways is planned to take over the running of the railways and specifically take over Network Rail's responsibilities as well as some functions currently carried out by the Department for Transport and Rail Delivery Group. The franchise model will be changed to one of concessions, although this will take some years to fully implement.

In London and on Merseyside concessions were already in place. These see the operator paid a fee to run the service, within tightly specified guidelines. Operators running a concession would not normally take commercial risks, although there are usually penalties and rewards in the contract.

Britain's national railway infrastructure is owned by a "not for dividend" company, Network Rail. In 2014 Network Rail was reclassified as a public sector company, being described by the Government as a "public sector arm's-length body of the Department for Transport".

Most stations and maintenance depots are leased to and operated by the Train Operating Companies (TOCs), but some larger stations are controlled by Network Rail. The only exception is the infrastructure on the Isle of Wight: The Island Line franchise uniquely included maintenance of the infrastructure as well as the operation of passenger services. Both the infrastructure and trains are operated by South Western Railway.

Trains are operated by TOCs over Network Rail tracks (termed the National Network), regulated by access agreements between the parties involved. In general, TOCs are responsible for the provision and maintenance of the trains and staff necessary for the direct operation of services, whilst

Network Rail is responsible for the provision and maintenance of the infrastructure and also for staff to regulate the operation of services.

The Department for Transport (DfT) is the authority for the national network. Transport Scotland has operated ScotRail since April 2022 and is also responsible for the Caledonian Sleeper franchises. In February 2021 the Welsh Government took over the operation of the Wales & Borders franchise (Transport for Wales) from KeolisAmey.

Each franchise was set up with the right to run specified services within a specified area for a period of time, in return for the right to charge fares and, where appropriate, to receive financial support from the Government. Subsidy was payable in respect of socially necessary services. Service standards are monitored by the DfT throughout the duration of the franchise. Franchisees earned revenue primarily from fares and from subsidy. They generally leased stations from Network Rail and earned rental income by sub-letting parts of them, for example to retailers.

TOC's and open access operator's main costs are the track access charges they pay to Network Rail, the costs of leasing stations and rolling stock and of employing staff. Franchisees may do light maintenance work on rolling stock or contract it out to other companies. Heavy maintenance is normally carried out by the Rolling Stock Leasing Companies, according to contracts.

DOMESTIC PASSENGER TRAIN OPERATORS

The majority of passenger trains are operated by Train Operating Companies, now supported by the Government through National Rail Contracts. For reference the date of the expiry of the original franchise is also given here (if later than the current NRC expiry date).

Name of franchise	*Operator*	*Trading Name*
Caledonian Sleeper	Scottish Government	**Caledonian Sleeper**

The original Sleeper franchise started in April 2015 when operation of the ScotRail and ScotRail Sleeper franchises was separated. Abellio won the ScotRail franchise and Serco the Caledonian Sleeper franchise. The Scottish Government took over the operation of the Sleeper from Abellio in 2023. Caledonian Sleeper operates four trains nightly between London Euston and Scotland using locomotives hired from GBRf. New CAF Mark 5 rolling stock was introduced during 2019.

Chiltern	Arriva (Deutsche Bahn)	**Chiltern Railways**

NRC until 1 April 2025 with the option to extend to December 2027

Chiltern Railways operates a frequent service between London Marylebone, Oxford, Banbury and Birmingham Snow Hill, with some peak trains extending to Kidderminster. There are also regular services from Marylebone to Stratford-upon-Avon and to Aylesbury Vale Parkway via Amersham (along the London Underground Metropolitan Line). The fleet consists of DMUs of Classes 165, and 168 plus a number of locomotive-hauled rakes used on some of the Birmingham route trains, worked by Class 68s hired from DRS.

Cross Country   Arriva (Deutsche Bahn)   **CrossCountry**
ERMA until 15 October 2027 with the option to extend to October 2031

CrossCountry operates a network of long distance services between Scotland, the North-East of England and Manchester to the South-West of England, Reading, Southampton, Bournemouth and Guildford, centred on Birmingham New Street. These trains are formed of diesel Class 220/221 Voyagers. Inter-urban services also link Nottingham, Leicester and Stansted Airport with Birmingham and Cardiff. These trains use Class 170 DMUs.

Crossrail   MTR   **Elizabeth Line**
Concession until 27 May 2025

This concession started in May 2015. Initially Crossrail took over the Liverpool Street–Shenfield stopping service from Greater Anglia, using a fleet of Class 315 EMUs, with the service branded "TfL Rail". The core Crossrail railway in central London started operating in May 2022 and since then the operation has been branded the "Elizabeth Line". Class 345 EMUs are now used on all services running from Reading/Heathrow Airport to Shenfield/Abbey Wood.

East Coast   DfT   **London North Eastern Railway**
Operated by DfT's "Operator of Last Resort" until June 2025

LNER operates frequent long distance trains on the East Coast Main Line between London King's Cross, Leeds, Lincoln, Harrogate, York, Newcastle-upon-Tyne and Edinburgh, with less frequent services to Bradford, Skipton, Hull, Middlesbrough, Glasgow, Stirling, Aberdeen and Inverness. A fleet of 65 Hitachi Class 800 and 801 "Azuma" trains (a mix of bi-mode and electric, 5- and 9-car units) operate the majority of services. A small number of Class 91 + Mark 4 sets have been retained and are mainly used on Leeds and some York services.

East Midlands   Transport UK Group   **East Midlands Railway**
NRC until 17 October 2026 with the option to extend to October 2030

EMR operates a mix of long distance high speed services on the Midland Main Line (MML), from London St Pancras to Sheffield, Nottingham (plus peak-hour trips to Corby) and Corby, and local and regional services ranging from the long distance Norwich–Liverpool route to Nottingham–Skegness, Nottingham–Mansfield–Worksop, Derby–Matlock and Newark Castle–Crewe. It also operates local services across Lincolnshire. Trains on the MML are worked by a fleet of Class 222 DMUs, whilst the local and regional fleet consists of DMU Classes 158 and 170. Class 360 EMUs operate services on the St Pancras–Corby route.

East Anglia   Transport UK Group (60%)/Mitsui Group (40%)   **Greater Anglia**
NRC until 19 September 2024 with option for a 2 year extension; original franchise was until 11 October 2025

Greater Anglia operates main line trains between London Liverpool Street, Ipswich and Norwich and local trains across Norfolk, Suffolk and parts of Cambridgeshire. It also runs local and commuter services into Liverpool Street from the Great Eastern (including Southend, Braintree and Clacton) and West Anglia (including Ely/Cambridge and Stansted Airport) routes. In 2019–20 a new fleet of Stadler EMUs and bi-mode units (Classes 745 and 755) was introduced on the GEML and in East Anglia, replacing older DMUs and loco-hauled trains. A large fleet of 133 new 5-car Class 720 Aventras now all over services out of Liverpool Street.

Essex Thameside   Trenitalia   **c2c**
NRC until 25 July 2025; original franchise was until 10 November 2029

c2c operates an intensive, principally commuter, service from London Fenchurch Street to Southend and Shoeburyness, via both Upminster and Tilbury. The fleet consists of 74 Class 357 EMUs and a fleet of 12 new 5-car Class 720 Aventras.

Great Western   First Group   **Great Western Railway**
NRC until 21 June 2025 with the option to extend to June 2028

Great Western Railway operates long distance trains from London Paddington to South Wales, the West Country and Worcester and Hereford. In addition, there are frequent trains along the Thames Valley corridor to Newbury/Bedwyn and Oxford, plus local and regional trains throughout the South-West including the Cornish, Devon and Thames Valley branches, the Reading–Gatwick North Downs Line and Cardiff–Portsmouth Harbour and Bristol–Weymouth regional routes. Long distance services are in the hands of a fleet of Class 800/802 bi-mode InterCity Express Trains. DMUs of Classes 165 and 166 are used on the Thames Valley branches and North Downs routes as well as on local services around Bristol and Exeter and across to Cardiff. Class 387 EMUs are used between Paddington, Reading, Didcot Parkway and Newbury. Classes 150, 158, 165 and 166 and a small fleet of short 4-car HSTs are used on local and regional trains in the South-West. A small fleet of Class 57s is maintained to work the overnight "Cornish Riviera" Sleeper service between London Paddington and Penzance formed of Mark 3 coaches.

London Rail   Arriva (Deutsche Bahn)   **London Overground**
Concession until 3 May 2026

London Overground operates services on the Richmond–Stratford North London Line and the Willesden Junction–Clapham Junction West London Line, plus the East London Line from Highbury & Islington to New Cross and New Cross Gate, with extensions to Clapham Junction (via Denmark Hill), Crystal Palace and West Croydon. It also runs services from London Euston to Watford Junction. All these use Class 378 EMUs, with Class 710s also used on the Watford Junction route. Class 710s operate services on the Gospel Oak–Barking Riverside line. London Overground also operates some suburban services from London Liverpool Street – to Chingford, Enfield Town and Cheshunt. These services mainly use Class 710/1s, with one of these units additionally used on the Romford–Upminster shuttle.

Merseyrail Electrics   Serco (50%)/Transport UK Group (50%)   **Merseyrail**
Concession until 22 July 2028. Under the control of Merseytravel PTE instead of the DfT
Due to be reviewed every five years to fit in with the Merseyside Local Transport Plan

Merseyrail operates services between Liverpool and Southport, Ormskirk, Kirkby, Hunts Cross, New Brighton, West Kirby, Chester and Ellesmere Port. A new fleet of Class 777 EMUs are currently replacing the Class 507 and 508 EMUs.

Northern   DfT   **Northern**
Operated by DfT's "Operator of Last Resort" until further notice

Northern operates a range of inter-urban, commuter and rural services throughout the North of England, including those around the cities of Leeds, Manchester, Sheffield, Liverpool and Newcastle. The network extends from Chathill in the north to Nottingham in the south, and Cleethorpes in the east to St Bees in the west. Long distance services include Leeds–Carlisle, Morpeth–Carlisle–Carlisle and York–Blackpool North. The route uses a large fleet of DMUs of Classes 150, 155, 156, 158, 170 and 195 plus EMU Classes 319, 323, 331 and 333. New fleets of DMUs (Class 195) and EMUs (Class 331) are used on a number of routes, and were followed by Class 769 bi-mode diesel electric units (converted from Class 319s) in 2021.

ScotRail   Scottish Government   **ScotRail**
Operated by the Scottish Government from April 2022, having taken over ScotRail from Abellio

ScotRail provides almost all passenger services within Scotland and also trains from Glasgow to Carlisle via Dumfries. The company operates a large fleet of DMUs of Classes 156, 158 and 170 and EMU Classes 318, 320, 334, 380 and 385. A fleet of 25 refurbished HSTs have been introduced onto InterCity services between Edinburgh/Glasgow and Aberdeen and Inverness and also between Inverness and Aberdeen. In 2021 five Class 153s were also introduced on the West Highland Line (mainly the Oban line) to provide more capacity and space for bikes and other luggage.

| **South Eastern** | DfT | **Southeastern** |

Operated by DfT's "Operator of Last Resort" until further notice.

Southeastern operates all services in the south-east London suburbs, the whole of Kent and part of Sussex, which are primarily commuter services to London. It also operates domestic High Speed trains on HS1 from London St Pancras to Ashford, Ramsgate, Dover and Faversham with additional peak services on other routes. EMUs of Classes 375, 376, 377, 465, 466 and 707 are used, along with Class 395s on the High Speed trains.

| **South Western** | First Group (70%)/MTR (30%) | **South Western Railway** |

NRC until 25 May 2025

South Western Railway operates trains from London Waterloo to destinations across the South and South-West including Woking, Basingstoke, Southampton, Portsmouth, Salisbury, Exeter, Reading and Weymouth, as well as suburban services from Waterloo. SWR also runs services between Ryde and Shanklin on the Isle of Wight, from November 2021 using a fleet of five third rail Vivarail Class 484 units (converted former LU D78 stock). The rest of the fleet consists of DMU Classes 158 and 159 and EMU Classes 444, 450, 455 and 458. A new fleet of Bombardier Class 701s are being delivered and should enter service from late 2023.

| **Thameslink, Southern &** | Govia (Go-Ahead/Keolis) | **Govia Thameslink Railway** |
| **Great Northern (TSGN)** | | |

NRC until 1 April 2025 with the option to extend to April 2028

TSGN is the largest operator in Great Britain (the former Southern franchise was combined with Thameslink/Great Northern in 2015). GTR uses four brands: "Thameslink" for trains between Cambridge North, Peterborough, Bedford and Rainham, Sevenoaks, East Grinstead, Brighton, Littlehampton and Horsham via central London and also on the Sutton/Wimbledon loop using Class 700 EMUs. "Great Northern" comprises services from London King's Cross and Moorgate to Welwyn Garden City, Hertford North, Peterborough, Cambridge and King's Lynn using Class 387 and 717 EMUs. "Southern" operates predominantly commuter services between London, Surrey and Sussex and "metro" services in South London, as well as services along the south Coast between Southampton, Brighton, Hastings and Ashford, plus the cross-London service from South Croydon to Milton Keynes. Class 171 DMUs are used on Ashford–Eastbourne and London Bridge–Uckfield services, whilst all other services are in the hands of Class 377 and 700 EMUs. Finally, Gatwick Express operates semi-fast trains between London Victoria, Gatwick Airport and Brighton using Class 387/2 EMUs.

| **Trans-Pennine Express** | DfT | **TransPennine Express** |

Operated by DfT's "Operator of Last Resort" until further notice.

TransPennine Express operates predominantly long distance inter-urban services linking major cities across the North of England, along with Edinburgh and Glasgow in Scotland. The main services are Manchester Airport–Saltburn, Liverpool–Hull, Manchester Piccadilly–York–Scarborough and Liverpool–Newcastle/Edinburgh along the North Trans-Pennine route via Huddersfield, Leeds and York, and Liverpool–Manchester Piccadilly–Cleethorpes along the South Trans-Pennine route via Sheffield. TPE also operates Manchester Airport–Edinburgh/Glasgow and Liverpool–Glasgow services. The fleet consists of Class 185 DMUs, plus three new fleets: Class 68s+Mark 5A (which are to be withdrawn in December 2023) used on the Scarborough route, Class 397s used on Manchester Airport/Liverpool–Scotland and Class 802 bi-mode units used mainly on Liverpool–Newcastle/Edinburgh.

Wales & Borders   Welsh Government   **Transport for Wales**
From February 2021 the Welsh Government took direct control of rail service operation. Infrastructure management continues to be managed by KeolisAmey.

Transport for Wales was procured by the Welsh Government and operates a mix of long distance, regional and local services throughout Wales, including the Valley Lines network of lines around Cardiff, and also through services to the English border counties and to Manchester and Birmingham. The fleet consists of DMUs of Classes 150, 153, 158, 170 and 175 and locomotive-hauled Mark 4 sets hauled by Class 67s. Rebuilt Class 230 diesel-battery units are used on the Wrexham–Bidston line and new Stadler (Class 231/398/756) and CAF (Class 197) fleets are being introduced across other routes by 2025.

West Coast Partnership   First Group (70%)/Trenitalia (30%)   **Avanti West Coast**
NRC until 18 October 2026 with the option to extend to October 2032

Avanti West Coast operates long distance services along the West Coast Main Line from London Euston to Birmingham/Wolverhampton, Manchester, Liverpool, Blackpool North and Glasgow/Edinburgh using Class 390 Pendolino EMUs. It also operates Class 221 Voyagers on the Euston–Chester–Holyhead route and a small number of trains from Wolverhampton to Shrewsbury and to Wrexham. New Hitachi Class 805 and 807 units are due into service from 2024.

West Midlands Trains   Transport UK Group (70%)/JR East (15%)/**West Midlands Railway/**
                                      Mitsui (15%)   **London Northwestern**
NRC until 19 September 2024 with option to extend to September 2026; original franchise ran until 31 March 2026

West Midlands Trains operates services under two brand names. West Midlands Railway trains are local and regional services around Birmingham, including to Stratford-upon-Avon, Worcester, Hereford, Redditch, Rugeley and Shrewsbury. WMR is managed by a consortium of 16 councils and the Department for Transport. London Northwestern is the brand used for long distance and regional services from London Euston to Northampton and Birmingham/Crewe and also between Birmingham and Liverpool, Bedford–Bletchley and Watford Junction–St Albans Abbey. The fleet consists of DMU Classes 139, 150 and 172 and EMU Classes 319, 323 and 350. New fleets of CAF Class 196 DMUs and Bombardier Class 730 EMUs are being introduced across a number of routes between 2022 and 2025.

NON-FRANCHISED SERVICES

The following operators run non-franchised, or "open access" services
(* special seasonal services):

Operator	Trading Name	Route
Heathrow Airport Holdings	Heathrow Express	London Paddington–Heathrow Airport

Heathrow Express is a frequent express passenger service between London
Paddington and Heathrow Airport using a sub-fleet of Great Western
Railway Class 387 EMUs (operated jointly with GWR).

| Hull Trains (part of First) | Hull Trains | London King's Cross–Hull |

Hull Trains operates seven trains a day on weekdays from Hull to London
King's Cross via the East Coast Main Line. Bi-mode Class 802s were
introduced in 2019–20. Two trains in each direction start back from and
extend to Beverley.

| Grand Central (part of Arriva) | Grand Central | London King's Cross–Sunderland/ Bradford Interchange |

Grand Central operates five trains a day from Sunderland and four from
Bradford Interchange to London King's Cross using Class 180 or 221 DMUs.

| Locomotive Services (TOC) | Locomotive Services | |

Locomotive Services runs various excursions across the network using
diesel, electric and steam locomotives operating under the brands Saphos
Trains (principally steam-hauled trips), Statesman Rail (diesel-locomotive
hauled trips and land cruises), Rail Charter Services, Midland Pullman (HST
tours using the luxury HST set) and Intercity (mainly electric locomotive-
hauled tours).

| First East Coast | Lumo | London King's Cross–Edinburgh |

Lumo started operating services from London to Edinburgh via the East
Coast Main Line in October 2021 and now operates five trains per day using
new electric Class 803 units.

| North Yorkshire Moors Railway Enterprises | North Yorkshire Moors Railway | Pickering–Grosmont–Whitby/ Battersby, Sheringham–Cromer* |

The North Yorkshire Moors Railway operates services on the national
network between Grosmont and Whitby as an extension of its Pickering–
Grosmont services and also operates services between Sheringham and
Cromer on behalf of the North Norfolk Railway.

| South Yorkshire Supertram | Stagecoach Supertram | Meadowhall South–Rotherham Parkgate |

South Yorkshire Supertram holds a passenger licence to allow the operation
of the pilot tram-train service linking Sheffield city centre with Rotherham
Central and Rotherham Parkgate.

Tyne & Wear PTE	Tyne & Wear Metro	Pelaw–Sunderland

Tyne & Wear Passenger Transport Executive holds a passenger license to allow the operation of its Metro service over Network Rail tracks between Pelaw and Sunderland.

Vintage Trains	Vintage Trains	Birmingham Snow Hill–Stratford-upon-Avon*

Vintage Trains operates steam-hauled services on a seasonal basis.

West Coast Railway Company	West Coast Railway Company	Fort William–Mallaig* York–Settle–Carlisle* Carnforth–York–Scarborough*

WCRC operates steam-hauled services on these routes on a seasonal basis and a range of other excursions across the network, including the Northern Belle luxury train.

INTERNATIONAL PASSENGER OPERATORS

Eurostar International operates passenger services between London St Pancras and mainland Europe. The company, established in 2010, is jointly owned by SNCF (the national operator of France): 55%, SNCB (the national operator of Belgium): 5% and Patina Rail: 40%. Patina Rail is made up of Canadian-based Caisse de dépôt et placement du Québec (CDPG) and UK-based Hermes Infrastructure (owning 30% and 10% respectively). This 40% was previously owned by the UK Government until it was sold in 2015.

In addition, a service for the conveyance of accompanied road vehicles through the Channel Tunnel is provided by the tunnel operating company, Eurotunnel. All Eurotunnel services are operated in top-and-tail mode by the powerful Class 9 Bo-Bo-Bo locomotives.

FREIGHT TRAIN OPERATORS

The following operators operate freight services or empty passenger stock workings under "open access" arrangements:

Colas Rail
DB Cargo (UK)
Devon & Cornwall Railways (DCR)
Direct Rail Services
Freightliner
GB Railfreight
LORAM (UK)
Rail Adventure
Rail Operations Group
Varamis Rail
West Coast Railway Company

In addition, Amey, Balfour Beatty Rail, Harsco Rail, Swietelsky Babcock Rail (SB Rail) and VolkerRail operate trains formed of On-Track Machines.

INTRODUCTION

This book contains details of all Electric Multiple Units, usually referred to as EMUs, which can run on Britain's national railway network.

The number of EMUs in operation has been steadily increasing in recent years as both more lines have been opened or have been electrified and as the number of passengers travelling on the network has increased. EMUs work a wide variety of services, from long distance Intercity (such as the Class 390 Pendolinos) to inter-urban and suburban duties.

LAYOUT OF INFORMATION

25 kV AC 50 Hz overhead EMUs and dual voltage EMUs are listed in numerical order of set numbers. Individual "loose" vehicles are listed in numerical order after vehicles formed into fixed formations.

750 V DC third rail EMUs are listed in numerical order of class number, then in numerical order of set number. Some of these use the former Southern Region four-digit set numbers. These are derived from theoretical six digit set numbers which are the four-digit set number prefixed by the first two numbers of the class.

Where sets or vehicles have been renumbered in recent years, former numbering detail is shown alongside current detail. Each entry is laid out as in the following example:

Set No.	Detail	Livery	Owner	Operator	Allocation	Formation
377120	s	**SN**	P	*SN*	SU	78520 77120 78920 78720

Codes: Codes are used to denote the livery, owner, operator and depot allocation of each Electric Multiple Unit. Details of these can be found in section 9 of this book. Where a unit or spare car is off-lease, the operator column is left blank.

Detail Differences: Detail differences which currently affect the areas and types of train which vehicles may work are shown, plus differences in interior layout. Where such differences occur within a class, these are shown either in the heading information or alongside the individual set or vehicle number.

Set Formations: Regular set formations are shown where these are normally maintained. Readers should note set formations might be temporarily varied from time to time to suit maintenance and/or operational requirements. Vehicles shown as "Spare" are not formed in any regular set formation.

Names: Only names carried with official sanction are listed. Names are shown in UPPER/lower case characters as actually shown on the name carried on the vehicle(s). Unless otherwise shown, complete units are regarded as named rather than just the individual car(s) which carry the name.

GENERAL INFORMATION

CLASSIFICATION AND NUMBERING

25kV AC 50Hz overhead and "Versatile" EMUs are classified in the series 300–399. 750 VDC third rail EMUs are classified in the series 400–599. More recently dual-voltage units have been numbered in the 700+ series and Hitachi IEP design units in the 800+ series. Most of the Class 8xx units are bi-mode units which can operate under both diesel or electric power. The hydrogen demonstrator unit (ex-Class 314) has been reserved Class 614 and the new units for the Tyne & Wear Metro, which shares Network Rail tracks in places, have been allocated Class 555.

Until 2014 EMU individual cars were numbered in the series 61000–78999, except for vehicles used on the Isle of Wight – which are numbered in a separate series, and the Class 378s, 380s and 395s, which took up the 38xxx and 39xxx series'.

For all new vehicles allocated by the Rolling Stock Library since 2014 6-digit vehicle numbers have been used.

Any vehicle constructed or converted to replace another vehicle following accident damage and carrying the same number as the original vehicle is denoted by the suffix[II] in this publication

WHEEL ARRANGEMENT

A system whereby the number of powered axles on a bogie or frame is denoted by a letter (A = 1, B = 2, C= 3 etc) and the number of unpowered axles is denoted by a number is used in this publication. The letter "o" after a letter indicates that each axle is individually powered.

UNITS OF MEASUREMENT

Principal details and dimensions are quoted for each class in metric and/or imperial units as considered appropriate bearing in mind common UK usage.

All dimensions and weights are quoted for vehicles in an "as new" condition with all necessary supplies (eg oil, water, sand) on board. Dimensions are quoted in the order Length – Width. All lengths quoted are over buffers or couplers as appropriate. Where two lengths are quoted, the first refers to outer vehicles in a set and the second to inner vehicles. All width dimensions quoted are maxima. All weights are shown as metric tonnes (t = tonnes).

Bogie Types are quoted in the format motored/non-motored (eg BP20/BT13 denotes BP20 motored bogies and BT non-motored bogies).

Unless noted to the contrary, all vehicles listed have bar couplers at non-driving ends.

Unless stated, traction motors power details refer to each motored car per unit.

Vehicles ordered under the auspices of BR were allocated a Lot (batch) number when ordered and these are quoted in class headings and sub-headings. Vehicles ordered since 1995 have no Lot Numbers, but the manufacturer and location that they were built is given.

OPERATING CODES

These codes are used by train operating company staff to describe the various different types of vehicles and normally appear on data panels on the inner (ie non driving) ends of vehicles.

A "B" prefix indicates a battery vehicle.
A "P" prefix indicates a trailer vehicle on which is mounted the pantograph, instead of the default case where the pantograph is mounted on a motor vehicle.

The first part of the code describes whether or not the car has a motor or a driving cab as follows:

DM Driving motor   DT Driving trailer   M Motor   T Trailer

The next letter is a "B" for cars with a brake compartment.
This is followed by the saloon details:

F   First   S Standard   C Composite   V Van

The next letter denotes the style of accommodation, which is "O" for Open for all EMU vehicles still in service.

Finally, vehicles with a buffet or kitchen area are suffixed RB or RMB for a miniature buffet counter.

Where two vehicles of the same type are formed within the same unit, the above codes may be suffixed by (A) and (B) to differentiate between vehicles.

A composite is a vehicle containing both First and Standard Class accommodation, whilst a brake vehicle is a vehicle containing separate specific accommodation for the conductor.

ACCOMMODATION

The information given in class headings and sub-headings is in the form F/S nT (or TD) nW. For example, 12/54 1T 1W denotes 12 First Class and 54 Standard Class seats, one toilet and one space for a wheelchair. A number in brackets (ie +2)) denotes tip-up seats (in addition to the fixed seats). The seating layout of open saloons is indicated as 2+1, 2+2 or 3+2. Where units have First Class accommodation as well as Standard Class and the layout is different for each class then these are shown separately prefixed by "1:" and "2:".

TD denotes a universal access toilet suitable for use by people with disabilities. By law all trains should have been fitted with such facilities by the start of 2020. All EMUs still in service are now fitted, or have been retrofitted, with a universal access toilet (this is not applicable for those suburban units that do not have toilet facilities).

ABBREVIATIONS

The following abbreviations are used throughout this publication:

AC	Alternating Current.
BR	British Railways.
BSI	Bergische Stahl Industrie.
DC	Direct Current.
EMU	Electric Multiple Unit.
Hz	Hertz.
kN	kilonewtons.
kW	kilowatts.
LT	London Transport.
LUL	London Underground Limited.
m	metres.
mph	miles per hour.
SR	BR Southern Region.
V	volts.

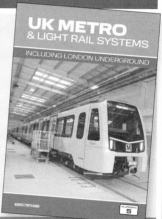

1. 25 kV AC 50 Hz OVERHEAD & DUAL VOLTAGE UNITS

Except where otherwise stated, all units in this section operate on 25 kV AC 50 Hz overhead only.

CLASS 318   BREL YORK

Outer suburban units.

Formation: DTS–MS–DTS.
Construction: Steel.
Traction Motors: Four Brush TM 2141 of 268 kW.
Wheel Arrangement: 2-2 + Bo-Bo + 2-2.
Braking: Disc.   **Dimensions:** 19.83/19.92 x 2.82 m.
Bogies: BP20 (MS), BT13 (others).   **Couplers:** Tightlock.
Gangways: Within unit.   **Control System:** Thyristor.
Doors: Sliding.   **Maximum Speed:** 90 mph.
Seating Layout: 3+2 facing.
Multiple Working: Within class & with Classes 317, 319, 320, 321 and 323.

77240–259. DTS. Lot No. 30999 1985–86. –/55 1TD 2W. 32.0 t.
77288. DTS. Lot No. 31020 1987. –/55 1TD 2W. 32.0 t.
62866–885. MS. Lot No. 30998 1985–86. –/79. 53.0 t.
62890. MS. Lot No. 31019 1987. –/79. 53.0 t.
77260–279. DTS. Lot No. 31000 1985–86. –/69(+2). 31.6 t.
77289. DTS. Lot No. 31021 1987. –/69(+2). 31.6 t.

318 250	**SR**	E	*SR*	GW	77240	62866	77260
318 251	**SR**	E	*SR*	GW	77241	62867	77261
318 252	**SR**	E	*SR*	GW	77242	62868	77262
318 253	**SR**	E	*SR*	GW	77243	62869	77263
318 254	**SR**	E	*SR*	GW	77244	62870	77264
318 255	**SR**	E	*SR*	GW	77245	62871	77265
318 256	**SR**	E	*SR*	GW	77246	62872	77266
318 257	**SR**	E	*SR*	GW	77247	62873	77267
318 258	**SR**	E	*SR*	GW	77248	62874	77268
318 259	**SR**	E	*SR*	GW	77249	62875	77269
318 260	**SR**	E	*SR*	GW	77250	62876	77270
318 261	**SR**	E	*SR*	GW	77251	62877	77271
318 262	**SR**	E	*SR*	GW	77252	62878	77272
318 263	**SR**	E	*SR*	GW	77253	62879	77273
318 264	**SR**	E	*SR*	GW	77254	62880	77274
318 265	**SR**	E	*SR*	GW	77255	62881	77275
318 266	**SR**	E	*SR*	GW	77256	62882	77276
318 267	**SR**	E	*SR*	GW	77257	62883	77277
318 268	**SR**	E	*SR*	GW	77258	62884	77278
318 269	**SR**	E	*SR*	GW	77259	62885	77279
318 270	**SR**	E	*SR*	GW	77288	62890	77289

CLASS 319   BREL YORK

Express and outer suburban units. Units shown * or † have a universal access toilet. Some units have been rebuilt as bi-modes (see Class 769 and Class 799) or converted to parcels units for Orion (see Class 768).

Formation: Various, see sub-class headings.
Systems: 25 kV AC overhead/750 V DC third rail.
Construction: Steel.
Traction Motors: Four GEC G315BZ of 268 kW.
Wheel Arrangement: 2-2 + Bo-Bo + 2-2 + 2-2.
Braking: Disc.   **Dimensions:** 20.17/20.16 x 2.82 m.
Bogies: P7-4 (MS), T3-7 (others).   **Couplers:** Tightlock.
Gangways: Within unit + end doors.   **Control System:** GTO chopper.
Doors: Sliding.   **Maximum Speed:** 100 mph.
Seating Layout: Various, see sub-class headings.
Multiple Working: Within class & with Classes 317, 318, 320, 321 and 323.

Class 319/0. DTS–MS–TS–DTS.

Seating Layout: 3+2 facing.

DTS(A). Lot No. 31022 (odd nos.) 1987–88. –/82. 28.2 t.
MS. Lot No. 31023 1987–88. –/82. 49.2 t.
TS. Lot No. 31024 1987–88. –/77 2T. 31.0 t.
DTS(B). Lot No. 31025 (even nos.) 1987–88. –/78. 28.1 t.

319011	**TL**	P		ZG	77311	62901	71782	77310

Class 319/2. DTS–MS–TS–DTC. Units converted from Class 319/0.

Seating Layout: 1: 2+1 facing, 2: 2+2/3+2 facing.

DTS. Lot No. 31022 (odd nos.) 1987–88. –/64. 30.0 t.
MS. Lot No. 31023 1987–88. –/73. 51.0 t.
TS. Lot No. 31024 1987–88. –/52 1TD 1T. 31.0 t.
DTC. Lot No. 31025 (even nos.) 1987–88. 18/36. 30.0 t.

319214	*	**TL**	P	*WM*	NN	77317	62904	71785	77316
319215	*	**TL**	P	*WM*	NN	77319	62905	71786	77318
319217	*	**TL**	P	*WM*	NN	77323	62907	71788	77322
319219	*	**TL**	P	*WM*	NN	77327	62909	71790	77326
319220	*	**TL**	P	*WM*	NN	77329	62910	71791	77328

Class 319/3. DTS–MS–TS–DTS. Converted from Class 319/1.

Refurbished with a new universal access toilet except 319373, which has been converted for carrying parcels and roller-cages for Orion (it was originally due to be renumbered 326001).
Seating Layout: 3+2 facing.

DTS(A). Lot No. 31063 1990. –/79. 29.0 t.
MS. Lot No. 31064 1990. –/81. 50.6 t.
TS. Lot No. 31065 1990. –/64 1TD 2W. 31.0 t.
DTS(B). Lot No. 31066 1990. –/79. 29.7 t.

319361	*	**NR**	P	*NO*	AN	77459	63043	71929	77458
319363	*	**NR**	P		LM	77463	63045	71931	77462
319366	*	**NR**	P	*NO*	AN	77469	63048	71934	77468
319367	*	**NR**	P	*NO*	AN	77471	63049	71935	77470
319368	*	**NR**	P	*NO*	AN	77473	63050	71936	77472
319369	*	**NR**	P	*NO*	AN	77475	63051	71937	77474
319370	*	**NR**	P	*NO*	AN	77477	63052	71938	77476
319371	*	**NR**	P		LM	77479	63053	71939	77478
319372	*	**TL**	P	*NO*	AN	77481	63054	71940	77480
319373		**ON**	P		CY	77483	63055	71941	77482
319375	*	**NR**	P	*NO*	AN	77487	63057	71943	77486
319377	*	**NR**	P		ZG	77491	63059	71945	77490
319378	*	**NR**	P	*NO*	AN	77493	63060	71946	77492
319379	*	**NR**	P	*NO*	AN	77495	63061	71947	77494
319380	*	**NR**	P		ZG	77497	63062	71948	77496
319381	*	**NR**	P	*NO*	AN	77973	63093	71979	77974
319383	*	**NR**	P	*NO*	AN	77977	63095	71981	77978
319384	*	**NR**	P	*NO*	AN	77979	63096	71982	77980
319385	*	**NR**	P	*NO*	AN	77981	63097	71983	77982
319386	*	**NR**	P	*NO*	AN	77983	63098	71984	77984

Class 319/4. DTC–MS–TS–DTS. Converted from Class 319/0. Refurbished with carpets. DTS(A) converted to composite.

319424/431/434/442/448/450/456/458 were converted to Class 769 bi-mode units for Northern.

319421/445/452 were converted to Class 769 bi-mode units for Transport for Wales. 319426 was rejected from this programme.

319422/423/425/427/428/430/432/435–440/443/444/446/447/449/459 were converted to Class 769 tri-mode units for Great Western Railway.

Non-standard livery: 319454 Porterbrook Innovation Hub (blue).

Seating Layout: 1: 2+1 facing 2: 2+2/3+2 facing.

77331–381. DTC. Lot No. 31022 (odd nos.) 1987–88. 12/51 (* 12/50). 30.0t (* 31.0 t).
77431–457. DTC. Lot No. 31038 (odd nos.) 1988. 12/51 (* 12/50). 30.0t (* 31.0 t).
62911–936. MS. Lot No. 31023 1987–88. –/74 (* –/75). 49.2t (* 52.4 t).
62961–974. MS. Lot No. 31039 1988. –/74 (* –/75). 49.2t (* 52.4 t).
71792–817. TS. Lot No. 31024 1987–88. –/67 2T (* –/58 1TD 2W). 31.0t (* 33.7 t).
71866–879. TS. Lot No. 31040 1988. –/67 2T (* –/58 1TD 2W). 31.0t (* 33.7 t).
77330–380. DTS. Lot No. 31025 (even nos.) 1987–88. –/71 1W (* –/73). 28.1t (* 30.7 t).
77430–456. DTS. Lot No. 31041 (even nos.) 1988. –/71 1W (* –/73). 28.1t (* 30.7 t).

319426	*	**NR**	P		ZN	77341	62916	71797	77290
319433	*	**LM**	P	*WM*	NN	77355	62923	71804	77354
319441	*	**LM**	P		CN	77371	62931	71812	77370
319454		**0**	P		LM	77445	62968	71873	77444
319457	*	**LM**	P	*WM*	NN	77451	62971	71876	77450

CLASS 320   BREL YORK

Suburban units. In 2016–19 ScotRail received 320401/403/404/411–418/420 (ex-Class 321s) which were refurbished and reformed as 3-cars.

Formation: DTS–MS–DTS.
Construction: Steel
Traction Motors: Four Brush TM2141B of 268 kW.
Wheel Arrangement: 2-2 + Bo-Bo + 2-2.
Braking: Disc.   **Dimensions:** 19.95 x 2.82 m.
Bogies: P7-4 (MS), T3-7 (others).   **Couplers:** Tightlock.
Gangways: Within unit.   **Control System:** Thyristor.
Doors: Sliding.   **Maximum Speed:** 90 mph.
Seating Layout: 3+2 facing.
Multiple Working: Within class & with Classes 317, 318, 319, 321 and 323.

Class 320/3. Original build.

DTS(A). Lot No. 31060 1990. –/51(+4) 1TD 2W. 31.7 t.
MS. Lot No. 31062 1990. –/78. 52.6 t.
DTS(B). Lot No. 31061 1990. –/73(+2). 31.6 t.

320 301	**SR**	E	*SR*	GW	77899	63021	77921
320 302	**SR**	E	*SR*	GW	77900	63022	77922
320 303	**SR**	E	*SR*	GW	77901	63023	77923
320 304	**SR**	E	*SR*	GW	77902	63024	77924
320 305	**SR**	E	*SR*	GW	77903	63025	77925
320 306	**SR**	E	*SR*	GW	77904	63026	77926
320 307	**SR**	E	*SR*	GW	77905	63027	77927
320 308	**SR**	E	*SR*	GW	77906	63028	77928
320 309	**SR**	E	*SR*	GW	77907	63029	77929
320 310	**SR**	E	*SR*	GW	77908	63030	77930
320 311	**SR**	E	*SR*	GW	77909	63031	77931
320 312	**SR**	E	*SR*	GW	77910	63032	77932
320 313	**SR**	E	*SR*	GW	77911	63033	77933
320 314	**SR**	E	*SR*	GW	77912	63034	77934
320 315	**SR**	E	*SR*	GW	77913	63035	77935
320 316	**SR**	E	*SR*	GW	77914	63036	77936
320 317	**SR**	E	*SR*	GW	77915	63037	77937
320 318	**SR**	E	*SR*	GW	77916	63038	77938
320 319	**SR**	E	*SR*	GW	77917	63039	77939
320 320	**SR**	E	*SR*	GW	77918	63040	77940
320 321	**SR**	E	*SR*	GW	77919	63041	77941
320 322	**SR**	E	*SR*	GW	77920	63042	77942

Class 320/4. Former London Midland Class 321s reduced to 3-car formation and refurbished as Class 320/4s by Wabtec Doncaster/Kilmarnock 2015–19.

The original vehicles 71966 and 77960 from 321418 (now 320418) and 78114 and 63082 from 321420 (now 320420) were written off after the Watford Junction accident in 1996. The undamaged vehicles were formed together as 321418 whilst four new vehicles were built in 1997, taking the same numbers as the scrapped vehicles, and these became the second 321420.

DTS(A). Lot No. 31060 1990. –/54(+4) 1TD 2W. 32.0 t.
MS. Lot No. 31062 1990. –/79. 52.2 t.
DTS(B). Lot No. 31061 1990. –/74(+2). 32.0 t.

320401	(321401)	**SR**	E	*SR*	GW	78095	63063	77943
320403	(321403)	**SR**	E	*SR*	GW	78097	63065	77945
320404	(321404)	**SR**	E	*SR*	GW	78098	63066	77946
320411	(321411)	**SR**	E	*SR*	GW	78105	63073	77953
320412	(321412)	**SR**	E	*SR*	GW	78106	63074	77954
320413	(321413)	**SR**	E	*SR*	GW	78107	63075	77955
320414	(321414)	**SR**	E	*SR*	GW	78108	63076	77956
320415	(321415)	**SR**	E	*SR*	GW	78109	63077	77957
320416	(321416)	**SR**	E	*SR*	GW	78110	63078	77958
320417	(321417)	**SR**	E	*SR*	GW	78111	63079	77959
320418	(321418)	**SR**	E	*SR*	GW	78112	63080	77962
320420	(321420)	**SR**	E	*SR*	GW	78114[II]	63082[II]	77960[II]

CLASS 321   BREL YORK

Outer suburban units. The remaining Greater Anglia units are due to be taken out of service during 2023.

Formation: DTC (DTS on Class 321/9)–MS–TS–DTS.
Construction: Steel.
Traction Motors: Four Brush TM2141C of 268 kW (* Four TSA010163 AC motors of 300 kW).
Wheel Arrangement: 2-2 + Bo-Bo + 2-2 + 2-2.
Braking: Disc (* and regenerative).   **Dimensions:** 19.95 x 2.82 m.
Bogies: P7-4 (MS), T3-7 (others).   **Couplers:** Tightlock.
Gangways: Within unit.
Control System: Thyristor (* IGBT Inverter).
Doors: Sliding.   **Maximum Speed:** 100 mph.
Seating Layout: 1: 2+2 facing, 2: 3+2 facing.
Multiple Working: Within class & with Classes 317, 318, 319, 320, and 323.

Class 321/3.

* "Renatus" rebuilt units with completely new interiors, air conditioning and Quantum seating, still arranged to a 3+2 layout in Standard Class. Fitted with new TSA AC traction motors.

† Converted to a freight carrying unit with all seats removed.

Non-standard livery: 321 334 Swift Express Freight (dark blue).

DTC. Lot No. 31053 1988–90. 16/57 (* 16/31(+4) 1TD 2W. 29.7 t (* 34.1 t).
MS. Lot No. 31054 1988–90. –/82 (* –/80). 51.5 t (* 53.8 t).
TS. Lot No. 31055 1988–90. –/75 2T (* –/78 1T). 29.1 t (* 31.7 t).
DTS. Lot No. 31056 1988–90. –/78 (* –/76). 29.7 t (* 32.8 t.)

321 301	*	**GR**	E		WB	78049	62975	71880	77853
321 302	*	**GR**	E		WA	78050	62976	71881	77854
321 303	*	**GR**	E		WB	78051	62977	71882	77855
321 304	*	**GR**	E		WB	78052	62978	71883	77856
321 305	*	**GR**	E		IL	78053	62979	71884	77857
321 306	*	**GR**	E		WA	78054	62980	71885	77858
321 307	*	**GR**	E		WA	78055	62981	71886	77859
321 308	*	**GR**	E		WA	78056	62982	71887	77860
321 309	*	**GR**	E		WB	78057	62983	71888	77861
321 310	*	**GR**	E		WB	78058	62984	71889	77862
321 311	*	**GR**	E		WA	78059	62985	71890	77863
321 312	*	**GR**	E		WA	78060	62986	71891	77864
321 313	*	**GR**	E		WB	78061	62987	71892	77865
321 314	*	**GR**	E		WA	78062	62988	71893	77866
321 315	*	**GR**	E		WB	78063	62989	71894	77867
321 316	*	**GR**	E		WB	78064	62990	71895	77868
321 317	*	**GR**	E		WB	78065	62991	71896	77869
321 318	*	**GR**	E		WB	78066	62992	71897	77870
321 319	*	**GR**	E		WA	78067	62993	71898	77871
321 320	*	**GR**	E		WB	78068	62994	71899	77872
321 321	*	**GR**	E		IL	78069	62995	71900	77873
321 322	*	**GR**	E		WB	78070	62996	71901	77874
321 323	*	**GR**	E		WB	78071	62997	71902	77875
321 324	*	**GR**	E		WB	78072	62998	71903	77876
321 325	*	**GR**	E		WB	78073	62999	71904	77877
321 326	*	**GR**	E		WA	78074	63000	71905	77878
321 327	*	**GR**	E		WB	78075	63001	71906	77879
321 328	*	**GR**	E		WB	78076	63002	71907	77880
321 329	*	**GR**	E		WB	78077	63003	71908	77881
321 330	*	**GR**	E		WB	78078	63004	71909	77882
321 332		**NC**	E		ZN	78080	63006	71911	77884
321 334	†	**O**	E	VA	GW	78082	63008	71913	77886
321 337		**NC**	E		WS	78085	63011	71916	77889
321 338		**NC**	E		ZN	78086	63012	71917	77890
321 339		**NC**	E		ZN	78087	63013	71918	77891
321 341		**NC**	E		ZN	78089	63015	71920	77893
321 342		**NC**	E		ZN	78090	63016	71921	77894

Class 321/4.

DTC. Lot No. 31067 1989–90. 28/40 (321 421–436 16/52, 321 439–444 16/56). 29.8 t.
MS. Lot No. 31068 1989–90. –/79 (321 439–444 –/82). 51.6 t.
TS. Lot No. 31069 1989–90. –/74 2T (321 439–444 –/75 2T). 29.2 t.
DTS. Lot No. 31070 1989–90. –/78. 29.8 t.

321 407	**FB**	E		ZN	78101	63069	71955	77949
321 419	**FB**	E		ZN	78113	63081	71967	77961
321 428	**NX**	E		ZN	78122	63090	71976	77970
321 429	**NX**	E		ZN	78123	63091	71977	77971
321 434	**NC**	ER		YA	78154	63128	72014	78303
321 440	**GA**	E		WS	78160	63134	72020	78309
321 443	**GA**	E		GA	78125	63099	71985	78274

CLASS 323 HUNSLET TRANSPORTATION PROJECTS

Suburban units.

Formation: DMS–PTS–DMS.
Construction: Welded aluminium alloy.
Traction Motors: Four Holec DMKT 52/24 asynchronous of 146 kW.
Wheel Arrangement: Bo-Bo + 2-2 + Bo-Bo.
Braking: Disc & regenerative.   **Dimensions:** 23.37/23.44 x 2.80 m.
Bogies: SRP BP62 (DMS), BT52 (PTS). **Couplers:** Tightlock.
Gangways: Within unit.   **Control System:** IGBT Inverter.
Doors: Sliding plug.   **Maximum Speed:** 90 mph.
Seating Layout: 3+2 facing/unidirectional.
Multiple Working: Within class & with Classes 317, 318, 319, 320 and 321.

DMS(B) vehicles 65003 and 65005 in 323 203/205 and 65019 and 65021 in 323 219/221 switched between units following accident damage and were not returned to their original sets, instead swapping numbers.

DMS(A). Lot No. 31112 Hunslet 1992–93. –/97. 41.0 t.
TS. Lot No. 31113 Hunslet 1992–93. –/81(+3) 1TD 2W. 39.3t.
DMS(B). Lot No. 31114 Hunslet 1992–93. –/97. 41.0 t.

323 201	**WI**	P	*WM*	SO	64001	72201	65001
323 202	**WI**	P	*WM*	SO	64002	72202	65002
323 203	**WI**	P	*WM*	SO	64003	72203	65003
323 204	**WI**	P	*WM*	SO	64004	72204	65004
323 205	**WI**	P	*WM*	SO	64005	72205	65005
323 206	**WI**	P	*WM*	SO	64006	72206	65006
323 207	**WI**	P	*WM*	SO	64007	72207	65007
323 208	**WI**	P	*WM*	SO	64008	72208	65008
323 209	**WI**	P	*WM*	SO	64009	72209	65009
323 210	**WI**	P	*WM*	SO	64010	72210	65010
323 211	**WI**	P	*WM*	SO	64011	72211	65011
323 212	**WI**	P	*WM*	SO	64012	72212	65012
323 213	**WI**	P	*WM*	SO	64013	72213	65013
323 214	**WI**	P	*WM*	SO	64014	72214	65014

323215	**WI**	P	*WM*	SO	64015	72215	65015
323216	**WI**	P	*WM*	SO	64016	72216	65016
323217	**WI**	P	*WM*	SO	64017	72217	65017
323218	**WI**	P	*WM*	SO	64018	72218	65018
323219	**WI**	P	*WM*	SO	64019	72219	65019
323220	**WI**	P	*WM*	SO	64020	72220	65020
323221	**CO**	P	*WM*	SO	64021	72221	65021
323222	**WI**	P	*WM*	SO	64022	72222	65022
323223	**NR**	P	*NO*	AN	64023	72223	65023
323224	**NR**	P	*NO*	AN	64024	72224	65024
323225	**NR**	P	*NO*	AN	64025	72225	65025
323226	**NR**	P	*NO*	AN	64026	72226	65026
323227	**NR**	P	*NO*	AN	64027	72227	65027
323228	**NR**	P	*NO*	AN	64028	72228	65028
323229	**NR**	P	*NO*	AN	64029	72229	65029
323230	**NR**	P	*NO*	AN	64030	72230	65030
323231	**NR**	P	*NO*	AN	64031	72231	65031
323232	**NR**	P	*NO*	AN	64032	72232	65032
323233	**NR**	P	*NO*	AN	64033	72233	65033
323234	**NR**	P	*NO*	AN	64034	72234	65034
323235	**NR**	P	*NO*	AN	64035	72235	65035
323236	**NR**	P	*NO*	AN	64036	72236	65036
323237	**NR**	P	*NO*	AN	64037	72237	65037
323238	**NR**	P	*NO*	AN	64038	72238	65038
323239	**NR**	P	*NO*	AN	64039	72239	65039
323240	**WI**	P	*WM*	SO	64040	72340	65040
323241	**WI**	P	*WM*	SO	64041	72341	65041
323242	**WI**	P	*WM*	SO	64042	72342	65042
323243	**WI**	P	*WM*	SO	64043	72343	65043

Names (carried on one side of TS):

323201	Duddeston	323214	Wylde Green
323202	Butlers Lane	323215	Gravelly Hill
323203	Aston	323216	University
323204	Selly Oak	323217	Chester Road
323205	Blake Street	323218	Lichfield City
323206	Barnt Green	323219	Kings Norton
323207	Bournville	323220	Lichfield Trent Valley
323208	Five Ways	323222	Redditch
323209	Birmingham New Street	323240	Erdington
323210	Shenstone	323241	Dave Pomroy 323 Fleet
323211	Four Oaks		Engineer 40 Years Service
323212	Bromsgrove	323242	Alvechurch
323213	Sutton Coldfield	323243	Longbridge

CLASS 325   ABB DERBY

Postal units based on Class 319s. Compatible with diesel or electric locomotive haulage. Built for dual voltage use, but 750 V DC third rail shoe gear has been removed as it is not required on current duties.

Formation: DTPMV–MPMV–TPMV–DTPMV.
System: 25 kV AC overhead.
Construction: Steel.
Traction Motors: Four GEC G315BZ of 268 kW.
Wheel Arrangement: 2-2 + Bo-Bo + 2-2 + 2-2.
Braking: Disc.   **Dimensions**: 19.33 x 2.82 m.
Bogies: P7-4 (MPMV), T3-7 (others).   **Couplers**: Drop-head buckeye.
Gangways: None.   **Control System**: GTO Chopper.
Doors: Roller shutter.   **Maximum Speed**: 100 mph.
Multiple Working: Within class.

DTPMV. Lot No. 31144 1995. 29.1 t.
MPMV. Lot No. 31145 1995. 49.5 t.
TPMV. Lot No. 31146 1995. 30.7 t.

325 001	**RM**	RM	*DB*	CE	68300	68340	68360	68301
325 002	**RM**	RM	*DB*	CE	68302	68341	68361	68303
325 003	**RM**	RM	*DB*	CE	68304	68342	68362	68305
325 004	**RM**	RM	*DB*	CE	68306	68343	68363	68307
325 005	**RM**	RM	*DB*	CE	68308	68344	68364	68309
325 006	**RM**	RM	*DB*	CE	68310	68345	68365	68311
325 007	**RM**	RM	*DB*	CE	68312	68346	68366	68313
325 008	**RM**	RM	*DB*	CE	68314	68347	68367	68315
325 009	**RM**	RM	*DB*	CE	68316	68349	68368	68317
325 011	**RM**	RM	*DB*	CE	68320	68350	68370	68321
325 012	**RM**	RM	*DB*	CE	68322	68351	68371	68323
325 013	**RM**	RM	*DB*	CE	68324	68352	68372	68325
325 014	**RM**	RM	*DB*	CE	68326	68353	68373	68327
325 015	**RM**	RM	*DB*	CE	68328	68354	68374	68329
325 016	**RM**	RM	*DB*	CE	68330	68355	68375	68331

Name (carried on one side of each DTPMV):

325 008   Peter Howarth CBE

CLASS 331   CIVITY   CAF

New Northern outer suburban units.

Formation: DMS–PTS–DMS or DMS–PTS–TS–DMS.
Construction: Aluminium.
Traction Motors: Four TSA asynchronous of 220 kW.
Wheel Arrangement: Bo-Bo + 2-2 + Bo-Bo or Bo-Bo + 2-2 + 2-2 + Bo-Bo.
Braking: Disc & regenerative.   **Dimensions:** 24.03/23.35 x 2.55 m.
Bogies: CAF.   **Couplers:** Dellner.
Gangways: Within unit.   **Control System:** IGBT Inverter.
Doors: Sliding plug.   **Maximum Speed:** 100 mph.
Heating & ventilation: Air conditioning.
Seating: 2+2 facing/unidirectional. **Multiple Working:** Within class.

Class 331/0. DMS–PTS–DMS. 3-car units. Used in North-West England.

DMS. CAF Zaragoza/Newport 2017–20. –/45(+8) 1TD 2W. 40.8 t.
PTS. CAF Zaragoza/Newport 2017–20. –/76(+4). 34.9 t.
DMS. CAF Zaragoza/Newport 2017–20. –/63(+7). 39.8 t.

331001	**NR**	E	*NO*	AN	463001	464001	466001
331002	**NR**	E	*NO*	AN	463002	464002	466002
331003	**NR**	E	*NO*	AN	463003	464003	466003
331004	**NR**	E	*NO*	AN	463004	464004	466004
331005	**NR**	E	*NO*	AN	463005	464005	466005
331006	**NR**	E	*NO*	AN	463006	464006	466006
331007	**NR**	E	*NO*	AN	463007	464007	466007
331008	**NR**	E	*NO*	AN	463008	464008	466008
331009	**NR**	E	*NO*	AN	463009	464009	466009
331010	**NR**	E	*NO*	AN	463010	464010	466010
331011	**NR**	E	*NO*	AN	463011	464011	466011
331012	**NR**	E	*NO*	AN	463012	464012	466012
331013	**NR**	E	*NO*	AN	463013	464013	466013
331014	**NR**	E	*NO*	AN	463014	464014	466014
331015	**NR**	E	*NO*	AN	463015	464015	466015
331016	**NR**	E	*NO*	AN	463016	464016	466016
331017	**NR**	E	*NO*	AN	463017	464017	466017
331018	**NR**	E	*NO*	AN	463018	464018	466018
331019	**NR**	E	*NO*	AN	463019	464019	466019
331020	**NR**	E	*NO*	AN	463020	464020	466020
331021	**NR**	E	*NO*	AN	463021	464021	466021
331022	**NR**	E	*NO*	AN	463022	464022	466022
331023	**NR**	E	*NO*	AN	463023	464023	466023
331024	**NR**	E	*NO*	AN	463024	464024	466024
331025	**NR**	E	*NO*	AN	463025	464025	466025
331026	**NR**	E	*NO*	AN	463026	464026	466026
331027	**NR**	E	*NO*	AN	463027	464027	466027
331028	**NR**	E	*NO*	AN	463028	464028	466028
331029	**NR**	E	*NO*	AN	463029	464029	466029
331030	**NR**	E	*NO*	AN	463030	464030	466030
331031	**NR**	E	*NO*	AN	463031	464031	466031

Class 331/1. DMS–PTS–TS–DMS. 4-car units. Used in West Yorkshire.

DMS. CAF Zaragoza/Newport 2017–19. –/45(+8) 1TD 2W. 40.8 t.
PTS. CAF Zaragoza/Newport 2017–19. –/76(+4). 34.9 t.
TS. CAF Zaragoza/Newport 2017–19. –/76(+4). 30.1 t.
DMS. CAF Zaragoza/Newport 2017–19. –/63(+7). 39.8 t.

331101	**NR**	E	*NO*	NL	463101	464101	465101	466101
331102	**NR**	E	*NO*	NL	463102	464102	465102	466102
331103	**NR**	E	*NO*	NL	463103	464103	465103	466103
331104	**NR**	E	*NO*	NL	463104	464104	465104	466104
331105	**NR**	E	*NO*	NL	463105	464105	465105	466105
331106	**NR**	E	*NO*	NL	463106	464106	465106	466106
331107	**NR**	E	*NO*	NL	463107	464107	465107	466107
331108	**NR**	E	*NO*	NL	463108	464108	465108	466108
331109	**NR**	E	*NO*	NL	463109	464109	465109	466109
331110	**NR**	E	*NO*	NL	463110	464110	465110	466110
331111	**NR**	E	*NO*	NL	463111	464111	465111	466111
331112	**NR**	E	*NO*	NL	463112	464112	465112	466112

Names (carried on driving cars):

331106   Proud to be Northern | 331110   Proud to be Northern

CLASS 333   CAF/SIEMENS

West Yorkshire area suburban units.

Formation: DMS–PTS–TS–DMS.
Construction: Steel.
Traction Motors: Two Siemens monomotors asynchronous of 350 kW.
Wheel Arrangement: B-B + 2-2 + 2-2 + B-B.
Braking: Disc.
Dimensions: 23.74/23.35 x 2.75 m.
Bogies: CAF.
Couplers: Dellner 10L.
Gangways: Within unit.
Control System: IGBT Inverter.
Doors: Sliding plug.
Maximum Speed: 100 mph.
Heating & ventilation: Air conditioning.
Multiple Working: Within class.
Seating Layout: 3+2 facing/unidirectional.

333001–008 were made up to 4-car units from 3-car units in 2002.

333009–016 were made up to 4-car units from 3-car units in 2003.

DMS(A). (odd Nos.) CAF Zaragoza 2001. –/90. 50.0 t.
PTS. CAF Zaragoza 2001. –/73(+7) 1TD 2W. 46.0 t.
TS. CAF Zaragoza 2002–03. –/100. 38.5 t.
DMS(B). (even Nos.) CAF Zaragoza 2001. –/90. 50.0 t.

333001	**NR**	A	*NO*	NL	78451	74461	74477	78452
333002	**NR**	A	*NO*	NL	78453	74462	74478	78454
333003	**NR**	A	*NO*	NL	78455	74463	74479	78456
333004	**NR**	A	*NO*	NL	78457	74464	74480	78458
333005	**NR**	A	*NO*	NL	78459	74465	74481	78460
333006	**NR**	A	*NO*	NL	78461	74466	74482	78462
333007	**NR**	A	*NO*	NL	78463	74467	74483	78464

333008	**NR**	A	*NO*	NL	78465	74468	74484	78466
333009	**NR**	A	*NO*	NL	78467	74469	74485	78468
333010	**NR**	A	*NO*	NL	78469	74470	74486	78470
333011	**NR**	A	*NO*	NL	78471	74471	74487	78472
333012	**NR**	A	*NO*	NL	78473	74472	74488	78474
333013	**NR**	A	*NO*	NL	78475	74473	74489	78476
333014	**NR**	A	*NO*	NL	78477	74474	74490	78478
333015	**NR**	A	*NO*	NL	78479	74475	74491	78480
333016	**NR**	A	*NO*	NL	78481	74476	74492	78482

CLASS 334   JUNIPER   ALSTOM BIRMINGHAM

Outer suburban units.

Formation: DMS–PTS–DMS.
Construction: Steel.
Traction Motors: Two Alstom ONIX 800 asynchronous of 270 kW.
Wheel Arrangement: 2-Bo + 2-2 + Bo-2.
Braking: Disc.   **Dimensions**: 21.01/19.94 x 2.80 m.
Bogies: Alstom LTB3/TBP3.   **Couplers**: Dellner.
Gangways: Within unit.   **Control System**: IGBT Inverter.
Doors: Sliding plug.   **Maximum Speed**: 90 mph.
Heating & ventilation: Air conditioning.
Seating Layout: 2+2 facing/unidirectional (3+2 in PTS).
Multiple Working: Within class.

Non-standard livery: 334006 Pride celebration colours (vehicle 64106).

DMS(A). Alstom Birmingham 1999–2001. –/64. 42.6 t.
PTS. Alstom Birmingham 1999–2001. –/55 1TD 1W. 39.4 t.
DMS(B). Alstom Birmingham 1999–2001. –/59(+3). 42.6 t.

334001	**SR**	E	*SR*	GW	64101	74301	65101
334002	**SR**	E	*SR*	GW	64102	74302	65102
334003	**SR**	E	*SR*	GW	64103	74303	65103
334004	**SR**	E	*SR*	GW	64104	74304	65104
334005	**SR**	E	*SR*	GW	64105	74305	65105
334006	**0**	E	*SR*	GW	64106	74306	65106
334007	**SR**	E	*SR*	GW	64107	74307	65107
334008	**SR**	E	*SR*	GW	64108	74308	65108
334009	**SR**	E	*SR*	GW	64109	74309	65109
334010	**SR**	E	*SR*	GW	64110	74310	65110
334011	**SR**	E	*SR*	GW	64111	74311	65111
334012	**SR**	E	*SR*	GW	64112	74312	65112
334013	**SR**	E	*SR*	GW	64113	74313	65113
334014	**SR**	E	*SR*	GW	64114	74314	65114
334015	**SR**	E	*SR*	GW	64115	74315	65115
334016	**SR**	E	*SR*	GW	64116	74316	65116
334017	**SR**	E	*SR*	GW	64117	74317	65117
334018	**SR**	E	*SR*	GW	64118	74318	65118
334019	**SR**	E	*SR*	GW	64119	74319	65119
334020	**SR**	E	*SR*	GW	64120	74320	65120

334021	**SR**	E	*SR*	GW	64121	74321	65121
334022	**SR**	E	*SR*	GW	64122	74322	65122
334023	**SR**	E	*SR*	GW	64123	74323	65123
334024	**SR**	E	*SR*	GW	64124	74324	65124
334025	**SR**	E	*SR*	GW	64125	74325	65125
334026	**SR**	E	*SR*	GW	64126	74326	65126
334027	**SR**	E	*SR*	GW	64127	74327	65127
334028	**SR**	E	*SR*	GW	64128	74328	65128
334029	**SR**	E	*SR*	GW	64129	74329	65129
334030	**SR**	E	*SR*	GW	64130	74330	65130
334031	**SR**	E	*SR*	GW	64131	74331	65131
334032	**SR**	E	*SR*	GW	64132	74332	65132
334033	**SR**	E	*SR*	GW	64133	74333	65133
334034	**SR**	E	*SR*	GW	64134	74334	65134
334035	**SR**	E	*SR*	GW	64135	74335	65135
334036	**SR**	E	*SR*	GW	64136	74336	65136
334037	**SR**	E	*SR*	GW	64137	74337	65137
334038	**SR**	E	*SR*	GW	64138	74338	65138
334039	**SR**	E	*SR*	GW	64139	74339	65139
334040	**SR**	E	*SR*	GW	64140	74340	65140

CLASS 345   AVENTRA   BOMBARDIER DERBY

These 9-car units are used on London's Crossrail (now branded as the Elizabeth Line), the core section of which opened in 2022. The design was marketed as "Aventra" by Bombardier and is a development of the successful Electrostar design. Some units initially operated as 7-car sets.

Formation: DMS–PMS–MS–MS–TS–MS–MS–PMS–DMS.
System: 25 kV AC overhead.
Construction: Aluminium.
Traction Motors: Two Bombardier asynchronous of 265 kW.
Wheel Arrangement: 2-Bo + Bo-2 + Bo-Bo + Bo-2 + 2-2 + 2-Bo + Bo-Bo + 2-Bo + Bo-2.

Braking: Disc & regenerative.	**Dimensions:** 23.62/22.50 m x 2.78 m.
Bogies: FLEXX B5000 inside-frame.	**Couplers:** Dellner.
Gangways: Within unit.	**Control System:** IGBT Inverter.
Doors: Sliding plug (three per vehicle).	**Maximum Speed:** 90 mph.

Heating & ventilation: Air conditioning.
Seating Layout: Mostly longitudinal, with some 2+2 facing.
Multiple Working: Within class.

Non-standard livery: 345055 Pride celebration colours (driving cars).

DMS(A). Bombardier Derby 2015–19. –/46. 39.0 t.
PMS(A). Bombardier Derby 2015–19. –/46(+6). 37.1 t.
MS(A). Bombardier Derby 2015–19. –/46(+6). 36.5 t.
MS(B). Bombardier Derby 2015–19. –/49(+3). 31.4 t.
TS. Bombardier Derby 2015–19. –/38(+12). 29.7 t.
MS(C). Bombardier Derby 2015–19. –/49(+3). 31.4 t.
MS(D). Bombardier Derby 2015–19. –/46(+6). 37.2 t.

PMS(B). Bombardier Derby 2015–19. –/46(+6). 37.1 t.
DMS(B). Bombardier Derby 2015–19. –/46. 39.0 t.

345001	**XR**	RF	*EL*	OC	340101	340201	340301	340401	340501
					340601	340701	340801	340901	
345002	**XR**	RF	*EL*	OC	340102	340202	340302	340402	340502
					340602	340702	340802	340902	
345003	**XR**	RF	*EL*	OC	340103	340203	340303	340403	340503
					340603	340703	340803	340903	
345004	**XR**	RF	*EL*	OC	340104	340204	340304	340404	340504
					340604	340704	340804	340904	
345005	**XR**	RF	*EL*	OC	340105	340205	340305	340405	340505
					340605	340705	340805	340905	
345006	**XR**	RF	*EL*	OC	340106	340206	340306	340406	340506
					340606	340706	340806	340906	
345007	**XR**	RF	*EL*	OC	340107	340207	340307	340407	340507
					340607	340707	340807	340907	
345008	**XR**	RF	*EL*	OC	340108	340208	340308	340408	340508
					340608	340708	340808	340908	
345009	**XR**	RF	*EL*	OC	340109	340209	340309	340409	340509
					340609	340709	340809	340909	
345010	**XR**	RF	*EL*	OC	340110	340210	340310	340410	340510
					340610	340710	340810	340910	
345011	**XR**	RF	*EL*	OC	340111	340211	340311	340411	340511
					340611	340711	340811	340911	
345012	**XR**	RF	*EL*	OC	340112	340212	340312	340412	340512
					340612	340712	340812	340912	
345013	**XR**	RF	*EL*	OC	340113	340213	340313	340413	340513
					340613	340713	340813	340913	
345014	**XR**	RF	*EL*	OC	340114	340214	340314	340414	340514
					340614	340714	340814	340914	
345015	**XR**	RF	*EL*	OC	340115	340215	340315	340415	340515
					340615	340715	340815	340915	
345016	**XR**	RF	*EL*	OC	340116	340216	340316	340416	340516
					340616	340716	340816	340916	
345017	**XR**	RF	*EL*	OC	340117	340217	340317	340417	340517
					340617	340717	340817	340917	
345018	**XR**	RF	*EL*	OC	340118	340218	340318	340418	340518
					340618	340718	340818	340918	
345019	**XR**	RF	*EL*	OC	340119	340219	340319	340419	340519
					340619	340719	340819	340919	
345020	**XR**	RF	*EL*	OC	340120	340220	340320	340420	340520
					340620	340720	340820	340920	
345021	**XR**	RF	*EL*	OC	340121	340221	340321	340421	340521
					340621	340721	340821	340921	
345022	**XR**	RF	*EL*	OC	340122	340222	340322	340422	340522
					340622	340722	340822	340922	
345023	**XR**	RF	*EL*	OC	340123	340223	340323	340423	340523
					340623	340723	340823	340923	
345024	**XR**	RF	*EL*	OC	340124	340224	340324	340424	340524
					340624	340724	340824	340924	

345 025	**XR**	RF	*EL*	OC	340125	340225	340325	340425	340525
					340625	340725	340825	340925	
345 026	**XR**	RF	*EL*	OC	340126	340226	340326	340426	340526
					340626	340726	340826	340926	
345 027	**XR**	RF	*EL*	OC	340127	340227	340327	340427	340527
					340627	340727	340827	340927	
345 028	**XR**	RF	*EL*	OC	340128	340228	340328	340428	340528
					340628	340728	340828	340928	
345 029	**XR**	RF	*EL*	OC	340129	340229	340329	340429	340529
					340629	340729	340829	340929	
345 030	**XR**	RF	*EL*	OC	340130	340230	340330	340430	340530
					340630	340730	340830	340930	
345 031	**XR**	RF	*EL*	OC	340131	340231	340331	340431	340531
					340631	340731	340831	340931	
345 032	**XR**	RF	*EL*	OC	340132	340232	340332	340432	340532
					340632	340732	340832	340932	
345 033	**XR**	RF	*EL*	OC	340133	340233	340333	340433	340533
					340633	340733	340833	340933	
345 034	**XR**	RF	*EL*	OC	340134	340234	340334	340434	340534
					340634	340734	340834	340934	
345 035	**XR**	RF	*EL*	OC	340135	340235	340335	340435	340535
					340635	340735	340835	340935	
345 036	**XR**	RF	*EL*	OC	340136	340236	340336	340436	340536
					340636	340736	340836	340936	
345 037	**XR**	RF	*EL*	OC	340137	340237	340337	340437	340537
					340637	340737	340837	340937	
345 038	**XR**	RF	*EL*	OC	340138	340238	340338	340438	340538
					340638	340738	340838	340938	
345 039	**XR**	RF	*EL*	OC	340139	340239	340339	340439	340539
					340639	340739	340839	340939	
345 040	**XR**	RF	*EL*	OC	340140	340240	340340	340440	340540
					340640	340740	340840	340940	
345 041	**XR**	RF	*EL*	OC	340141	340241	340341	340441	340541
					340641	340741	340841	340941	
345 042	**XR**	RF	*EL*	OC	340142	340242	340342	340442	340542
					340642	340742	340842	340942	
345 043	**XR**	RF	*EL*	OC	340143	340243	340343	340443	340543
					340643	340743	340843	340943	
345 044	**XR**	RF	*EL*	OC	340144	340244	340344	340444	340544
					340644	340744	340844	340944	
345 045	**XR**	RF	*EL*	OC	340145	340245	340345	340445	340545
					340645	340745	340845	340945	
345 046	**XR**	RF	*EL*	OC	340146	340246	340346	340446	340546
					340646	340746	340846	340946	
345 047	**XR**	RF	*EL*	OC	340147	340247	340347	340447	340547
					340647	340747	340847	340947	
345 048	**XR**	RF	*EL*	OC	340148	340248	340348	340448	340548
					340648	340748	340848	340948	
345 049	**XR**	RF	*EL*	OC	340149	340249	340349	340449	340549
					340649	340749	340849	340949	

345050	**XR**	RF	*EL*	OC	340150	340250	340350	340450	340550
					340650	340750	340850	340950	
345051	**XR**	RF	*EL*	OC	340151	340251	340351	340451	340551
					340651	340751	340851	340951	
345052	**XR**	RF	*EL*	OC	340152	340252	340352	340452	340552
					340652	340752	340852	340952	
345053	**XR**	RF	*EL*	OC	340153	340253	340353	340453	340553
					340653	340753	340853	340953	
345054	**XR**	RF	*EL*	OC	340154	340254	340354	340454	340554
					340654	340754	340854	340954	
345055	**0**	RF	*EL*	OC	340155	340255	340355	340455	340555
					340655	340755	340855	340955	
345056	**XR**	RF	*EL*	OC	340156	340256	340356	340456	340556
					340656	340756	340856	340956	
345057	**XR**	RF	*EL*	OC	340157	340257	340357	340457	340557
					340657	340757	340857	340957	
345058	**XR**	RF	*EL*	OC	340158	340258	340358	340458	340558
					340658	340758	340858	340958	
345059	**XR**	RF	*EL*	OC	340159	340259	340359	340459	340559
					340659	340759	340859	340959	
345060	**XR**	RF	*EL*	OC	340160	340260	340360	340460	340560
					340660	340760	340860	340960	
345061	**XR**	RF	*EL*	OC	340161	340261	340361	340461	340561
					340661	340761	340861	340961	
345062	**XR**	RF	*EL*	OC	340162	340262	340362	340462	340562
					340662	340762	340862	340962	
345063	**XR**	RF	*EL*	OC	340163	340263	340363	340463	340563
					340663	340763	340863	340963	
345064	**XR**	RF	*EL*	OC	340164	340264	340364	340464	340564
					340664	340764	340864	340964	
345065	**XR**	RF	*EL*	OC	340165	340265	340365	340465	340565
					340665	340765	340865	340965	
345066	**XR**	RF	*EL*	OC	340166	340266	340366	340466	340566
					340666	340766	340866	340966	
345067	**XR**	RF	*EL*	OC	340167	340267	340367	340467	340567
					340667	340767	340867	340967	
345068	**XR**	RF	*EL*	OC	340168	340268	340368	340468	340568
					340668	340768	340868	340968	
345069	**XR**	RF	*EL*	OC	340169	340269	340369	340469	340569
					340669	340769	340869	340969	
345070	**XR**	RF	*EL*	OC	340170	340270	340370	340470	340570
					340670	340770	340870	340970	

Names:

345004	Andy Byford
345024	Heidi Alexander

CLASS 350   DESIRO UK   SIEMENS

Outer suburban and long distance units. All now Standard Class only.

Formation: DMC–TC–PTS–DMC.
Systems: 25 kV AC overhead (350/1s built with 750 V DC, but equipment currently decommissioned).
Construction: Welded aluminium.
Traction Motors: 4 Siemens 1TB2016-0GB02 asynchronous of 250 kW.
Wheel Arrangement: Bo-Bo + 2-2 + 2-2 + Bo-Bo.
Braking: Disc & regenerative.   **Dimensions:** 20.34 x 2.79 m.
Bogies: SGP SF5000.   **Couplers:** Dellner 12.
Gangways: Throughout.   **Control System:** IGBT Inverter.
Doors: Sliding plug.   **Maximum Speed:** 110 mph.
Heating & ventilation: Air conditioning.
Seating Layout: Various, see sub-class headings.
Multiple Working: Within class.

Class 350/1. Original-build units owned by Angel Trains. Formerly part of an aborted South West Trains 5-car Class 450/2 order. 2+2 seating.

Seating Layout: 2+2 facing/unidirectional.

Advertising liveries:

350 104 Eurovision (various colours).
350 108 Anti-trespass rail safety (pink/blue – vehicle 63768).

DMS(A). Siemens Krefeld 2004–05. –/60. 48.7 t.
TC. Siemens Krefeld/Prague 2004–05. –/56 1T. 36.2 t.
PTS. Siemens Krefeld/Prague 2004–05. –/50(+9) 1TD 2W. 45.2 t.
DMS(B). Siemens Krefeld 2004–05. –/60. 49.2 t.

350 101	**LN**	A	*WM*	NN	63761	66811	66861	63711
350 102	**LN**	A	*WM*	NN	63762	66812	66862	63712
350 103	**LN**	A	*WM*	NN	63765	66813	66863	63713
350 104	**AL**	A	*WM*	NN	63764	66814	66864	63714
350 105	**LN**	A	*WM*	NN	63763	66815	66865	63715
350 106	**LN**	A	*WM*	NN	63766	66816	66866	63716
350 107	**LN**	A	*WM*	NN	63767	66817	66867	63717
350 108	**AL**	A	*WM*	NN	63768	66818	66865	63718
350 109	**LN**	A	*WM*	NN	63769	66819	66869	63719
350 110	**LN**	A	*WM*	NN	63770	66820	66870	63720
350 111	**LN**	A	*WM*	NN	63771	66821	66871	63721
350 112	**LN**	A	*WM*	NN	63772	66822	66872	63722
350 113	**LN**	A	*WM*	NN	63773	66823	66873	63723
350 114	**LN**	A	*WM*	NN	63774	66824	66874	63724
350 115	**LN**	A	*WM*	NN	63775	66825	66875	63725
350 116	**LN**	A	*WM*	NN	63776	66826	66876	63726
350 117	**LN**	A	*WM*	NN	63777	66827	66877	63727
350 118	**LN**	A	*WM*	NN	63778	66828	66878	63728
350 119	**LN**	A	*WM*	NN	63779	66829	66879	63729
350 120	**LN**	A	*WM*	NN	63780	66830	66880	63730
350 121	**LN**	A	*WM*	NN	63781	66831	66881	63731

350 122	**LN**	A	*WM*	NN	63782	66832	66882	63732
350 123	**LN**	A	*WM*	NN	63783	66833	66883	63733
350 124	**LN**	A	*WM*	NN	63784	66834	66884	63734
350 125	**LN**	A	*WM*	NN	63785	66835	66885	63735
350 126	**LN**	A	*WM*	NN	63786	66836	66886	63736
350 127	**LN**	A	*WM*	NN	63787	66837	66887	63737
350 128	**LN**	A	*WM*	NN	63788	66838	66888	63738
350 129	**LN**	A	*WM*	NN	63789	66839	66889	63739
350 130	**LN**	A	*WM*	NN	63790	66840	66890	63740

Class 350/2. Owned by Porterbrook Leasing.

Seating Layout: 3+2 facing/unidirectional (former First Class area 2+2).

350 233/246/264 are running with misformed formations, as shown.

DMS(A). Siemens Krefeld 2008–09. –/70. 43.7 t.
TC. Siemens Prague 2008–09. /66 1T. 35.3 t.
PTS. Siemens Prague 2008–09. –/61(+9) 1TD 2W. 42.9 t.
DMS(B). Siemens Krefeld 2008–09. –/70. 44.2 t.

350 231	**LI**	P	*WM*	NN	61431	65231	67531	61531
350 232	**LI**	P	*WM*	NN	61432	65232	67532	61532
350 233	**LM**	P	*WM*	NN	61433	65233	67533	61546
350 234	**LI**	P	*WM*	NN	61434	65234	67534	61534
350 235	**LM**	P	*WM*	NN	61435	65235	67535	61535
350 236	**LM**	P	*WM*	NN	61436	65236	67536	61536
350 237	**LM**	P	*WM*	NN	61437	65237	67537	61537
350 238	**LM**	P	*WM*	NN	61438	65238	67538	61538
350 239	**LI**	P	*WM*	NN	61439	65239	67539	61539
350 240	**LI**	P	*WM*	NN	61440	65240	67540	61540
350 241	**LM**	P	*WM*	NN	61441	65241	67541	61541
350 242	**LM**	P	*WM*	NN	61442	65242	67542	61542
350 243	**LM**	P	*WM*	NN	61443	65243	67543	61543
350 244	**LI**	P	*WM*	NN	61444	65244	67544	61544
350 245	**LI**	P	*WM*	NN	61445	65245	67545	61545
350 246	**LM**	P	*WM*	NN	61446	65246	67546	61564
350 247	**LM**	P	*WM*	NN	61447	65247	67547	61547
350 248	**LM**	P	*WM*	NN	61448	65248	67548	61548
350 249	**LM**	P	*WM*	NN	61449	65249	67549	61549
350 250	**LM**	P	*WM*	NN	61450	65250	67550	61550
350 251	**LM**	P	*WM*	NN	61451	65251	67551	61551
350 252	**LI**	P	*WM*	NN	61452	65252	67552	61552
350 253	**LI**	P	*WM*	NN	61453	65253	67553	61553
350 254	**LI**	P	*WM*	NN	61454	65254	67554	61554
350 255	**LM**	P	*WM*	NN	61455	65255	67555	61555
350 256	**LM**	P	*WM*	NN	61456	65256	67556	61556
350 257	**LI**	P	*WM*	NN	61457	65257	67557	61557
350 258	**LI**	P	*WM*	NN	61458	65258	67558	61558
350 259	**LI**	P	*WM*	NN	61459	65259	67559	61559
350 260	**LM**	P	*WM*	NN	61460	65260	67560	61560
350 261	**LM**	P	*WM*	NN	61461	65261	67561	61561
350 262	**LI**	P	*WM*	NN	61462	65262	67562	61562

350263	**LI**	P	*WM*	NN	61463	65263	67563	61563
350264	**LM**	P	*WM*	NN	61464	65264	67564	61533
350265	**LM**	P	*WM*	NN	61465	65265	67565	61565
350266	**LM**	P	*WM*	NN	61466	65266	67566	61566
350267	**LI**	P	*WM*	NN	61467	65267	67567	61567

Class 350/3. Owned by Angel Trains.

Seating Layout: 2+2 facing/unidirectional.

DMS(A). Siemens Krefeld 2014. –/60. 44.2 t.
TC. Siemens Krefeld 2014. –/60 1T. 36.3 t.
PTS. Siemens Krefeld 2014. –/50(+9) 1TD 2W. 44.0 t.
DMS(B). Siemens Krefeld 2014. –/60. 45.0 t.

350368	**LN**	A	*WM*	NN	60141	60511	60651	60151
350369	**LN**	A	*WM*	NN	60142	60512	60652	60152
350370	**LN**	A	*WM*	NN	60143	60513	60653	60153
350371	**LN**	A	*WM*	NN	60144	60514	60654	60154
350372	**LN**	A	*WM*	NN	60145	60515	60655	60155
350373	**LN**	A	*WM*	NN	60146	60516	60656	60156
350374	**LN**	A	*WM*	NN	60147	60517	60657	60157
350375	**LN**	A	*WM*	NN	60148	60518	60658	60158
350376	**LN**	A	*WM*	NN	60149	60519	60659	60159
350377	**LN**	A	*WM*	NN	60150	60520	60660	60160

Names (carried on one side of PTS):

350375 Vic Hall | 350377 Graham Taylor OBE

Class 350/4. Owned by Angel Trains. Previously operated by TransPennine Express before transfer to West Midlands Trains in 2019–20.

Seating Layout: 2+2 facing/unidirectional.

DMS(A). Siemens Krefeld 2013–14. –/56. 44.2 t.
TC. Siemens Krefeld 2013–14. –/48 1T. 36.2 t.
PTS. Siemens Krefeld 2013–14. –/42 1TD 1T. 44.6 t.
DMS(B). Siemens Krefeld 2013–14. –/56. 45.0 t.

350401	**LN**	A	*WM*	NN	60691	60901	60941	60671
350402	**LN**	A	*WM*	NN	60692	60902	60942	60672
350403	**LN**	A	*WM*	NN	60693	60903	60943	60673
350404	**LN**	A	*WM*	NN	60694	60904	60944	60674
350405	**LN**	A	*WM*	NN	60695	60905	60945	60675
350406	**LN**	A	*WM*	NN	60696	60906	60946	60676
350407	**LN**	A	*WM*	NN	60697	60907	60947	60677
350408	**LN**	A	*WM*	NN	60698	60908	60948	60678
350409	**LN**	A	*WM*	NN	60699	60909	60949	60679
350410	**LN**	A	*WM*	NN	60700	60910	60950	60680

CLASS 357 ELECTROSTAR
ADTRANZ/BOMBARDIER DERBY

Provision for 750 V DC supply if required.

Formation: DMS–MS–PTS–DMS.
Construction: Welded aluminium alloy underframe, sides and roof with steel ends. All sections bolted together.
Traction Motors: Two Adtranz asynchronous of 250 kW.
Wheel Arrangement: 2-Bo + 2-Bo + 2-2 + Bo-2.
Braking: Disc & regenerative.   **Dimensions:** 20.40/19.99 x 2.80 m.
Bogies: Adtranz P3-25/T3-25.   **Couplers:** Tightlock.
Gangways: Within unit.   **Control System:** IGBT Inverter.
Doors: Sliding plug.   **Maximum Speed:** 100 mph.
Heating & ventilation: Air conditioning.
Seating Layout: 3+2 facing/unidirectional.
Multiple Working: Within class.

Class 357/0. Owned by Porterbrook Leasing.

Advertising liveries:

357 008 Gold Geese (yellow).
357 016 British Transport Police Guardian app (dark blue).

DMS(A). Adtranz Derby 1999–2001. –/71. 40.7 t.
MS. Adtranz Derby 1999–2001. –/78. 36.7 t.
PTS. Adtranz Derby 1999–2001. –/58(+4) 1TD 2W. 39.5 t.
DMS(B). Adtranz Derby 1999–2001. –/71. 40.7 t.

357 001	C2	P	C2	EM	67651	74151	74051	67751
357 002	C2	P	C2	EM	67652	74152	74052	67752
357 003	C2	P	C2	EM	67653	74153	74053	67753
357 004	C2	P	C2	EM	67654	74154	74054	67754
357 005	C2	P	C2	EM	67655	74155	74055	67755
357 006	C2	P	C2	EM	67656	74156	74056	67756
357 007	C2	P	C2	EM	67657	74157	74057	67757
357 008	AL	P	C2	EM	67658	74158	74058	67758
357 009	C2	P	C2	EM	67659	74159	74059	67759
357 010	C2	P	C2	EM	67660	74160	74060	67760
357 011	C2	P	C2	EM	67661	74161	74061	67761
357 012	C2	P	C2	EM	67662	74162	74062	67762
357 013	C2	P	C2	EM	67663	74163	74063	67763
357 014	C2	P	C2	EM	67664	74164	74064	67764
357 015	C2	P	C2	EM	67665	74165	74065	67765
357 016	AL	P	C2	EM	67666	74166	74066	67766
357 017	C2	P	C2	EM	67667	74167	74067	67767
357 018	C2	P	C2	EM	67668	74168	74068	67768
357 019	C2	P	C2	EM	67669	74169	74069	67769
357 020	C2	P	C2	EM	67670	74170	74070	67770
357 021	C2	P	C2	EM	67671	74171	74071	67771
357 022	C2	P	C2	EM	67672	74172	74072	67772

357 023	**C2**	P	*C2*	EM	67673	74173	74073	67773
357 024	**C2**	P	*C2*	EM	67674	74174	74074	67774
357 025	**C2**	P	*C2*	EM	67675	74175	74075	67775
357 026	**C2**	P	*C2*	EM	67676	74176	74076	67776
357 027	**C2**	P	*C2*	EM	67677	74177	74077	67777
357 028	**C2**	P	*C2*	EM	67678	74178	74078	67778
357 029	**C2**	P	*C2*	EM	67679	74179	74079	67779
357 030	**C2**	P	*C2*	EM	67680	74180	74080	67780
357 031	**C2**	P	*C2*	EM	67681	74181	74081	67781
357 032	**C2**	P	*C2*	EM	67682	74182	74082	67782
357 033	**C2**	P	*C2*	EM	67683	74183	74083	67783
357 034	**C2**	P	*C2*	EM	67684	74184	74084	67784
357 035	**C2**	P	*C2*	EM	67685	74185	74085	67785
357 036	**C2**	P	*C2*	EM	67686	74186	74086	67786
357 037	**C2**	P	*C2*	EM	67687	74187	74087	67787
357 038	**C2**	P	*C2*	EM	67688	74188	74088	67788
357 039	**C2**	P	*C2*	EM	67689	74189	74089	67789
357 040	**C2**	P	*C2*	EM	67690	74190	74090	67790
357 041	**C2**	P	*C2*	EM	67691	74191	74091	67791
357 042	**C2**	P	*C2*	EM	67692	74192	74092	67792
357 043	**C2**	P	*C2*	EM	67693	74193	74093	67793
357 044	**C2**	P	*C2*	EM	67694	74194	74094	67794
357 045	**C2**	P	*C2*	EM	67695	74195	74095	67795
357 046	**C2**	P	*C2*	EM	67696	74196	74096	67796

Names (carried on DMS(A) and DMS(B) (one plate on each)):

357 001   BARRY FLAXMAN
357 002   ARTHUR LEWIS STRIDE 1841–1922
357 003   SOUTHEND city.on.sea
357 004   TONY AMOS
357 005   SOUTHEND: 2017 Alternative City of Culture
357 006   DIAMOND JUBILEE 1952–2012
357 007   Sir Andrew Foster
357 011   JOHN LOWING
357 018   Remembering our Fallen 88 1914–1918
357 028   London, Tilbury & Southend Railway 1854–2004
357 029   THOMAS WHITELEGG 1840–1922
357 030   ROBERT HARBEN WHITELEGG 1871–1957

Class 357/2. Owned by Angel Trains.

DMS(A). Bombardier Derby 2001–02. –/71. 40.7 t.
MS. Bombardier Derby 2001–02. –/78. 36.7 t.
PTS. Bombardier Derby 2001–02. –/58(+4) 1TD 2W. 39.5 t.
DMS(B). Bombardier Derby 2001–02. –/71. 40.7 t.

357 201	**C2**	A	*C2*	EM	68601	74701	74601	68701
357 202	**C2**	A	*C2*	EM	68602	74702	74602	68702
357 203	**C2**	A	*C2*	EM	68603	74703	74603	68703
357 204	**C2**	A	*C2*	EM	68604	74704	74604	68704
357 205	**C2**	A	*C2*	EM	68605	74705	74605	68705
357 206	**C2**	A	*C2*	EM	68606	74706	74606	68706

357 207	**C2**	A	*C2*	EM	68607	74707	74607	68707
357 208	**C2**	A	*C2*	EM	68608	74708	74608	68708
357 209	**C2**	A	*C2*	EM	68609	74709	74609	68709
357 210	**C2**	A	*C2*	EM	68610	74710	74610	68710
357 211	**C2**	A	*C2*	EM	68611	74711	74611	68711

Names (carried on DMS(A) and DMS(B) (one plate on each)):

357 201	KEN BIRD	357 206	MARTIN AUNGIER
357 202	KENNY MITCHELL	357 207	JOHN PAGE
357 203	HENRY PUMFRETT	357 208	DAVE DAVIS
357 204	DEREK FOWERS	357 209	JAMES SNELLING
357 205	JOHN D'SILVA		

Class 357/3. Owned by Angel Trains. In 2015–16 17 Class 357/2s (357 212–228) were reconfigured as "high density" units 357 312–328 with fewer seats and more standing room for shorter distance workings.

Seating Layout: 2+2 facing/unidirectional.

DMS(A). Bombardier Derby 2001–02. –/56. 40.7 t.
MS. Bombardier Derby 2001–02. –/60. 36.7 t.
PTS. Bombardier Derby 2001–02. –/50 1TD 2W. 39.5 t.
DMS(B). Bombardier Derby 2001–02. –/56. 40.7 t.

357 312	(357 212)	**C2**	A	*C2*	EM	68612	74712	74612	68712
357 313	(357 213)	**C2**	A	*C2*	EM	68613	74713	74613	68713
357 314	(357 214)	**C2**	A	*C2*	EM	68614	74714	74614	68714
357 315	(357 215)	**C2**	A	*C2*	EM	68615	74715	74615	68715
357 316	(357 216)	**C2**	A	*C2*	EM	68616	74716	74616	68716
357 317	(357 217)	**C2**	A	*C2*	EM	68617	74717	74617	68717
357 318	(357 218)	**C2**	A	*C2*	EM	68618	74718	74618	68718
357 319	(357 219)	**C2**	A	*C2*	EM	68619	74719	74619	68719
357 320	(357 220)	**C2**	A	*C2*	EM	68620	74720	74620	68720
357 321	(357 221)	**C2**	A	*C2*	EM	68621	74721	74621	68721
357 322	(357 222)	**C2**	A	*C2*	EM	68622	74722	74622	68722
357 323	(357 223)	**C2**	A	*C2*	EM	68623	74723	74623	68723
357 324	(357 224)	**C2**	A	*C2*	EM	68624	74724	74624	68724
357 325	(357 225)	**C2**	A	*C2*	EM	68625	74725	74625	68725
357 326	(357 226)	**C2**	A	*C2*	EM	68626	74726	74626	68726
357 327	(357 227)	**C2**	A	*C2*	EM	68627	74727	74627	68727
357 328	(357 228)	**C2**	A	*C2*	EM	68628	74728	74628	68728

Names (carried on DMS(A) and DMS(B) (one plate on each)):

357 313 UPMINSTER I.E.C.C.
357 317 ALLAN BURNELL
357 327 SOUTHEND UNITED

CLASS 360/0   DESIRO UK   SIEMENS

Outer suburban/express units. Originally operated by Greater Anglia, then transferred to East Midlands Railway to operate services between London St Pancras and Corby from May 2021.

Formation: DMC–PTS–TS–DMC.
Construction: Welded aluminium.
Traction Motors: Four Siemens 1TB2016-0GB02 asynchronous of 250 kW.
Wheel Arrangement: Bo-Bo + 2-2 + 2-2 + Bo-Bo.
Braking: Disc & regenerative.   **Dimensions:** 20.34 x 2.80 m.
Bogies: SGP SF5000.   **Couplers:** Dellner 12.
Gangways: Within unit.   **Control System:** IGBT Inverter.
Doors: Sliding plug.   **Maximum Speed:** 100 mph.
Heating & ventilation: Air conditioning.
Seating Layout: 1: 2+2 facing, 2: 3+2 facing/unidirectional.
Multiple Working: Within class.

DMC(A). Siemens Krefeld 2002–03. 8/59. 45.0 t.
PTS. Siemens Vienna 2002–03. –/60(+9) 1TD 2W. 43.6 t.
TS. Siemens Vienna 2002–03. –/78. 34.3 t.
DMC(B). Siemens Krefeld 2002–03. 8/59. 44.1 t.

360 101	**ER**	A	*EM*	BF	65551	72551	74551	68551
360 102	**ER**	A	*EM*	BF	65552	72552	74552	68552
360 103	**ER**	A	*EM*	BF	65553	72553	74553	68553
360 104	**ER**	A	*EM*	BF	65554	72554	74554	68554
360 105	**ER**	A	*EM*	BF	65555	72555	74555	68555
360 106	**ER**	A	*EM*	BF	65556	72556	74556	68556
360 107	**ER**	A	*EM*	BF	65557	72557	74557	68557
360 108	**ER**	A	*EM*	BF	65558	72558	74558	68558
360 109	**ER**	A	*EM*	BF	65559	72559	74559	68559
360 110	**ER**	A	*EM*	BF	65560	72560	74560	68560
360 111	**ER**	A	*EM*	BF	65561	72561	74561	68561
360 112	**ER**	A	*EM*	BF	65562	72562	74562	68562
360 113	**ER**	A	*EM*	BF	65563	72563	74563	68563
360 114	**ER**	A	*EM*	BF	65564	72564	74564	68564
360 115	**ER**	A	*EM*	BF	65565	72565	74565	68565
360 116	**ER**	A	*EM*	BF	65566	72566	74566	68566
360 117	**ER**	A	*EM*	BF	65567	72567	74567	68567
360 118	**ER**	A	*EM*	BF	65568	72568	74568	68568
360 119	**ER**	A	*EM*	BF	65569	72569	74569	68569
360 120	**ER**	A	*EM*	BF	65570	72570	74570	68570
360 121	**ER**	A	*EM*	BF	65571	72571	74571	68571

CLASS 360/2   DESIRO UK   SIEMENS

4-car Class 350 testbed units rebuilt for use by Heathrow Express on "Heathrow Connect" stopping services. The five Class 360/2s were stored in 2020, their duties having been taken over by Class 345s. 360 204/205 were scrapped in 2022 and 360 201–203 were sold to the Global Centre of Rail Excellence (GCRE) for use as test train units at the planned new test centre in South Wales.

Formation: DMS–PTS–TS–TS–DMS.
Construction: Welded aluminium.
Traction Motors: Four Siemens 1TB2016-0GB02 asynchronous of 250 kW.
Wheel Arrangement: Bo-Bo + 2-2 + 2-2 + 2-2 + Bo-Bo.
Braking: Disc & regenerative.   **Dimensions:** 20.34 x 2.80 m.
Bogies: SGP SF5000.   **Couplers:** Dellner 12.
Gangways: Within unit.   **Control System:** IGBT Inverter.
Doors: Sliding plug.   **Maximum Speed:** 100 mph.
Heating & ventilation: Air conditioning.
Seating Layout: 3+2 facing/unidirectional.
Multiple Working: Within class.

DMS(A). Siemens Krefeld 2002–06. –/63). 44.8 t.
PTS. Siemens Krefeld 2002–06. –/57(+9) 1TD 2W. 44.2 t.
TS(A). Siemens Krefeld 2005–06. –/74. 35.3 t.
TS(B). Siemens Krefeld 2002–06. –/74. 34.1 t.
DMS(B). Siemens Krefeld 2002–06. –/63. 44.4 t.

360 201	**HC**	GR	BR	78431	63421	72431	72421	78441
360 202	**HC**	GR	BR	78432	63422	72432	72422	78442
360 203	**HC**	GR	BR	78433	63423	72433	72423	78443

CLASS 375 ELECTROSTAR
ADTRANZ/BOMBARDIER DERBY

Express and outer suburban units. Southeastern declassified all First Class in its Class 375 units in 2022.

Formation: Various, see sub-class headings.
Systems: 25 kV AC overhead/750 V DC third rail (some third rail only with provision for retro-fitting of AC equipment).
Construction: Welded aluminium alloy underframe, sides and roof with steel ends. All sections bolted together.
Traction Motors: Two Adtranz asynchronous of 250 kW.
Wheel Arrangement: 2-Bo (+ 2-Bo) + 2-2 + Bo-2.
Braking: Disc & regenerative.   **Dimensions:** 20.40/19.99 x 2.80 m.
Bogies: Adtranz P3-25/T3-25.   **Couplers:** Dellner 12.
Gangways: Throughout.   **Control System:** IGBT Inverter.
Doors: Sliding plug.   **Maximum Speed:** 100 mph.
Heating & ventilation: Air conditioning.
Seating Layout: 2+2 facing/unidirectional (375/9: 3+2 facing/unidirectional).
Multiple Working: Within class and with Classes 376, 377, 378 and 379.

Class 375/3. Express units. 750 V DC only. DMS–TS–DMS.

DMS(A). Bombardier Derby 2001–02. –/60. 43.8 t.
TS. Bombardier Derby 2001–02. –/56 1TD 2W. 35.5 t.
DMS(B). Bombardier Derby 2001–02. –/60. 43.8 t.

375301	**SB**	E	*SE*	RM	67921	74351	67931
375302	**SB**	E	*SE*	RM	67922	74352	67932
375303	**SB**	E	*SE*	RM	67923	74353	67933
375304	**SB**	E	*SE*	RM	67924	74354	67934
375305	**SB**	E	*SE*	RM	67925	74355	67935
375306	**SB**	E	*SE*	RM	67926	74356	67936
375307	**SB**	E	*SE*	RM	67927	74357	67937
375308	**SB**	E	*SE*	RM	67928	74358	67938
375309	**SB**	E	*SE*	RM	67929	74359	67939
375310	**SB**	E	*SE*	RM	67930	74360	67940

Class 375/6. Express units. 25 kV AC/750 V DC. DMS–MS–PTS–DMS.

DMS(A). Adtranz Derby 1999–2001. –/60. 46.2 t.
MS. Adtranz Derby 1999–2001. –/66 1T. 40.5 t.
PTS. Adtranz Derby 1999–2001. –/56 1TD 2W. 40.7 t.
DMS(B). Adtranz Derby 1999–2001. –/60. 46.2 t.

375601	**SB**	E	*SE*	RM	67801	74251	74201	67851
375602	**SB**	E	*SE*	RM	67802	74252	74202	67852
375603	**SB**	E	*SE*	RM	67803	74253	74203	67853
375604	**SB**	E	*SE*	RM	67804	74254	74204	67854
375605	**SB**	E	*SE*	RM	67805	74255	74205	67855
375606	**SB**	E	*SE*	RM	67806	74256	74206	67856
375607	**SB**	E	*SE*	RM	67807	74257	74207	67857
375608	**SB**	E	*SE*	RM	67808	74258	74208	67858
375609	**SB**	E	*SE*	RM	67809	74259	74209	67859
375610	**SB**	E	*SE*	RM	67810	74260	74210	67860
375611	**SB**	E	*SE*	RM	67811	74261	74211	67861
375612	**SB**	E	*SE*	RM	67812	74262	74212	67862
375613	**SB**	E	*SE*	RM	67813	74263	74213	67863
375614	**SB**	E	*SE*	RM	67814	74264	74214	67864
375615	**SB**	E	*SE*	RM	67815	74265	74215	67865
375616	**SB**	E	*SE*	RM	67816	74266	74216	67866
375617	**SB**	E	*SE*	RM	67817	74267	74217	67867
375618	**SB**	E	*SE*	RM	67818	74268	74218	67868
375619	**SB**	E	*SE*	RM	67819	74269	74219	67869
375620	**SB**	E	*SE*	RM	67820	74270	74220	67870
375621	**SB**	E	*SE*	RM	67821	74271	74221	67871
375622	**SB**	E	*SE*	RM	67822	74272	74222	67872
375623	**SB**	E	*SE*	RM	67823	74273	74223	67873
375624	**SB**	E	*SE*	RM	67824	74274	74224	67874
375625	**SB**	E	*SE*	RM	67825	74275	74225	67875
375626	**SB**	E	*SE*	RM	67826	74276	74226	67876
375627	**SB**	E	*SE*	RM	67827	74277	74227	67877
375628	**SB**	E	*SE*	RM	67828	74278	74228	67878
375629	**SB**	E	*SE*	RM	67829	74279	74229	67879
375630	**SB**	E	*SE*	RM	67830	74280	74230	67880

Names (carried on one side of each MS or TS):

375619 Driver John Neve | 375623 Hospice in the Weald

Class 375/7. Express units. 750 V DC only. DMS–MS–TS–DMS.

DMS(A). Bombardier Derby 2001–02. –/60. 43.8 t.
MS. Bombardier Derby 2001–02. –/66 1T. 36.4 t.
TS. Bombardier Derby 2001–02. –/56 1TD 2W. 34.1 t.
DMS(B). Bombardier Derby 2001–02. –/60. 43.8 t.

375701	**SB**	E	*SE*	RM	67831	74281	74231	67881
375702	**SB**	E	*SE*	RM	67832	74282	74232	67882
375703	**SB**	E	*SE*	RM	67833	74283	74233	67883
375704	**SB**	E	*SE*	RM	67834	74284	74234	67884
375705	**SB**	E	*SE*	RM	67835	74285	74235	67885
375706	**SB**	E	*SE*	RM	67836	74286	74236	67886
375707	**SB**	E	*SE*	RM	67837	74287	74237	67887
375708	**SB**	E	*SE*	RM	67838	74288	74238	67888
375709	**SB**	E	*SE*	RM	67839	74289	74239	67889
375710	**SB**	E	*SE*	RM	67840	74290	74240	67890
375711	**SB**	E	*SE*	RM	67841	74291	74241	67891
375712	**SB**	E	*SE*	RM	67842	74292	74242	67892
375713	**SB**	E	*SE*	RM	67843	74293	74243	67893
375714	**SB**	E	*SE*	RM	67844	74294	74244	67894
375715	**SB**	E	*SE*	RM	67845	74295	74245	67895

Names (carried on one side of each MS or TS):

375701 Kent Air Ambulance Explorer | 375714   Rochester Cathedral
375710 Rochester Castle

Class 375/8. Express units. 750 V DC only. DMS–MS–TS–DMS.

375801–820 are fitted with de-icing equipment. TS weighs 36.5 t.

DMS(A). Bombardier Derby 2004. –/60. 43.3 t.
MS. Bombardier Derby 2004. –/66 1T. 39.8 t.
TS. Bombardier Derby 2004. –/52 1TD 2W. 35.9 t.
DMS(B). Bombardier Derby 2004. –/64. 43.3 t.

375801	**SB**	E	*SE*	RM	73301	79001	78201	73701
375802	**SB**	E	*SE*	RM	73302	79002	78202	73702
375803	**SB**	E	*SE*	RM	73303	79003	78203	73703
375804	**SB**	E	*SE*	RM	73304	79004	78204	73704
375805	**SB**	E	*SE*	RM	73305	79005	78205	73705
375806	**SB**	E	*SE*	RM	73306	79006	78206	73706
375807	**SB**	E	*SE*	RM	73307	79007	78207	73707
375808	**SB**	E	*SE*	RM	73308	79008	78208	73708
375809	**SB**	E	*SE*	RM	73309	79009	78209	73709
375810	**SB**	E	*SE*	RM	73310	79010	78210	73710
375811	**SB**	E	*SE*	RM	73311	79011	78211	73711
375812	**SB**	E	*SE*	RM	73312	79012	78212	73712
375813	**SB**	E	*SE*	RM	73313	79013	78213	73713
375814	**SB**	E	*SE*	RM	73314	79014	78214	73714
375815	**SB**	E	*SE*	RM	73315	79015	78215	73715

375816	**SB**	E	*SE*	RM	73316	79016	78216	73716
375817	**SB**	E	*SE*	RM	73317	79017	78217	73717
375818	**SB**	E	*SE*	RM	73318	79018	78218	73718
375819	**SB**	E	*SE*	RM	73319	79019	78219	73719
375820	**SB**	E	*SE*	RM	73320	79020	78220	73720
375821	**SB**	E	*SE*	RM	73321	79021	78221	73721
375822	**SB**	E	*SE*	RM	73322	79022	78222	73722
375823	**SB**	E	*SE*	RM	73323	79023	78223	73723
375824	**SB**	E	*SE*	RM	73324	79024	78224	73724
375825	**SB**	E	*SE*	RM	73325	79025	78225	73725
375826	**SB**	E	*SE*	RM	73326	79026	78226	73726
375827	**SB**	E	*SE*	RM	73327	79027	78227	73727
375828	**SB**	E	*SE*	RM	73328	79028	78228	73728
375829	**SB**	E	*SE*	RM	73329	79029	78229	73729
375830	**SB**	E	*SE*	RM	73330	79030	78230	73730

Names (carried on one side of each MS or TS):

375823 Ashford Proudly served by rail since 1842
375829 Verera Holmes (1889–1964) Women in Engineering

Class 375/9. Outer suburban units. 750 V DC only. DMS–MS–TS–DMS.

DMS(A). Bombardier Derby 2003–04. –/71. 43.4 t.
MS. Bombardier Derby 2003–04. –/73 1T. 39.3 t.
TS. Bombardier Derby 2003–04. –/62 1TD 2W. 35.6 t.
DMS(B). Bombardier Derby 2003–04. –/71. 43.4 t.

375901	**SB**	E	*SE*	RM	73331	79031	79061	73731
375902	**SB**	E	*SE*	RM	73332	79032	79062	73732
375903	**SB**	E	*SE*	RM	73333	79033	79063	73733
375904	**SB**	E	*SE*	RM	73334	79034	79064	73734
375905	**SB**	E	*SE*	RM	73335	79035	79065	73735
375906	**SB**	E	*SE*	RM	73336	79036	79066	73736
375907	**SB**	E	*SE*	RM	73337	79037	79067	73737
375908	**SB**	E	*SE*	RM	73338	79038	79068	73738
375909	**SB**	E	*SE*	RM	73339	79039	79069	73739
375910	**SB**	E	*SE*	RM	73340	79040	79070	73740
375911	**SB**	E	*SE*	RM	73341	79041	79071	73741
375912	**SB**	E	*SE*	RM	73342	79042	79072	73742
375913	**SB**	E	*SE*	RM	73343	79043	79073	73743
375914	**SB**	E	*SE*	RM	73344	79044	79074	73744
375915	**SB**	E	*SE*	RM	73345	79045	79075	73745
375916	**SB**	E	*SE*	RM	73346	79046	79076	73746
375917	**SB**	E	*SE*	RM	73347	79047	79077	73747
375918	**SB**	E	*SE*	RM	73348	79048	79078	73748
375919	**SB**	E	*SE*	RM	73349	79049	79079	73749
375920	**SB**	E	*SE*	RM	73350	79050	79080	73750
375921	**SB**	E	*SE*	RM	73351	79051	79081	73751
375922	**SB**	E	*SE*	RM	73352	79052	79082	73752
375923	**SB**	E	*SE*	RM	73353	79053	79083	73753
375924	**SB**	E	*SE*	RM	73354	79054	79084	73754
375925	**SB**	E	*SE*	RM	73355	79055	79085	73755

| 375 926 | **SB** | E | *SE* | RM | 73356 | 79056 | 79086 | 73756 |
| 375 927 | **SB** | E | *SE* | RM | 73357 | 79057 | 79087 | 73757 |

CLASS 376   ELECTROSTAR   BOMBARDIER DERBY

Inner suburban units.

Formation: DMS–MS–TS–MS–DMS.
System: 750 V DC third rail.
Construction: Welded aluminium alloy underframe, sides and roof with steel ends. All sections bolted together.
Traction Motors: Two Bombardier asynchronous of 200 kW.
Wheel Arrangement: 2-Bo + 2-Bo + 2-2 + Bo-2 + Bo-2.
Braking: Disc & regenerative.   **Dimensions:** 20.40/19.99 x 2.80 m.
Bogies: Bombardier P3-25/T3-25.   **Couplers:** Dellner 12.
Gangways: Within unit.   **Control System:** IGBT Inverter.
Doors: Sliding.   **Maximum Speed:** 75 mph.
Heating & ventilation: Pressure heating and ventilation.
Seating Layout: 2+2 low density facing.
Multiple Working: Within class and with Classes 375, 377, 378 and 379.

DMS(A). Bombardier Derby 2004–05. –/36(+6) 1W. 42.1 t.
MS. Bombardier Derby 2004–05. –/48. 36.2 t.
TS. Bombardier Derby 2004–05. –/48. 36.3 t.
DMS(B). Bombardier Derby 2004–05. –/36(+6) 1W. 42.1 t.

376 001	**CN**	E	*SE*	SG	61101	63301	64301	63501	61601
376 002	**CN**	E	*SE*	SG	61102	63302	64302	63502	61602
376 003	**CN**	E	*SE*	SG	61103	63303	64303	63503	61603
376 004	**CN**	E	*SE*	SG	61104	63304	64304	63504	61604
376 005	**CN**	E	*SE*	SG	61105	63305	64305	63505	61605
376 006	**CN**	E	*SE*	SG	61106	63306	64306	63506	61606
376 007	**CN**	E	*SE*	SG	61107	63307	64307	63507	61607
376 008	**CN**	E	*SE*	SG	61108	63308	64308	63508	61608
376 009	**CN**	E	*SE*	SG	61109	63309	64309	63509	61609
376 010	**CN**	E	*SE*	SG	61110	63310	64310	63510	61610
376 011	**CN**	E	*SE*	SG	61111	63311	64311	63511	61611
376 012	**CN**	E	*SE*	SG	61112	63312	64312	63512	61612
376 013	**CN**	E	*SE*	SG	61113	63313	64313	63513	61613
376 014	**CN**	E	*SE*	SG	61114	63314	64314	63514	61614
376 015	**CN**	E	*SE*	SG	61115	63315	64315	63515	61615
376 016	**CN**	E	*SE*	SG	61116	63316	64316	63516	61616
376 017	**CN**	E	*SE*	SG	61117	63317	64317	63517	61617
376 018	**CN**	E	*SE*	SG	61118	63318	64318	63518	61618
376 019	**CN**	E	*SE*	SG	61119	63319	64319	63519	61619
376 020	**CN**	E	*SE*	SG	61120	63320	64320	63520	61620
376 021	**CN**	E	*SE*	SG	61121	63321	64321	63521	61621
376 022	**CN**	E	*SE*	SG	61122	63322	64322	63522	61622
376 023	**CN**	E	*SE*	SG	61123	63323	64323	63523	61623
376 024	**CN**	E	*SE*	SG	61124	63324	64324	63524	61624
376 025	**CN**	E	*SE*	SG	61125	63325	64325	63525	61625
376 026	**CN**	E	*SE*	SG	61126	63326	64326	63526	61626

376 027	CN	E	SE	SG	61127 63327 64327 63527 61627
376 028	CN	E	SE	SG	61128 63328 64328 63528 61628
376 029	CN	E	SE	SG	61129 63329 64329 63529 61629
376 030	CN	E	SE	SG	61130 63330 64330 63530 61630
376 031	CN	E	SE	SG	61131 63331 64331 63531 61631
376 032	CN	E	SE	SG	61132 63332 64332 63532 61632
376 033	CN	E	SE	SG	61133 63333 64333 63533 61633
376 034	CN	E	SE	SG	61134 63334 64334 63534 61634
376 035	CN	E	SE	SG	61135 63335 64335 63535 61635
376 036	CN	E	SE	SG	61136 63336 64336 63536 61636

Name (carried on TSO): 376 001   Alan Doggett

CLASS 377   ELECTROSTAR   BOMBARDIER DERBY

Express and outer suburban units.

Formation: Various, see sub-class headings.
Systems: 25 kV AC overhead/750 V DC third rail or third rail only with provision for retro-fitting of AC equipment.
Construction: Welded aluminium alloy underframe, sides and roof with steel ends. All sections bolted together.
Traction Motors: Two Bombardier asynchronous of 250 kW.
Wheel Arrangement: 2-Bo + 2-2 + Bo-2 or 2-Bo + 2-Bo + 2-2 + Bo-2 or 2-Bo + 2-Bo + 2-2 + Bo-2 + Bo-2.
Braking: Disc & regenerative.   **Dimensions:** 20.39/20.00 x 2.80 m.
Bogies: Bombardier P3-25/T3-25.   **Couplers:** Dellner 12.
Gangways: Throughout.   **Control System:** IGBT Inverter.
Doors: Sliding plug.   **Maximum Speed:** 100 mph.
Heating & ventilation: Air conditioning.
Seating Layout: Various, see sub-class headings.
Multiple Working: Within class and with Classes 375, 376, 378, 379 and 387.

Class 377/1. 750 V DC only. DMC–MS–TS–DMC.
Seating layout: 1: 2+2 facing/unidirectional, 2: 2+2 facing/unidirectional (377 101–119), 3+2/2+2 facing/unidirectional (377 120–139), 3+2 (middle cars and 2+2 (end cars) facing/unidirectional (377 140–164).

DMC(A). Bombardier Derby 2002–03. 12/48 (s 12/56). 44.8 t.
MS. Bombardier Derby 2002–03. –/62 (s –/70, t –/69). 1T. 39.0 t.
TS. Bombardier Derby 2002–03. –/52 (s –/60, t –/57). 1TD 2W. 35.4 t.
DMC(B). Bombardier Derby 2002–03. 12/48 (s 12/56). 43.4 t.

377 101	SN	P	SN	SU	78501 77101 78901 78701
377 102	SN	P	SN	SU	78502 77102 78902 78702
377 103	SN	P	SN	SU	78503 77103 78903 78703
377 104	SN	P	SN	SU	78504 77104 78904 78704
377 105	SN	P	SN	SU	78505 77105 78905 78705
377 106	SN	P	SN	SU	78506 77106 78906 78706
377 107	SN	P	SN	SU	78507 77107 78907 78707
377 108	SN	P	SN	SU	78508 77108 78908 78708
377 109	SN	P	SN	SU	78509 77109 78909 78709
377 110	SN	P	SN	SU	78510 77110 78910 78710

377 111		**SN**	P	*SN*	SU	78511	77111	78911	78711
377 112		**SN**	P	*SN*	SU	78512	77112	78912	78712
377 113		**SN**	P	*SN*	SU	78513	77113	78913	78713
377 114		**SN**	P	*SN*	SU	78514	77114	78914	78714
377 115		**SN**	P	*SN*	SU	78515	77115	78915	78715
377 116		**SN**	P	*SN*	SU	78516	77116	78916	78716
377 117		**SN**	P	*SN*	SU	78517	77117	78917	78717
377 118		**SN**	P	*SN*	SU	78518	77118	78918	78718
377 119		**SN**	P	*SN*	SU	78519	77119	78919	78719
377 120	s	**SN**	P	*SN*	SU	78520	77120	78920	78720
377 121	s	**SN**	P	*SN*	SU	78521	77121	78921	78721
377 122	s	**SN**	P	*SN*	SU	78522	77122	78922	78722
377 123	s	**SN**	P	*SN*	SU	78523	77123	78923	78723
377 124	s	**SN**	P	*SN*	SU	78524	77124	78924	78724
377 125	s	**SN**	P	*SN*	SU	78525	77125	78925	78725
377 126	s	**SN**	P	*SN*	SU	78526	77126	78926	78726
377 127	s	**SN**	P	*SN*	SU	78527	77127	78927	78727
377 128	s	**SN**	P	*SN*	SU	78528	77128	78928	78728
377 129	s	**SN**	P	*SN*	SU	78529	77129	78929	78729
377 130	s	**SN**	P	*SN*	SU	78530	77130	78930	78730
377 131	s	**SN**	P	*SN*	SU	78531	77131	78931	78731
377 132	s	**SN**	P	*SN*	SU	78532	77132	78932	78732
377 133	s	**SN**	P	*SN*	SU	78533	77133	78933	78733
377 134	s	**SN**	P	*SN*	SU	78534	77134	78934	78734
377 135	s	**SN**	P	*SN*	SU	78535	77135	78935	78735
377 136	s	**SN**	P	*SN*	SU	78536	77136	78936	78736
377 137	s	**SN**	P	*SN*	SU	78537	77137	78937	78737
377 138	s	**SN**	P	*SN*	SU	78538	77138	78938	78738
377 139	s	**SN**	P	*SN*	SU	78539	77139	78939	78739
377 140	t	**SN**	P	*SN*	SU	78540	77140	78940	78740
377 141	t	**SN**	P	*SN*	SU	78541	77141	78941	78741
377 142	t	**SN**	P	*SN*	SU	78542	77142	78942	78742
377 143	t	**SN**	P	*SN*	SU	78543	77143	78943	78743
377 144	t	**SN**	P	*SN*	SU	78544	77144	78944	78744
377 145	t	**SN**	P	*SN*	SU	78545	77145	78945	78745
377 146	t	**SN**	P	*SN*	SU	78546	77146	78946	78746
377 147	t	**SN**	P	*SN*	SU	78547	77147	78947	78747
377 148	t	**SN**	P	*SN*	SU	78548	77148	78948	78748
377 149	t	**SN**	P	*SN*	SU	78549	77149	78949	78749
377 150	t	**SN**	P	*SN*	SU	78550	77150	78950	78750
377 151	t	**SN**	P	*SN*	SU	78551	77151	78951	78751
377 152	t	**SN**	P	*SN*	SU	78552	77152	78952	78752
377 153	t	**SN**	P	*SN*	SU	78553	77153	78953	78753
377 154	t	**SN**	P	*SN*	SU	78554	77154	78954	78754
377 155	t	**SN**	P	*SN*	SU	78555	77155	78955	78755
377 156	t	**SN**	P	*SN*	SU	78556	77156	78956	78756
377 157	t	**SN**	P	*SN*	SU	78557	77157	78957	78757
377 158	t	**SN**	P	*SN*	SU	78558	77158	78958	78758
377 159	t	**SN**	P	*SN*	SU	78559	77159	78959	78759
377 160	t	**SN**	P	*SN*	SU	78560	77160	78960	78760
377 161	t	**SN**	P	*SN*	SU	78561	77161	78961	78761

377 162	t	**SN**	P	*SN*	SU	78562	77162	78962	78762
377 163	t	**SN**	P	*SN*	SU	78563	77163	78963	78763
377 164	t	**SN**	P	*SN*	SU	78564	77164	78964	78764

Class 377/2. 25 kV AC/750 V DC. DMC–MS–PTS–DMC. Dual-voltage units.
Seating layout: 1: 2+2 facing/unidirectional, 2: 2+2 and 3+2 facing/
unidirectional (3+2 seating in middle cars only).

DMC(A). Bombardier Derby 2003–04. 12/48. 44.2 t.
MS. Bombardier Derby 2003–04. –/69 1T. 39.8 t.
PTS. Bombardier Derby 2003–04. –/57 1TD 2W. 40.1 t.
DMC(B). Bombardier Derby 2003–04. 12/48. 44.2 t.

377 201	**SN**	P	*SN*	SU	78571	77171	78971	78771
377 202	**SN**	P	*SN*	SU	78572	77172	78972	78772
377 203	**SN**	P	*SN*	SU	78573	77173	78973	78773
377 204	**SN**	P	*SN*	SU	78574	77174	78974	78774
377 205	**SN**	P	*SN*	SU	78575	77175	78975	78775
377 206	**SN**	P	*SN*	SU	78576	77176	78976	78776
377 207	**SN**	P	*SN*	SU	78577	77177	78977	78777
377 208	**SN**	P	*SN*	SU	78578	77178	78978	78778
377 209	**SN**	P	*SN*	SU	78579	77179	78979	78779
377 210	**SN**	P	*SN*	SU	78580	77180	78980	78780
377 211	**SN**	P	*SN*	SU	78581	77181	78981	78781
377 212	**SN**	P	*SN*	SU	78582	77182	78982	78782
377 213	**SN**	P	*SN*	SU	78583	77183	78983	78783
377 214	**SN**	P	*SN*	SU	78584	77184	78984	78784
377 215	**SN**	P	*SN*	SU	78585	77185	78985	78785

Class 377/3. 750 V DC only. DMC–TS–DMC.
Seating Layout: 1: 2+2 facing/unidirectional, 2: 2+2 facing/unidirectional.

Units built as Class 375, but renumbered in the Class 377/3 range when
fitted with Dellner couplers.

DMC(A). Bombardier Derby 2001–02. 12/48. 43.5 t.
TS. Bombardier Derby 2001–02. –/56 1TD 2W. 35.4 t.
DMC(B). Bombardier Derby 2001–02. 12/48. 43.5 t.

377 301	(375 311)	**SN**	P	*SN*	SU	68201	74801	68401
377 302	(375 312)	**SN**	P	*SN*	SU	68202	74802	68402
377 303	(375 313)	**SN**	P	*SN*	SU	68203	74803	68403
377 304	(375 314)	**SN**	P	*SN*	SU	68204	74804	68404
377 305	(375 315)	**SN**	P	*SN*	SU	68205	74805	68405
377 306	(375 316)	**SN**	P	*SN*	SU	68206	74806	68406
377 307	(375 317)	**SN**	P	*SN*	SU	68207	74807	68407
377 308	(375 318)	**SN**	P	*SN*	SU	68208	74808	68408
377 309	(375 319)	**SN**	P	*SN*	SU	68209	74809	68409
377 310	(375 320)	**SN**	P	*SN*	SU	68210	74810	68410
377 311	(375 321)	**SN**	P	*SN*	SU	68211	74811	68411
377 312	(375 322)	**SN**	P	*SN*	SU	68212	74812	68412
377 313	(375 323)	**SN**	P	*SN*	SU	68213	74813	68413
377 314	(375 324)	**SN**	P	*SN*	SU	68214	74814	68414
377 315	(375 325)	**SN**	P	*SN*	SU	68215	74815	68415

377316	(375326)	**SN**	P	*SN*	SU	68216	74816	68416
377317	(375327)	**SN**	P	*SN*	SU	68217	74817	68417
377318	(375328)	**SN**	P	*SN*	SU	68218	74818	68418
377319	(375329)	**SN**	P	*SN*	SU	68219	74819	68419
377320	(375330)	**SN**	P	*SN*	SU	68220	74820	68420
377321	(375331)	**SN**	P	*SN*	SU	68221	74821	68421
377322	(375332)	**SN**	P	*SN*	SU	68222	74822	68422
377323	(375333)	**SN**	P	*SN*	SU	68223	74823	68423
377324	(375334)	**SN**	P	*SN*	SU	68224	74824	68424
377325	(375335)	**SN**	P	*SN*	SU	68225	74825	68425
377326	(375336)	**SN**	P	*SN*	SU	68226	74826	68426
377327	(375337)	**SN**	P	*SN*	SU	68227	74827	68427
377328	(375338)	**SN**	P	*SN*	SU	68228	74828	68428

Class 377/4. 750 V DC only. DMC–MS–TS–DMC.
Seating Layout: 1: 2+2 facing/two seats longitudinal, 2: 2+2 and 3+2 facing/unidirectional (3+2 seating in middle cars only).

377442 operated as 3-car 377342 between 2016 and 2021 after fire damage to MS vehicle 78842 in 2016.

DMC(A). Bombardier Derby 2004–05. 10/48. 43.1 t.
MS. Bombardier Derby 2004–05. –/69 1T. 39.3 t.
TS. Bombardier Derby 2004–05. –/56 1TD 2W. 35.3 t.
DMC(B). Bombardier Derby 2004–05. 10/48. 43.2 t.

377401	**SN**	P	*SN*	SU	73401	78801	78601	73801
377402	**SN**	P	*SN*	SU	73402	78802	78602	73802
377403	**SN**	P	*SN*	SU	73403	78803	78603	73803
377404	**SN**	P	*SN*	SU	73404	78804	78604	73804
377405	**SN**	P	*SN*	SU	73405	78805	78605	73805
377406	**SN**	P	*SN*	SU	73406	78806	78606	73806
377407	**SN**	P	*SN*	SU	73407	78807	78607	73807
377408	**SN**	P	*SN*	SU	73408	78808	78608	73808
377409	**SN**	P	*SN*	SU	73409	78809	78609	73809
377410	**SN**	P	*SN*	SU	73410	78810	78610	73810
377411	**SN**	P	*SN*	SU	73411	78811	78611	73811
377412	**SN**	P	*SN*	SU	73412	78812	78612	73812
377413	**SN**	P	*SN*	SU	73413	78813	78613	73813
377414	**SN**	P	*SN*	SU	73414	78814	78614	73814
377415	**SN**	P	*SN*	SU	73415	78815	78615	73815
377416	**SN**	P	*SN*	SU	73416	78816	78616	73816
377417	**SN**	P	*SN*	SU	73417	78817	78617	73817
377418	**SN**	P	*SN*	SU	73418	78818	78618	73818
377419	**SN**	P	*SN*	SU	73419	78819	78619	73819
377420	**SN**	P	*SN*	SU	73420	78820	78620	73820
377421	**SN**	P	*SN*	SU	73421	78821	78621	73821
377422	**SN**	P	*SN*	SU	73422	78822	78622	73822
377423	**SN**	P	*SN*	SU	73423	78823	78623	73823
377424	**SN**	P	*SN*	SU	73424	78824	78624	73824
377425	**SN**	P	*SN*	SU	73425	78825	78625	73825
377426	**SN**	P	*SN*	SU	73426	78826	78626	73826
377427	**SN**	P	*SN*	SU	73427	78827	78627	73827

377 428	**SN**	P	*SN*	SU	73428	78828	78628	73828
377 429	**SN**	P	*SN*	SU	73429	78829	78629	73829
377 430	**SN**	P	*SN*	SU	73430	78830	78630	73830
377 431	**SN**	P	*SN*	SU	73431	78831	78631	73831
377 432	**SN**	P	*SN*	SU	73432	78832	78632	73832
377 433	**SN**	P	*SN*	SU	73433	78833	78633	73833
377 434	**SN**	P	*SN*	SU	73434	78834	78634	73834
377 435	**SN**	P	*SN*	SU	73435	78835	78635	73835
377 436	**SN**	P	*SN*	SU	73436	78836	78636	73836
377 437	**SN**	P	*SN*	SU	73437	78837	78637	73837
377 438	**SN**	P	*SN*	SU	73438	78838	78638	73838
377 439	**SN**	P	*SN*	SU	73439	78839	78639	73839
377 440	**SN**	P	*SN*	SU	73440	78840	78640	73840
377 441	**SN**	P	*SN*	SU	73441	78841	78641	73841
377 442	**SN**	P	*SN*	SU	73442	78842	78642	73842
377 443	**SN**	P	*SN*	SU	73443	78843	78643	73843
377 444	**SN**	P	*SN*	SU	73444	78844	78644	73844
377 445	**SN**	P	*SN*	SU	73445	78845	78645	73845
377 446	**SN**	P	*SN*	SU	73446	78846	78646	73846
377 447	**SN**	P	*SN*	SU	73447	78847	78647	73847
377 448	**SN**	P	*SN*	SU	73448	78848	78648	73848
377 449	**SN**	P	*SN*	SU	73449	78849	78649	73849
377 450	**SN**	P	*SN*	SU	73450	78850	78650	73850
377 451	**SN**	P	*SN*	SU	73451	78851	78651	73851
377 452	**SN**	P	*SN*	SU	73452	78852	78652	73852
377 453	**SN**	P	*SN*	SU	73453	78853	78653	73853
377 454	**SN**	P	*SN*	SU	73454	78854	78654	73854
377 455	**SN**	P	*SN*	SU	73455	78855	78655	73855
377 456	**SN**	P	*SN*	SU	73456	78856	78656	73856
377 457	**SN**	P	*SN*	SU	73457	78857	78657	73857
377 458	**SN**	P	*SN*	SU	73458	78858	78658	73858
377 459	**SN**	P	*SN*	SU	73459	78859	78659	73859
377 460	**SN**	P	*SN*	SU	73460	78860	78660	73860
377 461	**SN**	P	*SN*	SU	73461	78861	78661	73861
377 462	**SN**	P	*SN*	SU	73462	78862	78662	73862
377 463	**SN**	P	*SN*	SU	73463	78863	78663	73863
377 464	**SN**	P	*SN*	SU	73464	78864	78664	73864
377 465	**SN**	P	*SN*	SU	73465	78865	78665	73865
377 466	**SN**	P	*SN*	SU	73466	78866	78666	73866
377 467	**SN**	P	*SN*	SU	73467	78867	78667	73867
377 468	**SN**	P	*SN*	SU	73468	78868	78668	73868
377 469	**SN**	P	*SN*	SU	73469	78869	78669	73869
377 470	**SN**	P	*SN*	SU	73470	78870	78670	73870
377 471	**SN**	P	*SN*	SU	73471	78871	78671	73871
377 472	**SN**	P	*SN*	SU	73472	78872	78672	73872
377 473	**SN**	P	*SN*	SU	73473	78873	78673	73873
377 474	**SN**	P	*SN*	SU	73474	78874	78674	73874
377 475	**SN**	P	*SN*	SU	73475	78875	78675	73875

Class 377/5. 25kV AC/750V DC. DMC–MS–PTS–DMS. Dual-voltage units sub-leased from Southern. Details as Class 377/2 unless stated.

DMC. Bombardier Derby 2008–09. 10/48. 43.1 t.
MS. Bombardier Derby 2008–09. –/69 1T. 40.3 t.
PTS. Bombardier Derby 2008–09. –/56 1TD 2W. 40.6 t.
DMS. Bombardier Derby 2008–09. –/58. 44.9 t.

377501	**FB**	P	*SE*	RM	73501	75901	74901	73601
377502	**FB**	P	*SE*	RM	73502	75902	74902	73602
377503	**FB**	P	*SE*	RM	73503	75903	74903	73603
377504	**FB**	P	*SE*	RM	73504	75904	74904	73604
377505	**FB**	P	*SE*	RM	73505	75905	74905	73605
377506	**FB**	P	*SE*	RM	73506	75906	74906	73606
377507	**FB**	P	*SE*	RM	73507	75907	74907	73607
377508	**FB**	P	*SE*	RM	73508	75908	74908	73608
377509	**FB**	P	*SE*	RM	73509	75909	74909	73609
377510	**FB**	P	*SE*	RM	73510	75910	74910	73610
377511	**FB**	P	*SE*	RM	73511	75911	74911	73611
377512	**FB**	P	*SE*	RM	73512	75912	74912	73612
377513	**FB**	P	*SE*	RM	73513	75913	74913	73613
377514	**FB**	P	*SE*	RM	73514	75914	74914	73614
377515	**FB**	P	*SE*	RM	73515	75915	74915	73615
377516	**FB**	P	*SE*	RM	73516	75916	74916	73616
377517	**FB**	P	*SE*	RM	73517	75917	74917	73617
377518	**FB**	P	*SE*	RM	73518	75918	74918	73618
377519	**FB**	P	*SE*	RM	73519	75919	74919	73619
377520	**FB**	P	*SE*	RM	73520	75920	74920	73620
377521	**FB**	P	*SE*	RM	73521	75921	74921	73621
377522	**FB**	P	*SE*	RM	73522	75922	74922	73622
377523	**FB**	P	*SE*	RM	73523	75923	74923	73623

Class 377/6. 750V DC. DMS–MS–TS–MS–DMS. 5-car suburban units fitted with Fainsa seating. Technically the same as the 377/5s but using the slightly modified Class 379-style bodyshell.

Seating Layout: 2+2 facing/unidirectional.

DMS. Bombardier Derby 2012–13. 24/36. 44.7 t.
MS. Bombardier Derby 2012–13. –/64 1T. 38.8 t.
TS. Bombardier Derby 2012–13. –/46(+2) 1TD 2W. 37.8 t.
MS. Bombardier Derby 2012–13. –/66. 38.3 t.
DMS. Bombardier Derby 2012–13. –/62. 44.7 t.

377601	**SN**	P	*SN*	SU	70101	70201	70301	70401	70501
377602	**SN**	P	*SN*	SU	70102	70202	70302	70402	70502
377603	**SN**	P	*SN*	SU	70103	70203	70303	70403	70503
377604	**SN**	P	*SN*	SU	70104	70204	70304	70404	70504
377605	**SN**	P	*SN*	SU	70105	70205	70305	70405	70505
377606	**SN**	P	*SN*	SU	70106	70206	70306	70406	70506
377607	**SN**	P	*SN*	SU	70107	70207	70307	70407	70507
377608	**SN**	P	*SN*	SU	70108	70208	70308	70408	70508
377609	**SN**	P	*SN*	SU	70109	70209	70309	70409	70509
377610	**SN**	P	*SN*	SU	70110	70210	70310	70410	70510

377611	**SN**	P	*SN*	SU	70111	70211	70311	70411	70511
377612	**SN**	P	*SN*	SU	70112	70212	70312	70412	70512
377613	**SN**	P	*SN*	SU	70113	70213	70313	70413	70513
377614	**SN**	P	*SN*	SU	70114	70214	70314	70414	70514
377615	**SN**	P	*SN*	SU	70115	70215	70315	70415	70515
377616	**SN**	P	*SN*	SU	70116	70216	70316	70416	70516
377617	**SN**	P	*SN*	SU	70117	70217	70317	70417	70517
377618	**SN**	P	*SN*	SU	70118	70218	70318	70418	70518
377619	**SN**	P	*SN*	SU	70119	70219	70319	70419	70519
377620	**SN**	P	*SN*	SU	70120	70220	70320	70420	70520
377621	**SN**	P	*SN*	SU	70121	70221	70321	70421	70521
377622	**SN**	P	*SN*	SU	70122	70222	70322	70422	70522
377623	**SN**	P	*SN*	SU	70123	70223	70323	70423	70523
377624	**SN**	P	*SN*	SU	70124	70224	70324	70424	70524
377625	**SN**	P	*SN*	SU	70125	70225	70325	70425	70525
377626	**SN**	P	*SN*	SU	70126	70226	70326	70426	70526

Class 377/7. 25 kV AC/750 V DC. DMS–MS–TS–MS–DMS. Dual-voltage units.

DMS. Bombardier Derby 2013–14. 24/36. 45.6 t.
MS. Bombardier Derby 2013–14. –/64 1T. 41.0 t.
PTS. Bombardier Derby 2013–14. –/46(+2) 1TD 2W. 40.9 t.
MS. Bombardier Derby 2013–14. –/66. 39.6 t.
DMS. Bombardier Derby 2013–14. –/62. 45.2 t.

377701	**SN**	P	*SN*	SU	65201	70601	65601	70701	65401
377702	**SN**	P	*SN*	SU	65202	70602	65602	70702	65402
377703	**SN**	P	*SN*	SU	65203	70603	65603	70703	65403
377704	**SN**	P	*SN*	SU	65204	70604	65604	70704	65404
377705	**SN**	P	*SN*	SU	65205	70605	65605	70705	65405
377706	**SN**	P	*SN*	SU	65206	70606	65606	70706	65406
377707	**SN**	P	*SN*	SU	65207	70607	65607	70707	65407
377708	**SN**	P	*SN*	SU	65208	70608	65608	70708	65408

CLASS 378   CAPITALSTAR   BOMBARDIER DERBY

These suburban Electrostars are designated "Capitalstars" by TfL.

Formation: DMS–MS–TS–MS–DMS or DMS–MS–PTS–MS–DMS.
System: Class 378/1 750 V DC third rail only. Class 378/2 25 kV AC overhead and 750 V DC third rail.
Construction: Welded aluminium alloy underframe, sides and roof with steel ends. All sections bolted together.
Traction Motors: Three Bombardier asynchronous of 200 kW.
Wheel Arrangement: 1A-Bo + 1A-Bo + 2-2 + Bo-1A + Bo-1A.
Braking: Disc & regenerative.   **Dimensions**: 20.46/20.14 x 2.80 m.
Bogies: Bombardier P3-25/T3-25.   **Couplers**: Dellner 12.
Gangways: Within unit + end doors. **Control System**: IGBT Inverter.
Doors: Sliding.   **Maximum Speed**: 75 mph.
Heating & ventilation: Air conditioning.
Seating Layout: Longitudinal ("tube style") low density.

Multiple Working: Within class and with Classes 375, 376, 377 and 379.

57 extra MSs (in the 384xx number series) were delivered 2014–15 to make all units up to 5-cars.

Class 378/1. 750V DC. DMS–MS–TS–MS–DMS. Third rail only units used on the East London Line. Provision for retro-fitting as dual voltage.

378150–154 are fitted with de-icing equipment.

DMS(A). Bombardier Derby 2009–10. –/36. 43.1 t.
MS(A). Bombardier Derby 2009–10. –/40. 39.3 t.
TS. Bombardier Derby 2009–10. –/34(+6) 2W. 34.3 t.
MS(B). Bombardier Derby 2014–15. –/40. 40.2 t.
DMS(B). Bombardier Derby 2009–10. –/36. 42.7 t.

378135	**LD**	QW	*LO*	NG	38035	38235	38335	38435	38135
378136	**LD**	QW	*LO*	NG	38036	38236	38336	38436	38136
378137	**LO**	QW	*LO*	NG	38037	38237	38337	38437	38137
378138	**LO**	QW	*LO*	NG	38038	38238	38338	38438	38138
378139	**LO**	QW	*LO*	NG	38039	38239	38339	38439	38139
378140	**LO**	QW	*LO*	NG	38040	38240	38340	38440	38140
378141	**LO**	QW	*LO*	NG	38041	38241	38341	38441	38141
378142	**LO**	QW	*LO*	NG	38042	38242	38342	38442	38142
378143	**LO**	QW	*LO*	NG	38043	38243	38343	38443	38143
378144	**LO**	QW	*LO*	NG	38044	38244	38344	38444	38144
378145	**LO**	QW	*LO*	NG	38045	38245	38345	38445	38145
378146	**LO**	QW	*LO*	NG	38046	38246	38346	38446	38146
378147	**LD**	QW	*LO*	NG	38047	38247	38347	38447	38147
378148	**LO**	QW	*LO*	NG	38048	38248	38348	38448	38148
378149	**LO**	QW	*LO*	NG	38049	38249	38349	38449	38149
378150	**LD**	QW	*LO*	NG	38050	38250	38350	38450	38150
378151	**LO**	QW	*LO*	NG	38051	38251	38351	38451	38151
378152	**LO**	QW	*LO*	NG	38052	38252	38352	38452	38152
378153	**LO**	QW	*LO*	NG	38053	38253	38353	38453	38153
378154	**LO**	QW	*LO*	NG	38054	38254	38354	38454	38154

Names (carried on DMS(A)):

378135 Daks Hamilton | 378136   Transport for London

Class 378/2. 25kV AC/750V DC. DMS–MS–PTS–MS–DMS. Dual-voltage units mainly used on North London Railway services. 378201–224 were built as 3-car units 378001–024, extended to 4-car units in 2010 and then extended to 5-cars in 2014–15.

Fitted with tripcocks for operation on the tracks shared with London Underground between Queens Park and Harrow & Wealdstone.

378216–220 are fitted with de-icing equipment.

Non-standard livery: 378205 Pride celebration colours.

DMS(A). Bombardier Derby 2008–11. –/36. 43.4 t.
MS(A). Bombardier Derby 2008–11. –/40. 39.6 t.
PTS. Bombardier Derby 2008–11. –/34(+6) 2W. 39.2 t.

MS(B). Bombardier Derby 2014–15. –/40. 40.4 t.
DMS(B). Bombardier Derby 2008–11. –/36. 43.1 t.

378 201	**L0**	QW	*L0*	NG	38001	38201	38301	38401	38101
378 202	**L0**	QW	*L0*	NG	38002	38202	38302	38402	38102
378 203	**L0**	QW	*L0*	NG	38003	38203	38303	38403	38103
378 204	**L0**	QW	*L0*	NG	38004	38204	38304	38404	38104
378 205	**0**	QW	*L0*	NG	38005	38205	38305	38405	38105
378 206	**LD**	QW	*L0*	NG	38006	38206	38306	38406	38106
378 207	**L0**	QW	*L0*	NG	38007	38207	38307	38407	38107
378 208	**L0**	QW	*L0*	NG	38008	38208	38308	38408	38108
378 209	**L0**	QW	*L0*	NG	38009	38209	38309	38409	38109
378 210	**L0**	QW	*L0*	NG	38010	38210	38310	38410	38110
378 211	**LD**	QW	*L0*	NG	38011	38211	38311	38411	38111
378 212	**L0**	QW	*L0*	NG	38012	38212	38312	38412	38112
378 213	**L0**	QW	*L0*	NG	38013	38213	38313	38413	38113
378 214	**L0**	QW	*L0*	NG	38014	38214	38314	38414	38114
378 215	**L0**	QW	*L0*	NG	38015	38215	38315	38415	38115
378 216	**L0**	QW	*L0*	NG	38016	38216	38316	38416	38116
378 217	**L0**	QW	*L0*	NG	38017	38217	38317	38417	38117
378 218	**L0**	QW	*L0*	NG	38018	38218	38318	38418	38118
378 219	**L0**	QW	*L0*	NG	38019	38219	38319	38419	38119
378 220	**L0**	QW	*L0*	NG	38020	38220	38320	38420	38120
378 221	**L0**	QW	*L0*	NG	38021	38221	38321	38421	38121
378 222	**L0**	QW	*L0*	NG	38022	38222	38322	38422	38122
378 223	**L0**	QW	*L0*	NG	38023	38223	38323	38423	38123
378 224	**L0**	QW	*L0*	NG	38024	38224	38324	38424	38124
378 225	**L0**	QW	*L0*	NG	38025	38225	38325	38425	38125
378 226	**L0**	QW	*L0*	NG	38026	38226	38326	38426	38126
378 227	**L0**	QW	*L0*	NG	38027	38227	38327	38427	38127
378 228	**L0**	QW	*L0*	NG	38028	38228	38328	38428	38128
378 229	**L0**	QW	*L0*	NG	38029	38229	38329	38429	38129
378 230	**L0**	QW	*L0*	NG	38030	38230	38330	38430	38130
378 231	**L0**	QW	*L0*	NG	38031	38231	38331	38431	38131
378 232	**LD**	QW	*L0*	NG	38032	38232	38332	38432	38132
378 233	**L0**	QW	*L0*	NG	38033	38233	38333	38433	38133
378 234	**L0**	QW	*L0*	NG	38034	38234	38334	38434	38134
378 255	**L0**	QW	*L0*	NG	38055	38255	38355	38455	38155
378 256	**L0**	QW	*L0*	NG	38056	38256	38356	38456	38156
378 257	**L0**	QW	*L0*	NG	38057	38257	38357	38457	38157

Names (carried on DMS(A)):

378 204	Professor Sir Peter Hall	378 232	Jeff Langston
378 211	Gary Hunter	378 233	Ian Brown CBE

CLASS 379   ELECTROSTAR   BOMBARDIER DERBY

Express Electrostars built for Liverpool Street–Stansted Airport and Liverpool Street–Cambridge services. The whole fleet was stored in 2022 after being replaced on Greater Anglia by Class 720s.

Formation: DMS–MS–PTS–DMC.
System: 25 kV AC overhead.
Construction: Welded aluminium alloy underframe, sides and roof with steel ends. All sections bolted together.
Traction Motors: Two Bombardier asynchronous of 200 kW.
Wheel Arrangement: 2-Bo + 2-Bo + 2-2 + Bo-2.
Braking: Disc & regenerative.   **Dimensions:** 20.00 x 2.80 m.
Bogies: Bombardier P3-25/T3-25.   **Couplers:** Dellner 12.
Gangways: Throughout.   **Control System:** IGBT Inverter.
Doors: Sliding plug.   **Maximum Speed:** 100 mph.
Heating & ventilation: Air conditioning.
Seating Layout: 1: 2+1 facing. 2: 2+2 facing/unidirectional.
Multiple Working: Within class and with Classes 375, 376, 377 and 378.

DMS. Bombardier Derby 2010–11. –/60. 42.1 t.
MS. Bombardier Derby 2010–11. –/62 1T. 38.6 t.
PTS. Bombardier Derby 2010–11. –/43(+2) 1TD 2W. 40.9 t.
DMC. Bombardier Derby 2010–11. 20/24. 42.3 t.

379001	**NC**	AK	WS	61201	61701	61901	62101
379002	**NC**	AK	WS	61202	61702	61902	62102
379003	**NC**	AK	WS	61203	61703	61903	62103
379004	**NC**	AK	WS	61204	61704	61904	62104
379005	**NC**	AK	WS	61205	61705	61905	62105
379006	**NC**	AK	WS	61206	61706	61906	62106
379007	**NC**	AK	WS	61207	61707	61907	62107
379008	**NC**	AK	WS	61208	61708	61908	62108
379009	**NC**	AK	WS	61209	61709	61909	62109
379010	**NC**	AK	WS	61210	61710	61910	62110
379011	**NC**	AK	WS	61211	61711	61911	62111
379012	**NC**	AK	WS	61212	61712	61912	62112
379013	**NC**	AK	WS	61213	61713	61913	62113
379014	**NC**	AK	WS	61214	61714	61914	62114
379015	**NC**	AK	WS	61215	61715	61915	62115
379016	**NC**	AK	WS	61216	61716	61916	62116
379017	**NC**	AK	WS	61217	61717	61917	62117
379018	**NC**	AK	WS	61218	61718	61918	62118
379019	**NC**	AK	WS	61219	61719	61919	62119
379020	**NC**	AK	WS	61220	61720	61920	62120
379021	**NC**	AK	WS	61221	61721	61921	62121
379022	**NC**	AK	WS	61222	61722	61922	62122
379023	**NC**	AK	WS	61223	61723	61923	62123
379024	**NC**	AK	WS	61224	61724	61924	62124
379025	**NC**	AK	WS	61225	61725	61925	62125
379026	**NC**	AK	WS	61226	61726	61926	62126
379027	**NC**	AK	WS	61227	61727	61927	62127

379028	**NC**	AK		WS	61228	61728	61928	62128
379029	**NC**	AK		WS	61229	61729	61929	62129
379030	**NC**	AK		WS	61230	61730	61930	62130

CLASS 380   DESIRO UK   SIEMENS

ScotRail units mainly used on Strathclyde area services.

Formation: DMS–PTS–DMS or DMS–PTS–TS–DMS.
System: 25 kV AC overhead.
Construction: Welded aluminium with steel ends.
Traction Motors: Four Siemens ITB2016-0GB02 asynchronous of 250 kW.
Wheel Arrangement: Bo-Bo + 2-2 (+2-2) + Bo-Bo

Braking: Disc & regenerative.	**Dimensions:** 23.78/23.57 x 2.80 m.
Bogies: SGP SF5000.	**Couplers:** Voith.
Gangways: Throughout.	**Control System:** IGBT Inverter.
Doors: Sliding plug.	**Maximum Speed:** 100 mph.
Heating & ventilation: Air conditioning.	**Seating Layout:** 2+2 facing/unidirectional.

Multiple Working: Within class.

DMS(A). Siemens Krefeld 2009–10. –/70. 45.0t.
PTS. Siemens Krefeld 2009–10. –/57(+12) 1TD 2W. 42.7t.
TS. Siemens Krefeld 2009–10. –/74 1T. 34.8t.
DMS(B). Siemens Krefeld 2009–10. –/64(+5). 44.9t.

Class 380/0. 3-car units. **Formation:** DMS–PTS–DMS.

380001	**SR**	E	*SR*	GW	38501	38601	38701
380002	**SR**	E	*SR*	GW	38502	38602	38702
380003	**SR**	E	*SR*	GW	38503	38603	38703
380004	**SR**	E	*SR*	GW	38504	38604	38704
380005	**SR**	E	*SR*	GW	38505	38605	38705
380006	**SR**	E	*SR*	GW	38506	38606	38706
380007	**SR**	E	*SR*	GW	38507	38607	38707
380008	**SR**	E	*SR*	GW	38508	38608	38708
380009	**SR**	E	*SR*	GW	38509	38609	38709
380010	**SR**	E	*SR*	GW	38510	38610	38710
380011	**SR**	E	*SR*	GW	38511	38611	38711
380012	**SR**	E	*SR*	GW	38512	38612	38712
380013	**SR**	E	*SR*	GW	38513	38613	38713
380014	**SR**	E	*SR*	GW	38514	38614	38714
380015	**SR**	E	*SR*	GW	38515	38615	38715
380016	**SR**	E	*SR*	GW	38516	38616	38716
380017	**SR**	E	*SR*	GW	38517	38617	38717
380018	**SR**	E	*SR*	GW	38518	38618	38718
380019	**SR**	E	*SR*	GW	38519	38619	38719
380020	**SR**	E	*SR*	GW	38520	38620	38720
380021	**SR**	E	*SR*	GW	38521	38621	38721
380022	**SR**	E	*SR*	GW	38522	38622	38722

Class 380/1. 4-car units. **Formation:** DMS–PTS–TS–DMS.

380 101	**SR**	E	*SR*	GW	38551	38651	38851	38751
380 102	**SR**	E	*SR*	GW	38552	38652	38852	38752
380 103	**SR**	E	*SR*	GW	38553	38653	38853	38753
380 104	**SR**	E	*SR*	GW	38554	38654	38854	38754
380 105	**SR**	E	*SR*	GW	38555	38655	38855	38755
380 106	**SR**	E	*SR*	GW	38556	38656	38856	38756
380 107	**SR**	E	*SR*	GW	38557	38657	38857	38757
380 108	**SR**	E	*SR*	GW	38558	38658	38858	38758
380 109	**SR**	E	*SR*	GW	38559	38659	38859	38759
380 110	**SR**	E	*SR*	GW	38560	38660	38860	38760
380 111	**SR**	E	*SR*	GW	38561	38661	38861	38761
380 112	**SR**	E	*SR*	GW	38562	38662	38862	38762
380 113	**SR**	E	*SR*	GW	38563	38663	38863	38763
380 114	**SR**	E	*SR*	GW	38564	38664	38864	38764
380 115	**SR**	E	*SR*	GW	38565	38665	38865	38765
380 116	**SR**	E	*SR*	GW	38566	38666	38866	38766

CLASS 385   AT200   HITACHI

3- and 4-car ScotRail units, financed by Caledonian Rail Leasing.

Formation: DMS–PTS–DMS or DMC–PTS–TS–DMS.
System: 25 kV AC overhead.
Construction: Aluminium.
Traction Motors: Four Hitachi asynchronous of 250 kW.
Wheel Arrangement: Bo-Bo + 2-2 + Bo-2 or Bo-Bo + 2-2 + 2-2 + Bo-Bo.
Braking: Disc & regenerative.
Dimensions: 23.18/22.08 x 2.74 m.   **Couplers:** Dellner.
Bogies: Hitachi.   **Control System:** IGBT Inverter.
Gangways: Throughout.   **Maximum Speed:** 100 mph.
Doors: Sliding plug.   **Multiple Working:** Within class only.
Heating & ventilation: Air conditioning.
Seating Layout: 1: 2+1 facing. 2: 2+2 facing/unidirectional.

Class 385/0. 3-car units. Standard Class only. **Formation:** DMS–PTS–DMS.

DMS(A): Hitachi Newton Aycliffe/Kasado 2016–18. –/48(+9) 1TD 2W. 44.6 t.
PTS: Hitachi Newton Aycliffe/Kasado 2016–18. –/80. 38.4 t.
DMS(B): Hitachi Newton Aycliffe/Kasado 2016–18. –62(+5) 1T. 42.0 t.

385001	**SR**	CL	*SR*	EC	441001	442001	444001
385002	**SR**	CL	*SR*	EC	441002	442002	444002
385003	**SR**	CL	*SR*	EC	441003	442003	444003
385004	**SR**	CL	*SR*	EC	441004	442004	444004
385005	**SR**	CL	*SR*	EC	441005	442005	444005
385006	**SR**	CL	*SR*	EC	441006	442006	444006
385007	**SR**	CL	*SR*	EC	441007	442007	444007
385008	**SR**	CL	*SR*	EC	441008	442008	444008
385009	**SR**	CL	*SR*	EC	441009	442009	444009
385010	**SR**	CL	*SR*	EC	441010	442010	444010
385011	**SR**	CL	*SR*	EC	441011	442011	444011

385012	**SR**	CL	*SR*	EC	441012	442012	444012	
385013	**SR**	CL	*SR*	EC	441013	442013	444013	
385014	**SR**	CL	*SR*	EC	441014	442014	444014	
385015	**SR**	CL	*SR*	EC	441015	442015	444015	
385016	**SR**	CL	*SR*	EC	441016	442016	444016	
385017	**SR**	CL	*SR*	EC	441017	442017	444017	
385018	**SR**	CL	*SR*	EC	441018	442018	444018	
385019	**SR**	CL	*SR*	EC	441019	442019	444019	
385020	**SR**	CL	*SR*	EC	441020	442020	444020	
385021	**SR**	CL	*SR*	EC	441021	442021	444021	
385022	**SR**	CL	*SR*	EC	441022	442022	444022	
385023	**SR**	CL	*SR*	EC	441023	442023	444023	
385024	**SR**	CL	*SR*	EC	441024	442024	444024	
385025	**SR**	CL	*SR*	EC	441025	442025	444025	
385026	**SR**	CL	*SR*	EC	441026	442026	444026	
385027	**SR**	CL	*SR*	EC	441027	442027	444027	
385028	**SR**	CL	*SR*	EC	441028	442028	444028	
385029	**SR**	CL	*SR*	EC	441029	442029	444029	
385030	**SR**	CL	*SR*	EC	441030	442030	444030	
385031	**SR**	CL	*SR*	EC	441031	442031	444031	
385032	**SR**	CL	*SR*	EC	441032	442032	444032	
385033	**SR**	CL	*SR*	EC	441033	442033	444033	
385034	**SR**	CL	*SR*	EC	441034	442034	444034	
385035	**SR**	CL	*SR*	EC	441035	442035	444035	
385036	**SR**	CL	*SR*	EC	441036	442036	444036	
385037	**SR**	CL	*SR*	EC	441037	442037	444037	
385038	**SR**	CL	*SR*	EC	441038	442038	444038	
385039	**SR**	CL	*SR*	EC	441039	442039	444039	
385040	**SR**	CL	*SR*	EC	441040	442040	444040	
385041	**SR**	CL	*SR*	EC	441041	442041	444041	
385042	**SR**	CL	*SR*	EC	441042	442042	444042	
385043	**SR**	CL	*SR*	EC	441043	442043	444043	
385044	**SR**	CL	*SR*	EC	441044	442044	444044	
385045	**SR**	CL	*SR*	EC	441045	442045	444045	
385046	**SR**	CL	*SR*	EC	441046	442046	444046	

Class 385/1. 4-car units. Standard Class and First Class seating.
Formation: DMC–PTS–TS–DMS.

DMC: Hitachi Newton Aycliffe/Kasado 2016–18. 20/15(+9) 1TD 2W. 44.7 t.
PTS: Hitachi Newton Aycliffe/Kasado 2016–18. –/80. 38.4 t.
TS: Hitachi Newton Aycliffe/Kasado 2016–18. –/80. 31.5 t.
DMS: Hitachi Newton Aycliffe/Kasado 2016–18. –62(+5) 1T. 44.5 t.

385101	**SR**	CL	*SR*	EC	441101	442101	443101	444101
385102	**SR**	CL	*SR*	EC	441102	442102	443102	444102
385103	**SR**	CL	*SR*	EC	441103	442103	443103	444103
385104	**SR**	CL	*SR*	EC	441104	442104	443104	444104
385105	**SR**	CL	*SR*	EC	441105	442105	443105	444105
385106	**SR**	CL	*SR*	EC	441106	442106	443106	444106
385107	**SR**	CL	*SR*	EC	441107	442107	443107	444107
385108	**SR**	CL	*SR*	EC	441108	442108	443108	444108

385 109	**SR**	CL	*SR*	EC	441109	442109	443109	444109
385 110	**SR**	CL	*SR*	EC	441110	442110	443110	444110
385 111	**SR**	CL	*SR*	EC	441111	442111	443111	444111
385 112	**SR**	CL	*SR*	EC	441112	442112	443112	444112
385 113	**SR**	CL	*SR*	EC	441113	442113	443113	444113
385 114	**SR**	CL	*SR*	EC	441114	442114	443114	444114
385 115	**SR**	CL	*SR*	EC	441115	442115	443115	444115
385 116	**SR**	CL	*SR*	EC	441116	442116	443116	444116
385 117	**SR**	CL	*SR*	EC	441117	442117	443117	444117
385 118	**SR**	CL	*SR*	EC	441118	442118	443118	444118
385 119	**SR**	CL	*SR*	EC	441119	442119	443119	444119
385 120	**SR**	CL	*SR*	EC	441120	442120	443120	444120
385 121	**SR**	CL	*SR*	EC	441121	442121	443121	444121
385 122	**SR**	CL	*SR*	EC	441122	442122	443122	444122
385 123	**SR**	CL	*SR*	EC	441123	442123	443123	444123
385 124	**SR**	CL	*SR*	EC	441124	442124	443124	444124

CLASS 387   ELECTROSTAR   BOMBARDIER DERBY

The first 29 110 mph Class 387/1s were delivered in 2014–15 for Thameslink. In 2016–17 these transferred to Great Northern for services from King's Cross to Cambridge/King's Lynn and Peterborough.

A further 27 Class 387/2 units were delivered to Southern for Gatwick Express services in 2016 but some have been used by Great Northern.

Great Western Railway took 45 Class 387/1s for services between London Paddington and Reading, Didcot Parkway and Newbury and these now also operate a small number of services to Cardiff Central. 387 130–141 have been fitted with ETCS and are dedicated to the Heathrow Express service.

Part of a speculative order by Porterbrook Leasing, c2c had six Class 387/3s on lease but these are now used by Great Northern.

Formation: DMC/DMS–MS–PTS–DMS.
System: 25 kV AC overhead and 750 V DC third rail.
Construction: Welded aluminium alloy underframe, sides and roof with steel ends. All sections bolted together.
Traction Motors: Two Bombardier asynchronous of 250 kW.
Wheel Arrangement: 2-Bo + 2-Bo + 2-2 + Bo-2.
Braking: Disc & regenerative.   **Dimensions**: 20.39/20.00 x 2.80 m.
Bogies: Bombardier P3-25/T3-25.   **Couplers**: Dellner 12.
Gangways: Throughout.   **Control System**: IGBT Inverter.
Doors: Sliding plug.   **Maximum Speed**: 110 mph.
Heating & ventilation: Air conditioning.
Seating Layout: 2+2 facing/unidirectional.
Multiple Working: Within class and with Class 377.

Class 387/1. Units built for Thameslink, now used by Great Northern.

DMC. Bombardier Derby 2014–15. 22/34. 46.0 t.
MS. Bombardier Derby 2014–15. –/62 1T. 41.3 t.
PTS. Bombardier Derby 2014–15. –/45(+2) 1TD 2W. 41.6 t.
DMS. Bombardier Derby 2014–15. –/60. 45.9 t.

387 101	**TG**	P	*GN*	HE	421101	422101	423101	424101
387 102	**TG**	P	*GN*	HE	421102	422102	423102	424102
387 103	**TG**	P	*GN*	HE	421103	422103	423103	424103
387 104	**TG**	P	*GN*	HE	421104	422104	423104	424104
387 105	**TG**	P	*GN*	HE	421105	422105	423105	424105
387 106	**TG**	P	*GN*	HE	421106	422106	423106	424106
387 107	**TG**	P	*GN*	HE	421107	422107	423107	424107
387 108	**TG**	P	*GN*	HE	421108	422108	423108	424108
387 109	**TG**	P	*GN*	HE	421109	422109	423109	424109
387 110	**TG**	P	*GN*	HE	421110	422110	423110	424110
387 111	**TG**	P	*GN*	HE	421111	422111	423111	424111
387 112	**TG**	P	*GN*	HE	421112	422112	423112	424112
387 113	**TG**	P	*GN*	HE	421113	422113	423113	424113
387 114	**TG**	P	*GN*	HE	421114	422114	423114	424114
387 115	**TG**	P	*GN*	HE	421115	422115	423115	424115
387 116	**TG**	P	*GN*	HE	421116	422116	423116	424116
387 117	**TG**	P	*GN*	HE	421117	422117	423117	424117
387 118	**TG**	P	*GN*	HE	421118	422118	423118	424118
387 119	**TG**	P	*GN*	HE	421119	422119	423119	424119
387 120	**TG**	P	*GN*	HE	421120	422120	423120	424120
387 121	**TG**	P	*GN*	HE	421121	422121	423121	424121
387 122	**TG**	P	*GN*	HE	421122	422122	423122	424122
387 123	**TG**	P	*GN*	HE	421123	422123	423123	424123
387 124	**TG**	P	*GN*	HE	421124	422124	423124	424124
387 125	**TG**	P	*GN*	HE	421125	422125	423125	424125
387 126	**TG**	P	*GN*	HE	421126	422126	423126	424126
387 127	**TG**	P	*GN*	HE	421127	422127	423127	424127
387 128	**TG**	P	*GN*	HE	421128	422128	423128	424128
387 129	**TG**	P	*GN*	HE	421129	422129	423129	424129

Name (carried on DMC): 387 124 Paul McCann

Class 387/1. Heathrow Express units. Fitted with First Class and a modified seating layout with more luggage space and fewer seats for use on Paddington–Heathrow Airport Heathrow Express services. ETCS fitted.

DMC. Bombardier Derby 2016–17. 22/20. 46.0 t.
MS. Bombardier Derby 2016–17. –/54 1T. 41.3 t.
PTS. Bombardier Derby 2016–17. –/39(+2) 1TD 2W. 41.6 t.
DMS. Bombardier Derby 2016–17. –/52. 45.9 t.

387 130	**HX**	P	*HE*	RG	421130	422130	423130	424130
387 131	**HX**	P	*HE*	RG	421131	422131	423131	424131
387 132	**HX**	P	*HE*	RG	421132	422132	423132	424132
387 133	**HX**	P	*HE*	RG	421133	422133	423133	424133
387 134	**HX**	P	*HE*	RG	421134	422134	423134	424134
387 135	**HX**	P	*HE*	RG	421135	422135	423135	424135

387 136	**HX**	P	*HE*	RG	421136	422136	423136	424136
387 137	**HX**	P	*HE*	RG	421137	422137	423137	424137
387 138	**HX**	P	*HE*	RG	421138	422138	423138	424138
387 139	**HX**	P	*HE*	RG	421139	422139	423139	424139
387 140	**HX**	P	*HE*	RG	421140	422140	423140	424140
387 141	**HX**	P	*HE*	RG	421141	422141	423141	424141

Names (carried on end cars):

387 130	SAN FRANCISCO	387 136	PARIS
387 131	SYDNEY	387 137	AMSTERDAM
387 132	NEW YORK	387 138	LAS VEGAS
387 133	TOKYO	387 139	DUBLIN
387 134	BARCELONA	387 140	LONDON
387 135	ROME	387 141	PRAGUE

Class 387/1. Great Western Railway or Great Northern units.

DMS(A). Bombardier Derby 2016–17. –/56. 46.0 t.
MS. Bombardier Derby 2016–17. –/62 1T. 41.3 t.
PTS. Bombardier Derby 2016–17. –/45(+2) 1TD 2W. 41.6 t.
DMS(B). Bombardier Derby 2016–17. –/60. 45.9 t.

387 142	**GW**	P	*GW*	RG	421142	422142	423142	424142
387 143	**GW**	P	*GW*	RG	421143	422143	423143	424143
387 144	**GW**	P	*GW*	RG	421144	422144	423144	424144
387 145	**GW**	P	*GW*	RG	421145	422145	423145	424145
387 146	**GW**	P	*GW*	RG	421146	422146	423146	424146
387 147	**GW**	P	*GW*	RG	421147	422147	423147	424147
387 148	**GW**	P	*GW*	RG	421148	422148	423148	424148
387 149	**GW**	P	*GW*	RG	421149	422149	423149	424149
387 150	**GW**	P	*GW*	RG	421150	422150	423150	424150
387 151	**GW**	P	*GW*	RG	421151	422151	423151	424151
387 152	**GW**	P	*GW*	RG	421152	422152	423152	424152
387 153	**GW**	P	*GW*	RG	421153	422153	423153	424153
387 154	**GW**	P	*GW*	RG	421154	422154	423154	424154
387 155	**GW**	P	*GW*	RG	421155	422155	423155	424155
387 156	**GW**	P	*GW*	RG	421156	422156	423156	424156
387 157	**GW**	P	*GW*	RG	421157	422157	423157	424157
387 158	**GW**	P	*GW*	RG	421158	422158	423158	424158
387 159	**GW**	P	*GW*	RG	421159	422159	423159	424159
387 160	**GW**	P	*GW*	RG	421160	422160	423160	424160
387 161	**GW**	P	*GW*	RG	421161	422161	423161	424161
387 162	**GW**	P	*GW*	RG	421162	422162	423162	424162
387 163	**GW**	P	*GW*	RG	421163	422163	423163	424163
387 164	**GW**	P	*GW*	RG	421164	422164	423164	424164
387 165	**GW**	P	*GW*	RG	421165	422165	423165	424165
387 166	**GW**	P	*GW*	RG	421166	422166	423166	424166
387 167	**GW**	P	*GW*	RG	421167	422167	423167	424167
387 168	**GW**	P	*GW*	RG	421168	422168	423168	424168
387 169	**GW**	P	*GW*	RG	421169	422169	423169	424169
387 170	**GW**	P	*GW*	RG	421170	422170	423170	424170
387 171	**GW**	P	*GW*	RG	421171	422171	423171	424171

387 172	**GW**	P	*GN*	HE	421172	422172	423172	424172
387 173	**GW**	P	*GN*	HE	421173	422173	423173	424173
387 174	**GW**	P	*GN*	HE	421174	422174	423174	424174

Class 387/2. Southern units built for use Gatwick Express-branded services on the London Victoria–Gatwick Airport–Brighton route, but also used on other Southern routes.

DMC. Bombardier Derby 2015–16. 22/34. 46.0 t.
MS. Bombardier Derby 2015–16. –/60 1T. 41.3 t.
PTS. Bombardier Derby 2015–16. –/45(+2) 1TD 2W. 41.6 t.
DMS. Bombardier Derby 2015–16. –/60. 45.9 t.

387 201	**GX**	P	*GN*	HE	421201	422201	423201	424201
387 202	**GX**	P	*SN*	SL	421202	422202	423202	424202
387 203	**GX**	P	*SN*	SL	421203	422203	423203	424203
387 204	**GX**	P	*SN*	SL	421204	422204	423204	424204
387 205	**GX**	P	*SN*	SL	421205	422205	423205	424205
387 206	**GX**	P	*SN*	SL	421206	422206	423206	424206
387 207	**GX**	P	*SN*	SL	421207	422207	423207	424207
387 208	**GX**	P	*SN*	SL	421208	422208	423208	424208
387 209	**GX**	P	*SN*	SL	421209	422209	423209	424209
387 210	**GX**	P	*SN*	SL	421210	422210	423210	424210
387 211	**GX**	P	*SN*	SL	421211	422211	423211	424211
387 212	**GX**	P	*SN*	SL	421212	422212	423212	424212
387 213	**GX**	P	*SN*	SL	421213	422213	423213	424213
387 214	**GX**	P	*SN*	SL	421214	422214	423214	424214
387 215	**GX**	P	*SN*	SL	421215	422215	423215	424215
387 216	**GX**	P	*SN*	SL	421216	422216	423216	424216
387 217	**GX**	P	*SN*	SL	421217	422217	423217	424217
387 218	**GX**	P	*SN*	SL	421218	422218	423218	424218
387 219	**GX**	P	*SN*	SL	421219	422219	423219	424219
387 220	**GX**	P	*SN*	SL	421220	422220	423220	424220
387 221	**GX**	P	*SN*	SL	421221	422221	423221	424221
387 222	**GX**	P	*SN*	SL	421222	422222	423222	424222
387 223	**GX**	P	*SN*	SL	421223	422223	423223	424223
387 224	**GX**	P	*SN*	SL	421224	422224	423224	424224
387 225	**GX**	P	*SN*	SL	421225	422225	423225	424225
387 226	**GX**	P	*SN*	SL	421226	422226	423226	424226
387 227	**GX**	P	*SN*	SL	421227	422227	423227	424227

Class 387/3. Former c2c units now used by Great Northern.

DMS(A). Bombardier Derby 2016. –/56. 46.0 t.
MS. Bombardier Derby 2016. –/62 1T. 41.3 t.
PTS. Bombardier Derby 2016. –/45(+2) 1TD 2W. 41.6 t.
DMS(B). Bombardier Derby 2016. –/60. 45.9 t.

387 301	**C2**	P	*GN*	HE	421301	422301	423301	424301
387 302	**C2**	P	*GN*	HE	421302	422302	423302	424302
387 303	**C2**	P	*GN*	HE	421303	422303	423303	424303
387 304	**C2**	P	*GN*	HE	421304	422304	423304	424304
387 305	**C2**	P	*GN*	HE	421305	422305	423305	424305
387 306	**C2**	P	*GN*	HE	421306	422306	423306	424306

CLASS 390   PENDOLINO   ALSTOM

Tilting units used on the West Coast Main Line.

Formation: As listed below.
Construction: Welded aluminium alloy.
Traction Motors: Two Alstom ONIX 800 of 425 kW.
Wheel Arrangement: 1A-A1 + 1A-A1 + 2-2 + 1A-A1 (+ 2-2 + 1A-A1) + 2-2 + 1A-A1 + 2-2 + 1A-A1 + 1A-A1.
Braking: Disc, rheostatic & regenerative.
Dimensions: 24.80/23.90 x 2.73 m.
Couplers: Dellner 12.
Bogies: Fiat-SIG.
Control System: IGBT Inverter.
Gangways: Within unit.
Maximum Speed: 125 mph.
Doors: Sliding plug.
Heating & ventilation: Air conditioning.
Seating Layout: 1: 2+1 facing/unidirectional, 2: 2+2 facing/unidirectional.
Multiple Working: Within class. Can also be controlled from Class 57/3 locos.

Units up to 390034 were delivered as 8-car sets, without the TS (688xx). During 2004–05 these units were increased to 9-cars.

62 extra vehicles were built 2010–12 to lengthen 31 sets to 11-cars. On renumbering units were renumbered by adding 100 to the set number. Four new complete 11-car units were also delivered. All these extra vehicles were built at Savigliano, Italy (all original Pendolino vehicles were built at Birmingham).

The 9-car units had their MF(B) converted to an MS in 2015 to give them a better balance of Standard to First Class seating.

390033 was written off in the Lambrigg accident of February 2007.

Non-standard liveries:

390 119 Pride celebration colours.
390 121 Race Against Climate Change (various colours).

Class 390/0. Original build 9-car units.

* Refurbished units.

Formation: DMRF–MF–PTF–MS–TS–MS–PTSRMB–MS–DMS.

DMRBF: Alstom Birmingham/Savigliano 2001–05. 18/–. 56.3 t.
MF: Alstom Birmingham/Savigliano 2001–05. 37/–(+2) 1TD 1W. 52.3 t.
PTF: Alstom Birmingham/Savigliano 2001–05. 44/– 1T. 51.2 t.
MS: Alstom Birmingham/Savigliano 2001–05. –/76 1T. 52.3 t.
TS: Alstom Birmingham/Savigliano 2001–05. –/76 1T. 45.5 t.
MS: Alstom Birmingham/Savigliano 2001–05. –/62(+4) 1TD 1W. 52.0 t.
PTSRMB: Alstom Birmingham/Savigliano 2001–05. –/48. 53.2 t.
MS: Alstom Birmingham/Savigliano 2001–05. –/62(+2) 1TD 1W. 52.5 t.
DMS: Alstom Birmingham/Savigliano 2001–05. –/46 1T. 54.5 t.

390 001	**AT**	A	*AW* MA	69101 69401 69501 69601 68801
				69701 69801 69901 69201
390 002	**AT**	A	*AW* MA	69102 69402 69502 69602 68802
				69702 69802 69902 69202
390 005	**AT**	A	*AW* MA	69105 69405 69505 69605 68805
				69705 69805 69905 69205

390 006		**AT**	A	*AW* MA	69106 69406 69506 69606 68806
					69706 69806 69906 69206
390 008		**AT**	A	*AW* MA	69108 69408 69508 69608 68808
					69708 69808 69908 69208
390 009	*	**AT**	A	*AW* MA	69109 69409 69509 69609 68809
					69709 69809 69909 69209
390 010		**AT**	A	*AW* MA	69110 69410 69510 69610 68810
					69710 69810 69910 69210
390 011		**AT**	A	*AW* MA	69111 69411 69511 69611 68811
					69711 69811 69911 69211
390 013		**AT**	A	*AW* MA	69113 69413 69513 69613 68813
					69713 69813 69913 69213
390 016		**AT**	A	*AW* MA	69116 69416 69516 69616 68816
					69716 69816 69916 69216
390 020		**AT**	A	*AW* MA	69120 69420 69520 69620 68820
					69720 69820 69920 69220
390 039		**AT**	A	*AW* MA	69139 69439 69539 69639 68839
					69739 69839 69939 69239
390 040		**AT**	A	*AW* MA	69140 69440 69540 69640 68840
					69740 69840 69940 69240
390 042		**AT**	A	*AW* MA	69142 69442 69542 69642 68842
					69742 69842 69942 69242
390 043		**AT**	A	*AW* MA	69143 69443 69543 69643 68843
					69743 69843 69943 69243
390 044	*	**AT**	A	*AW* MA	69144 69444 69544 69644 68844
					69744 69844 69944 69244
390 045	*	**AT**	A	*AW* MA	69145 69445 69545 69645 68845
					69745 69845 69945 69245
390 046		**AT**	A	*AW* MA	69146 69446 69546 69646 68846
					69746 69846 69946 69246
390 047		**AT**	A	*AW* MA	69147 69447 69547 69647 68847
					69747 69847 69947 69247
390 049		**AT**	A	*AW* MA	69149 69449 69549 69649 68849
					69749 69849 69949 69249
390 050	*	**AT**	A	*AW* MA	69150 69450 69550 69650 68850
					69750 69850 69950 69250

Class 390/1. Original build 9-car units later extended to 11-cars, except 390 154–157 which were built new (in Italy) as 11-cars. All units have been refurbished at Alstom Widnes which included converting an MF coach to an MS and removing a number of Standard Class seats to provide additional luggage space.

Formation: DMRF–MF–PTF–MS–TS–MS–TS–MS–PTSRMB–MS–DMS.

DMRBF: Alstom Birmingham/Savigliano 2001–05/2010–12. 18/–. 56.3 t.
MF: Alstom Birmingham/Savigliano 2001–05/2010–12. 37/–(+2) 1TD 1W. 52.3 t.
PTF: Alstom Birmingham/Savigliano 2001–05/2010–12. 44/– 1T. 51.2 t.
MS: Alstom Birmingham/Savigliano 2001–05/2010–12. –/74 1T. 52.3 t.
TS: Alstom Savigliano 2010–12. –/72 1T. 49.2 t.
MS: Alstom Savigliano 2010–12. –/74 1T. 52.2 t.
TS: Alstom Birmingham/Savigliano 2001–05/2010–12. –/74 1T. 45.5 t.

MS: Alstom Birmingham/Savigliano 2001–05/2010–12. –/60(+4) 1TD 1W. 52.0 t.
PTSRMB: Alstom Birmingham/Savigliano 2001–05/2010–12. –/48. 53.2 t.
MS: Alstom Birmingham/Savigliano 2001–05/2010–12. –/60(+2) 1TD 1W. 52.5 t.
DMS: Alstom Birmingham/Savigliano 2001–05/2010–12. –/46 1T. 54.5 t.

390 103	**AT**	A	*AW* MA	69103 69403 69503 69603 65303 68903					
				68803 69703 69803 69903 69203					
390 104	**AT**	A	*AW* MA	69104 69404 69504 69604 65304 68904					
				68804 69704 69804 69904 69204					
390 107	**AT**	A	*AW* MA	69107 69407 69507 69607 65307 68907					
				68807 69707 69807 69907 69207					
390 112	**AT**	A	*AW* MA	69112 69412 69512 69612 65312 68912					
				68812 69712 69812 69912 69212					
390 114	**AT**	A	*AW* MA	69114 69414 69514 69614 65314 68914					
				68814 69714 69814 69914 69214					
390 115	**AT**	A	*AW* MA	69115 69415 69515 69615 65315 68915					
				68815 69715 69815 69915 69215					
390 117	**AT**	A	*AW* MA	69117 69417 69517 69617 65317 68917					
				68817 69717 69817 69917 69217					
390 118	**AT**	A	*AW* MA	69118 69418 69518 69618 65318 68918					
				68818 69718 69818 69918 69218					
390 119	**0**	A	*AW* MA	69119 69419 69519 69619 65319 68919					
				68819 69719 69819 69919 69219					
390 121	**0**	A	*AW* MA	69121 69421 69521 69621 65321 68921					
				68821 69721 69821 69921 69221					
390 122	**AT**	A	*AW* MA	69122 69422 69522 69622 65322 68922					
				68822 69722 69822 69922 69222					
390 123	**AT**	A	*AW* MA	69123 69423 69523 69623 65323 68923					
				68823 69723 69823 69923 69223					
390 124	**AT**	A	*AW* MA	69124 69424 69524 69624 65324 68924					
				68824 69724 69824 69924 69224					
390 125	**AT**	A	*AW* MA	69125 69425 69525 69625 65325 68925					
				68825 69725 69825 69925 69225					
390 126	**AT**	A	*AW* MA	69126 69426 69526 69626 65326 68926					
				68826 69726 69826 69926 69226					
390 127	**AT**	A	*AW* MA	69127 69427 69527 69627 65327 68927					
				68827 69727 69827 69927 69227					
390 128	**AT**	A	*AW* MA	69128 69428 69528 69628 65328 68928					
				68828 69728 69828 69928 69228					
390 129	**AT**	A	*AW* MA	69129 69429 69529 69629 65329 68929					
				68829 69729 69829 69929 69229					
390 130	**AT**	A	*AW* MA	69130 69430 69530 69630 65330 68930					
				68830 69730 69830 69930 69230					
390 131	**AT**	A	*AW* MA	69131 69431 69531 69631 65331 68931					
				68831 69731 69831 69931 69231					
390 132	**AT**	A	*AW* MA	69132 69432 69532 69632 65332 68932					
				68832 69732 69832 69932 69232					
390 134	**AT**	A	*AW* MA	69134 69434 69534 69634 65334 68934					
				68834 69734 69834 69934 69234					
390 135	**AT**	A	*AW* MA	69135 69435 69535 69635 65335 68935					
				68835 69735 69835 69935 69235					

▲ ScotRail-liveried 318 261 and 320 315 arrive at Partick with the 12.47 Dalmuir–Larkhall on 09/06/23. **Robert Pritchard**

▼ Swift Express Freight-liveried 321 334, operated by Varamis Rail, passes Symington with 1M04 17.34 Mossend Down Yard–Birmingham International parcels service on 04/09/23. **Robin Ralston**

▲ Northern-liveried 323 236 is seen at Mauldeth Road with the 15.36 Manchester Piccadilly–Crewe on 29/05/23. **Robert Pritchard**

▼ Northern-liveried 331 023 and 331 027 (nearest camera) are seen between Manchester Oxford Road and Piccadilly stations with the 10.26 Blackpool North–Manchester Airport on 29/05/23. **Robert Pritchard**

▲ ScotRail-liveried 334025 and 334028 arrive at Hyndland with the 13.24 Helensburgh Central–Edinburgh on 09/06/23. **Robert Pritchard**

▼ Elizabeth Line-liveried 345066 passes West Ealing with the 13.57 Reading–London Paddington on 17/10/22. **Robert Pritchard**

▲ London Northwestern Railway-liveried 350 107 leaves Wolverhampton with the 11.52 Crewe–Birmingham New Street on 14/10/22. **Robert Pritchard**

▼ c2c-liveried 357 322 and 357 022 pass Shadwell DLR station with the 11.53 London Fenchurch Street–Grays on 04/05/23. **Robert Pritchard**

▲ Southeastern-liveried 375310 leaves Maidstone Barracks with the 10.00 Paddock Wood–Strood on 07/04/23. **Robert Pritchard**

▼ Still in their original Connex livery, 376004 and 376018 leave Abbey Wood with the 12.23 London Cannon Street–Cannon Street loop service on 24/05/22. **Robert Pritchard**

▲ ScotRail-liveried 380 020 leaves Glasgow Central with the 17.10 to Cathcart on 09/06/23. **Robert Pritchard**

▼ ScotRail-liveried 385 006 pauses at Bishopbriggs with the 08.49 Glasgow Queen Street–Alloa on 09/06/23. **Robert Pritchard**

▲ Great Western Railway-liveried 387152 and 387166 pass Langley with the 11.08 Didcot Parkway–London Paddington on 18/10/22.	**Robert Pritchard**

▼ Avanti West Coast-liveried 390152 passes South Kenton with the 13.43 Liverpool Lime Street–London Euston on 04/05/23.	**Robert Pritchard**

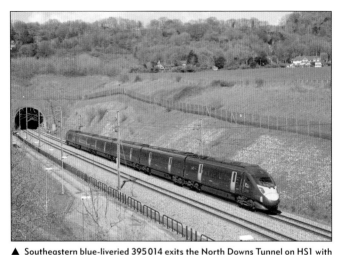

▲ Southeastern blue-liveried 395014 exits the North Downs Tunnel on HS1 with the 12.37 London St Pancras–Margate on 07/04/23. **Robert Pritchard**

▼ TransPennine Express-liveried 397006 passes Wandel with the 18.11 Edinburgh–Manchester Airport on 02/08/22. **Robin Ralston**

▲ Four of the new Transport for Wales Class 398 tram-trains are seen at the new Taffs Wells depot on 18/07/23, with 398006 and 398007 in the foreground.
Courtesy Transport for Wales

▼ South Western Railway-liveried 450090 leads old South West Trains blue-liveried 450121 through Ashford (Surrey) with the 14.20 London Waterloo–Reading on 18/10/22.
Robert Pritchard

▲ Southeastern suburban-liveried 465159 arrives at Rochester with the 16.42 London Victoria–Gillingham on 08/04/23.　　**Robert Pritchard**

▼ South Western Railway-liveried 484003 calls at Sandown with the 12.44 Ryde Pier Head–Shanklin on 15/11/21.　　**Robert Pritchard**

▲ Thameslink-liveried 700 154 arrives at Luton Airport Parkway with the 11.34 Bedford–Three Bridges on 25/03/23. **Robert Pritchard**

▼ South Western Railway-liveried new Aventra 701 017 passes Putney with a 5Q22 11.15 London Waterloo–Waterloo mileage accumulation run on 10/11/22. **Alex Ayre**

▲ London Overground-liveried 710 102 arrives at Hackney Downs with the 14.10 Chingford–London Liverpool Street on 13/08/23. **Robert Pritchard**

▼ Govia Thameslink-liveried 717 010 is seen at London King's Cross with a service to Stevenage on 29/07/23. **Ian Beardsley**

▲ Greater Anglia-liveried 720 129 and 720 522 arrive at Stratford with the 11.50 Southend Victoria–London Liverpool Street on 17/06/23. **Robert Pritchard**

▼ West Midlands Railway-liveried 730 018 is seen at Milton Keynes Central whilst on display to the press on 30/06/23. **Robert Pritchard**

▲ Greater Anglia-liveried 745006 arrives at Colchester with the 13.41 Ipswich–London Liverpool Street on 16/10/22. **Robert Pritchard**

▼ HydroFlex prototype unit 799201 (converted from 319382) is seen at Besford, being hauled from Gloucester Yard to Long Marston via Worcester on 05/09/23. **Dave Gommersall**

▲ Great Western Railway-liveried 800008 (with Pride stripes) and 800032 pass Slough with the 11.30 Bristol Temple Meads–London Paddington on 18/10/22.
Robert Pritchard

▼ LNER Azuma-liveried 801210 passes East Linton with the 11.00 Edinburgh–London King's Cross on 19/04/23.
Robin Ralston

▲ Lumo-liveried 803 002 passes Sunderland Bridge with the 10.45 London King's Cross–Edinburgh on 22/06/22. **Alex Ayre**

▼ Class 374 Eurostar 4005/06 is seen on HS1 near Harrietsham with the 14.43 Paris Nord–London St Pancras on 09/04/23. **Robert Pritchard**

390 136	**AT**	A	*AW* MA	69136	69436	69536	69636	65336	68936
				68836	69736	69836	69936	69236	
390 137	**AT**	A	*AW* MA	69137	69437	69537	69637	65337	68937
				68837	69737	69837	69937	69237	
390 138	**AT**	A	*AW* MA	69138	69438	69538	69638	65338	68938
				68838	69738	69838	69938	69238	
390 141	**AT**	A	*AW* MA	69141	69441	69541	69641	65341	68941
				68841	69741	69841	69941	69241	
390 148	**AT**	A	*AW* MA	69148	69448	69548	69648	65348	68948
				68848	69748	69848	69948	69248	
390 151	**AT**	A	*AW* MA	69151	69451	69551	69651	65351	68951
				68851	69751	69851	69951	69251	
390 152	**AT**	A	*AW* MA	69152	69452	69552	69652	65352	68952
				68852	69752	69852	69952	69252	
390 153	**AT**	A	*AW* MA	69153	69453	69553	69653	65353	68953
				68853	69753	69853	69953	69253	
390 154	**AT**	A	*AW* MA	69154	69454	69554	69654	65354	68954
				68854	69754	69854	69954	69254	
390 155	**AT**	A	*AW* MA	69155	69455	69555	69655	65355	68955
				68855	69755	69855	69955	69255	
390 156	**AT**	A	*AW* MA	69156	69456	69556	69656	65356	68956
				68856	69756	69856	69956	69256	
390 157	**AT**	A	*AW* MA	69157	69457	69557	69657	65357	68957
				68857	69757	69857	69957	69257	

Names (carried on MF No. 696xx):

390001	Bee Together	390119	PROGRESS
390002	Stephen Sutton	390121	OPPORTUNITY
390005	City of Wolverhampton	390122	Penny the Pendolino
390006	Rethink Mental Illness	390128	City of Preston
390008	CHARLES RENNIE MACKINTOSH	390129	City of Stoke-on-Trent
390009	Treaty of Union	390130	City of Edinburgh
390010	Cumbrian Spirit	390131	City of Liverpool
390011	City of Lichfield	390132	City of Birmingham
390013	Blackpool Belle	390134	City of Carlisle
390039	Lady Godiva	390135	City of Lancaster
390044	Royal Scot	390136	City of Coventry
390045	BIRMINGHAM PRIDE	390138	City of London
390103	ASQUITH XAVIER	390148	Flying Scouseman
390104	Alstom Pendolino	390151	Unknown Soldier
390114	City of Manchester	390155	RAILWAY BENEFIT FUND
390115	Crewe – All Change	390156	Pride and Prosperity
390117	Blue Peter	390157	Chad Varah

CLASS 395   JAVELIN   HITACHI JAPAN

6-car dual-voltage units used on Southeastern High Speed trains from London St Pancras.

Formation: PDTS–MS–MS–MS–MS–PDTS.
Systems: 25 kV AC overhead/750 V DC third rail.
Construction: Aluminium.
Traction Motors: Four Hitachi asynchronous of 210 kW.
Wheel Arrangement: 2-2 + Bo-Bo + Bo-Bo + Bo-Bo + Bo-Bo + 2-2.
Braking: Disc, rheostatic & regenerative.
Dimensions: 20.88/20.0 x 2.81 m.   **Couplers:** Scharfenberg.
Bogies: Hitachi.   **Control System:** IGBT Inverter.
Gangways: Within unit.   **Maximum Speed:** 140 mph.
Doors: Single-leaf sliding.   **Multiple Working:** Within class only.
Heating & ventilation: Air conditioning.
Seating Layout: 2+2 facing/unidirectional (mainly unidirectional).

PDTS(A): Hitachi Kasado, Japan 2006–09. –/28(+12) 1TD 2W. 46.7 t.
MS: Hitachi Kasado, Japan 2006–09. –/66. 45.0 t–45.7 t.
PDTS(B): Hitachi Kasado, Japan 2006–09. –/48 1T. 46.7 t.

395 001	**SB**	E	*SE*	AD	39011	39012	39013	39014	39015	39016
395 002	**SB**	E	*SE*	AD	39021	39022	39023	39024	39025	39026
395 003	**SB**	E	*SE*	AD	39031	39032	39033	39034	39035	39036
395 004	**SB**	E	*SE*	AD	39041	39042	39043	39044	39045	39046
395 005	**SB**	E	*SE*	AD	39051	39052	39053	39054	39055	39056
395 006	**SB**	E	*SE*	AD	39061	39062	39063	39064	39065	39066
395 007	**SB**	E	*SE*	AD	39071	39072	39073	39074	39075	39076
395 008	**SB**	E	*SE*	AD	39081	39082	39083	39084	39085	39086
395 009	**SB**	E	*SE*	AD	39091	39092	39093	39094	39095	39096
395 010	**SB**	E	*SE*	AD	39101	39102	39103	39104	39105	39106
395 011	**SB**	E	*SE*	AD	39111	39112	39113	39114	39115	39116
395 012	**SB**	E	*SE*	AD	39121	39122	39123	39124	39125	39126
395 013	**SB**	E	*SE*	AD	39131	39132	39133	39134	39135	39136
395 014	**SB**	E	*SE*	AD	39141	39142	39143	39144	39145	39146
395 015	**SB**	E	*SE*	AD	39151	39152	39153	39154	39155	39156
395 016	**SB**	E	*SE*	AD	39161	39162	39163	39164	39165	39166
395 017	**SB**	E	*SE*	AD	39171	39172	39173	39174	39175	39176
395 018	**SB**	E	*SE*	AD	39181	39182	39183	39184	39185	39186
395 019	**SB**	E	*SE*	AD	39191	39192	39193	39194	39195	39196
395 020	**SB**	E	*SE*	AD	39201	39202	39203	39204	39205	39206
395 021	**SB**	E	*SE*	AD	39211	39212	39213	39214	39215	39216
395 022	**SB**	E	*SE*	AD	39221	39222	39223	39224	39225	39226
395 023	**SB**	E	*SE*	AD	39231	39232	39233	39234	39235	39236
395 024	**SB**	E	*SE*	AD	39241	39242	39243	39244	39245	39246
395 025	**SB**	E	*SE*	AD	39251	39252	39253	39254	39255	39256
395 026	**SB**	E	*SE*	AD	39261	39262	39263	39264	39265	39266
395 027	**SB**	E	*SE*	AD	39271	39272	39273	39274	39275	39276
395 028	**SB**	E	*SE*	AD	39281	39282	39283	39284	39285	39286
395 029	**SB**	E	*SE*	AD	39291	39292	39293	39294	39295	39296

Names (carried on end cars):

395001	Dame Kelly Holmes	395018	THE VICTORY Javelin
395002	Sebastian Coe	395019	Jessica Ennis
395003	Sir Steve Redgrave	395020	Jason Kenny
395004	Sir Chris Hoy	395021	Ed Clancy MBE
395005	Dame Tanni Grey-Thompson	395022	Alistair Brownlee
395006	Daley Thompson	395023	Ellie Simmonds
395007	Steve Backley	395024	Jonnie Peacock
395008	Ben Ainslie	395025	Victoria Pendleton
395009	Rebecca Adlington	395026	Marc Woods
395010	Duncan Goodhew	395027	Hannah Cockcroft
395011	Katherine Grainger	395028	Laura Trott
395012	HORNBY Visitor Centre Margate, Kent	395029	David Weir
395013	Dina Asher-Smith		
395014			

CLASS 397   CIVITY   CAF

TransPennine Express units mainly used on the West Coast Main Line
Manchester Airport–Edinburgh/Glasgow services.

Formation: DMF–PTS–MS–PTS–DMS.
Construction: Aluminium.
Traction Motors: Four TSA of 220 kW.
Wheel Arrangement:
Braking: Disc and regenerative.   **Dimensions:** 24.03/23.35 x 2.71 m.
Bogies: CAF.   **Couplers:** Dellner.
Gangways: Within unit.   **Control System:** IGBT Inverter.
Doors: Sliding plug.   **Maximum Speed:** 125 mph.
Heating & ventilation: Air conditioning.
Seating: 1: 2+1 facing/unidirectional; 2: 2+2 facing/unidirectional.
Multiple Working: Within class.

DMF. CAF Beasain 2017–19. 24/– 1TD 2W. 41.4 t.
PTS(A). CAF Beasain 2017–19. –/76. 34.5 t.
MS. CAF Beasain 2017–19. –/68 2T. 36.6 t.
PTS(B). CAF Beasain 2017–19. –/76. 34.9 t.
DMS. CAF Beasain 2017–19. –/44(+8) 1T. 39.2 t.

397001	**TP**	E	*TP*	MA	471001	472001	473001	474001	475001
397002	**TP**	E	*TP*	MA	471002	472002	473002	474002	475002
397003	**TP**	E	*TP*	MA	471003	472003	473003	474003	475003
397004	**TP**	E	*TP*	MA	471004	472004	473004	474004	475004
397005	**TP**	E	*TP*	MA	471005	472005	473005	474005	475005
397006	**TP**	E	*TP*	MA	471006	472006	473006	474006	475006
397007	**TP**	E	*TP*	MA	471007	472007	473007	474007	475007
397008	**TP**	E	*TP*	MA	471008	472008	473008	474008	475008
397009	**TP**	E	*TP*	MA	471009	472009	473009	474009	475009
397010	**TP**	E	*TP*	MA	471010	472010	473010	474010	475010
397011	**TP**	E	*TP*	MA	471011	472011	473011	474011	475011
397012	**TP**	E	*TP*	MA	471012	472012	473012	474012	475012

CLASS 398   CITYLINK   STADLER

New 3-car Citylink bi-mode electric/battery metro tram-train units currently being delivered for Transport for Wales for use on the Cardiff Valley Lines (Aberdare, Merthyr Tydfil, Treherbert and the Cardiff City Line). Due to enter service from 2024 working from the new depot at Taff's Well.

Formation: DMS–TS–DMS.
Systems: 25 kV AC overhead/battery.
Construction: Steel.
Traction Motors: 4 x 140 kW (per unit).
Wheel Arrangement: Bo-2-2-Bo.   **Weight:** 76.8 t.
Braking: Disc, regenerative & emergency track.
Dimensions: 40.00 x 2.65 m (full set).
Bogies: Stadler.   **Couplers:**
Gangways: Within unit.   **Control System:** IGBT Inverter.
Doors: Sliding plug.   **Maximum Speed:** 60 mph.
Seating Layout: 2+2 unidirectional/facing.   **Multiple Working:** Within class only.

DMS(A): Stadler, Valencia 2020–24. –/34(+7).
MS: Stadler, Valencia 2020–24. –/36(+14).
DMS(B): Stadler, Valencia 2020–24. –/34(+7).

398001	**TW**	SM		999051	999151	999251
398002	**TW**	SM		999052	999152	999252
398003	**TW**	SM		999053	999153	999253
398004	**TW**	SM		999054	999154	999254
398005	**TW**	SM		999055	999155	999255
398006	**TW**	SM		999056	999156	999256
398007	**TW**	SM		999057	999157	999257
398008	**TW**	SM		999058	999158	999258
398009	**TW**	SM		999059	999159	999259
398010	**TW**	SM		999060	999160	999260
398011	**TW**	SM		999061	999161	999261
398012	**TW**	SM		999062	999162	999262
398013	**TW**	SM		999063	999163	999263
398014	**TW**	SM		999064	999164	999264
398015	**TW**	SM		999065	999165	999265
398016	**TW**	SM		999066	999166	999266
398017	**TW**	SM		999067	999167	999267
398018	**TW**	SM		999068	999168	999268
398019	**TW**	SM		999069	999169	999269
398020	**TW**	SM		999070	999170	999270
398021	**TW**	SM		999071	999171	999271
398022	**TW**	SM		999072	999172	999272
398023	**TW**	SM		999073	999173	999273
398024	**TW**	SM		999074	999174	999274
398025	**TW**	SM		999075	999175	999275
398026	**TW**	SM		999076	999176	999276
398027	**TW**	SM		999077	999177	999277
398028	**TW**	SM		999078	999178	999278
398029	**TW**	SM		999079	999179	999279

398 030	**TW**	SM		999080	999180	999280
398 031	**TW**	SM		999081	999181	999281
398 032	**TW**	SM		999082	999182	999282
398 033	**TW**	SM		999083	999183	999283
398 034	**TW**	SM		999084	999184	999284
398 035	**TW**	SM		999085	999185	999285
398 036	**TW**	SM		999086	999186	999286

CLASS 399   CITYLINK   VOSSLOH/STADLER

The Class 399s are tram-trains used on the pilot Sheffield–Rotherham Parkgate tram-train service. This launched in 2018, operated by Stagecoach Supertram. They are dual-voltage 750 V DC/25 kV AC (although currently only operating on 750 V DC). For operation on Network Rail lines EMU running numbers 399 201–207 are carried (as well as vehicle numbers in the 999xxx series), in addition to the Stagecoach Supertram fleet numbers 201–207.

Following two separate accidents in autumn 2018 units 399 202 and 399 204 are operating in mixed formations, as shown.

At the time of writing units 399 201–205 have tram-train wheel profiles for operating on the National Rail network to Rotherham Parkgate. 399 206/207 can only operate on the tramway network, but could be modified to operate to Rotherham if required, 399 206 having been modified to operate to Rotherham in 2018–20 to cover for the accident-damaged 399 204.

Formation: DMS–MS–DMS.
Systems: 750 V DC/25 kV AC overhead.
Construction: Steel.
Traction Motors: Six VEM of 145 kW (per unit).
Wheel Arrangement: Bo-2-Bo-Bo.   **Weight:** 64 t.
Braking: Disc, regenerative & emergency track.
Dimensions: 37.20 x 2.65 m (full set). **Couplers:** Albert (emergency use).
Bogies: Vossloh.   **Control System:** IGBT Inverter.
Gangways: Within unit.   **Maximum Speed:** 60 mph.
Doors: Sliding plug.   **Multiple Working:** Within class only.
Seating Layout: 2+2 facing/unidirectional.

DMS(A): Vossloh, Valencia 2014–15. –/22(+4) 1W.
MS: Vossloh, Valencia 2014–15. –/44.
DMS(B): Vossloh, Valencia 2014–15. –/22(+4) 1W.

399 201	**SD**	SY	*SY*	NU	999001	999101	999201
399 202	**SD**	SY	*SY*	NU	999002	999102	999204
399 203	**SD**	SY	*SY*	NU	999003	999103	999203
399 204	**SD**	SY	*SY*	NU	999004	999104	999202
399 205	**SD**	SY	*SY*	NU	999005	999105	999205
399 206	**SD**	SY	*SY*	NU	999006	999106	999206
399 207	**SD**	SY	*SY*	NU	999007	999107	999207

Name (carried on cars 999002 and 999204):

399 202   Theo – The Children's Hospital Charity

2. 750 V DC THIRD RAIL EMUs

These classes use the third rail system at 750 V DC (unless stated). Outer couplers are buckeyes on units built before 1982 with bar couplers within the units. Newer units generally have Dellner outer couplers.

CLASS 444   DESIRO UK   SIEMENS

Express units.

Formation: DMS–TS–TS–TS–DMC.
Construction: Aluminium.
Traction Motors: Four Siemens 1TB2016-0GB02 asynchronous of 250 kW.
Wheel Arrangement: Bo-Bo + 2-2 + 2-2 + 2-2 + Bo-Bo.
Braking: Disc, rheostatic & regenerative. **Dimensions:** 23.57 x 2.69 m.
Bogies: SGP SF5000.   **Couplers:** Dellner 12.
Gangways: Throughout.   **Control System:** IGBT Inverter.
Doors: Single-leaf sliding plug.   **Maximum Speed:** 100 mph.
Heating & Ventilation: Air conditioning.
Seating Layout: 1: 2+2 facing/unidirectional, 2: 2+2 facing/unidirectional.
Multiple Working: Within class and with Class 450.

DMS. Siemens Vienna/Krefeld 2003–04. –/76. 51.0t.
TS 67101–145. Siemens Vienna/Krefeld 2003–04. –/76 1T. 40.3t.
TS 67151–195. Siemens Vienna/Krefeld 2003–04. –/76 1T. 36.8t.
TS. Siemens Vienna/Krefeld 2003–04. –/59 1TD 1T 2W. 42.1t.
DMC. Siemens Vienna/Krefeld 2003–04. 32/40. 51.3t.

444001	SW	A	SW	NT	63801	67101	67151	67201	63851
444002	SW	A	SW	NT	63802	67102	67152	67202	63852
444003	SW	A	SW	NT	63803	67103	67153	67203	63853
444004	ST	A	SW	NT	63804	67104	67154	67204	63854
444005	SW	A	SW	NT	63805	67105	67155	67205	63855
444006	SW	A	SW	NT	63806	67106	67156	67206	63856
444007	SW	A	SW	NT	63807	67107	67157	67207	63857
444008	SW	A	SW	NT	63808	67108	67158	67208	63858
444009	SW	A	SW	NT	63809	67109	67159	67209	63859
444010	SW	A	SW	NT	63810	67110	67160	67210	63860
444011	SW	A	SW	NT	63811	67111	67161	67211	63861
444012	SW	A	SW	NT	63812	67112	67162	67212	63862
444013	SW	A	SW	NT	63813	67113	67163	67213	63863
444014	SW	A	SW	NT	63814	67114	67164	67214	63864
444015	SW	A	SW	NT	63815	67115	67165	67215	63865
444016	SW	A	SW	NT	63816	67116	67166	67216	63866
444017	SW	A	SW	NT	63817	67117	67167	67217	63867
444018	SW	A	SW	NT	63818	67118	67168	67218	63868
444019	SW	A	SW	NT	63819	67119	67169	67219	63869
444020	SW	A	SW	NT	63820	67120	67170	67220	63870
444021	SW	A	SW	NT	63821	67121	67171	67221	63871
444022	SW	A	SW	NT	63822	67122	67172	67222	63872
444023	SW	A	SW	NT	63823	67123	67173	67223	63873

444024	**SW**	A	*SW*	NT	63824	67124	67174	67224	63874
444025	**SW**	A	*SW*	NT	63825	67125	67175	67225	63875
444026	**ST**	A	*SW*	NT	63826	67126	67176	67226	63876
444027	**SW**	A	*SW*	NT	63827	67127	67177	67227	63877
444028	**SW**	A	*SW*	NT	63828	67128	67178	67228	63878
444029	**SW**	A	*SW*	NT	63829	67129	67179	67229	63879
444030	**SW**	A	*SW*	NT	63830	67130	67180	67230	63880
444031	**SW**	A	*SW*	NT	63831	67131	67181	67231	63881
444032	**SW**	A	*SW*	NT	63832	67132	67182	67232	63882
444033	**SW**	A	*SW*	NT	63833	67133	67183	67233	63883
444034	**SW**	A	*SW*	NT	63834	67134	67184	67234	63884
444035	**SW**	A	*SW*	NT	63835	67135	67185	67235	63885
444036	**SW**	A	*SW*	NT	63836	67136	67186	67236	63886
444037	**SW**	A	*SW*	NT	63837	67137	67187	67237	63887
444038	**SW**	A	*SW*	NT	63838	67138	67188	67238	63888
444039	**ST**	A	*SW*	NT	63839	67139	67189	67239	63889
444040	**SW**	A	*SW*	NT	63840	67140	67190	67240	63890
444041	**SW**	A	*SW*	NT	63841	67141	67191	67241	63891
444042	**SW**	A	*SW*	NT	63842	67142	67192	67242	63892
444043	**SW**	A	*SW*	NT	63843	67143	67193	67243	63893
444044	**ST**	A	*SW*	NT	63844	67144	67194	67244	63894
444045	**ST**	A	*SW*	NT	63845	67145	67195	67245	63895

Names (carried on TSRMB):

444001	NAOMI HOUSE	444023	The Alex Wardle Foundation
444012	DESTINATION WEYMOUTH	444038	SOUTH WESTERN RAILWAY
444018	THE FAB 444	444040	THE D-DAY STORY PORTSMOUTH

CLASS 450   DESIRO UK   SIEMENS

Outer suburban units.

Formation: DMC–TS–TS–DMC.
Construction: Aluminium.
Traction Motors: Four Siemens 1TB2016-0GB02 asynchronous of 250 kW.
Wheel Arrangement: Bo-Bo + 2-2 + 2-2 + Bo-Bo.
Braking: Disc, rheostatic & regenerative. **Dimensions:** 20.34 x 2.79 m.
Bogies: SGP SF5000. **Couplers:** Dellner 12.
Gangways: Throughout. **Control System:** IGBT Inverter.
Doors: Sliding plug. **Maximum Speed:** 100 mph.
Heating & Ventilation: Air conditioning.
Seating Layout: 1: 2+2 facing/unidirectional, 2: 3+2 facing/unidirectional.
Multiple Working: Within class and with Class 444.

Advertising livery: 450067 Keyworkers (blue on driving cars).

450043–070 were numbered 450543–570 between 2007/08 and 2019. They were renumbered back into the 450/0 series in 2019.

DMC(A). Siemens Krefeld/Vienna 2002–06. 8/62. 48.0 t.
TS(A). Siemens Krefeld/Vienna 2002–06. –/70(+4) 1T. 35.8 t.
TS(B). Siemens Krefeld/Vienna 2002–06. –/61(+9) 1TD 2W. 39.8 t.
DMC(B). Siemens Krefeld/Vienna 2002–06. 8/62. 48.6 t.

450001	**SW**	A	*SW*	NT	63201	64201	68101	63601
450002	**SW**	A	*SW*	NT	63202	64202	68102	63602
450003	**SW**	A	*SW*	NT	63203	64203	68103	63603
450004	**SW**	A	*SW*	NT	63204	64204	68104	63604
450005	**SW**	A	*SW*	NT	63205	64205	68105	63605
450006	**SW**	A	*SW*	NT	63206	64206	68106	63606
450007	**SW**	A	*SW*	NT	63207	64207	68107	63607
450008	**SW**	A	*SW*	NT	63208	64208	68108	63608
450009	**SW**	A	*SW*	NT	63209	64209	68109	63609
450010	**SW**	A	*SW*	NT	63210	64210	68110	63610
450011	**SW**	A	*SW*	NT	63211	64211	68111	63611
450012	**SW**	A	*SW*	NT	63212	64212	68112	63612
450013	**SW**	A	*SW*	NT	63213	64213	68113	63613
450014	**SW**	A	*SW*	NT	63214	64214	68114	63614
450015	**SW**	A	*SW*	NT	63215	64215	68115	63615
450016	**SW**	A	*SW*	NT	63216	64216	68116	63616
450017	**SW**	A	*SW*	NT	63217	64217	68117	63617
450018	**SW**	A	*SW*	NT	63218	64218	68118	63618
450019	**SW**	A	*SW*	NT	63219	64219	68119	63619
450020	**SW**	A	*SW*	NT	63220	64220	68120	63620
450021	**SW**	A	*SW*	NT	63221	64221	68121	63621
450022	**SW**	A	*SW*	NT	63222	64222	68122	63622
450023	**SW**	A	*SW*	NT	63223	64223	68123	63623
450024	**SW**	A	*SW*	NT	63224	64224	68124	63624
450025	**SW**	A	*SW*	NT	63225	64225	68125	63625
450026	**SW**	A	*SW*	NT	63226	64226	68126	63626
450027	**SW**	A	*SW*	NT	63227	64227	68127	63627
450028	**SW**	A	*SW*	NT	63228	64228	68128	63628
450029	**SW**	A	*SW*	NT	63229	64229	68129	63629
450030	**SW**	A	*SW*	NT	63230	64230	68130	63630
450031	**SD**	A	*SW*	NT	63231	64231	68131	63631
450032	**SW**	A	*SW*	NT	63232	64232	68132	63632
450033	**SW**	A	*SW*	NT	63233	64233	68133	63633
450034	**SW**	A	*SW*	NT	63234	64234	68134	63634
450035	**SW**	A	*SW*	NT	63235	64235	68135	63635
450036	**SW**	A	*SW*	NT	63236	64236	68136	63636
450037	**SW**	A	*SW*	NT	63237	64237	68137	63637
450038	**SW**	A	*SW*	NT	63238	64238	68138	63638
450039	**SW**	A	*SW*	NT	63239	64239	68139	63639
450040	**SW**	A	*SW*	NT	63240	64240	68140	63640
450041	**SW**	A	*SW*	NT	63241	64241	68141	63641
450042	**SW**	A	*SW*	NT	63242	64242	68142	63642
450043	**SW**	A	*SW*	NT	63243	64243	68143	63643
450044	**SW**	A	*SW*	NT	63244	64244	68144	63644
450045	**SW**	A	*SW*	NT	63245	64245	68145	63645
450046	**SW**	A	*SW*	NT	63246	64246	68146	63646
450047	**SW**	A	*SW*	NT	63247	64247	68147	63647
450048	**SW**	A	*SW*	NT	63248	64248	68148	63648
450049	**SW**	A	*SW*	NT	63249	64249	68149	63649
450050	**SW**	A	*SW*	NT	63250	64250	68150	63650
450051	**SW**	A	*SW*	NT	63251	64251	68151	63651

450 052	**SW**	A	*SW*	NT	63252	64252	68152	63652
450 053	**SW**	A	*SW*	NT	63253	64253	68153	63653
450 054	**SW**	A	*SW*	NT	63254	64254	68154	63654
450 055	**SW**	A	*SW*	NT	63255	64255	68155	63655
450 056	**SW**	A	*SW*	NT	63256	64256	68156	63656
450 057	**SW**	A	*SW*	NT	63257	64257	68157	63657
450 058	**SW**	A	*SW*	NT	63258	64258	68158	63658
450 059	**SD**	A	*SW*	NT	63259	64259	68159	63659
450 060	**SW**	A	*SW*	NT	63260	64260	68160	63660
450 061	**SW**	A	*SW*	NT	63261	64261	68161	63661
450 062	**SW**	A	*SW*	NT	63262	64262	68162	63662
450 063	**SW**	A	*SW*	NT	63263	64263	68163	63663
450 064	**SW**	A	*SW*	NT	63264	64264	68164	63664
450 065	**SW**	A	*SW*	NT	63265	64265	68165	63665
450 066	**SW**	A	*SW*	NT	63266	64266	68166	63666
450 067	**AL**	A	*SW*	NT	63267	64267	68167	63667
450 068	**SW**	A	*SW*	NT	63268	64268	68168	63668
450 069	**SW**	A	*SW*	NT	63269	64269	68169	63669
450 070	**SW**	A	*SW*	NT	63270	64270	68170	63670
450 071	**SW**	A	*SW*	NT	63271	64271	68171	63671
450 072	**SW**	A	*SW*	NT	63272	64272	68172	63672
450 073	**SW**	A	*SW*	NT	63273	64273	68173	63673
450 074	**SW**	A	*SW*	NT	63274	64274	68174	63674
450 075	**SW**	A	*SW*	NT	63275	64275	68175	63675
450 076	**SW**	A	*SW*	NT	63276	64276	68176	63676
450 077	**SW**	A	*SW*	NT	63277	64277	68177	63677
450 078	**SW**	A	*SW*	NT	63278	64278	68178	63678
450 079	**SW**	A	*SW*	NT	63279	64279	68179	63679
450 080	**SW**	A	*SW*	NT	63280	64280	68180	63680
450 081	**SW**	A	*SW*	NT	63281	64281	68181	63681
450 082	**SW**	A	*SW*	NT	63282	64282	68182	63682
450 083	**SW**	A	*SW*	NT	63283	64283	68183	63683
450 084	**SW**	A	*SW*	NT	63284	64284	68184	63684
450 085	**SD**	A	*SW*	NT	63285	64285	68185	63685
450 086	**SW**	A	*SW*	NT	63286	64286	68186	63686
450 087	**SW**	A	*SW*	NT	63287	64287	68187	63687
450 088	**SW**	A	*SW*	NT	63288	64288	68188	63688
450 089	**SW**	A	*SW*	NT	63289	64289	68189	63689
450 090	**SW**	A	*SW*	NT	63290	64290	68190	63690
450 091	**SW**	A	*SW*	NT	63291	64291	68191	63691
450 092	**SW**	A	*SW*	NT	63292	64292	68192	63692
450 093	**SW**	A	*SW*	NT	63293	64293	68193	63693
450 094	**SW**	A	*SW*	NT	63294	64294	68194	63694
450 095	**SW**	A	*SW*	NT	63295	64295	68195	63695
450 096	**SW**	A	*SW*	NT	63296	64296	68196	63696
450 097	**SW**	A	*SW*	NT	63297	64297	68197	63697
450 098	**SW**	A	*SW*	NT	63298	64298	68198	63698
450 099	**SD**	A	*SW*	NT	63299	64299	68199	63699
450 100	**SW**	A	*SW*	NT	63300	64300	68200	63700
450 101	**SW**	A	*SW*	NT	63701	66851	66801	63751
450 102	**SW**	A	*SW*	NT	63702	66852	66802	63752

450 103	**SW**	A	*SW*	NT	63703	66853	66803	63753
450 104	**SW**	A	*SW*	NT	63704	66854	66804	63754
450 105	**SW**	A	*SW*	NT	63705	66855	66805	63755
450 106	**SW**	A	*SW*	NT	63706	66856	66806	63756
450 107	**SW**	A	*SW*	NT	63707	66857	66807	63757
450 108	**SW**	A	*SW*	NT	63708	66858	66808	63758
450 109	**SW**	A	*SW*	NT	63709	66859	66809	63759
450 110	**SW**	A	*SW*	NT	63710	66860	66810	63760
450 111	**SW**	A	*SW*	NT	63921	66901	66921	63901
450 112	**SD**	A	*SW*	NT	63922	66902	66922	63902
450 113	**SW**	A	*SW*	NT	63923	66903	66923	63903
450 114	**SW**	A	*SW*	NT	63924	66904	66924	63904
450 115	**SW**	A	*SW*	NT	63925	66905	66925	63905
450 116	**SD**	A	*SW*	NT	63926	66906	66926	63906
450 117	**SW**	A	*SW*	NT	63927	66907	66927	63907
450 118	**SD**	A	*SW*	NT	63928	66908	66928	63908
450 119	**SW**	A	*SW*	NT	63929	66909	66929	63909
450 120	**SW**	A	*SW*	NT	63930	66910	66930	63910
450 121	**SW**	A	*SW*	NT	63931	66911	66931	63911
450 122	**SW**	A	*SW*	NT	63932	66912	66932	63912
450 123	**SW**	A	*SW*	NT	63933	66913	66933	63913
450 124	**SW**	A	*SW*	NT	63934	66914	66934	63914
450 125	**SD**	A	*SW*	NT	63935	66915	66935	63915
450 126	**SW**	A	*SW*	NT	63936	66916	66936	63916
450 127	**SW**	A	*SW*	NT	63937	66917	66937	63917

Names (carried on DMSO(B)):

450015 DESIRO
450042 TRELOAR COLLEGE
450100 Transport Benevolent Fund CIO 1923–2023
450114 FAIRBRIDGE investing in the future
450127 DAVE GUNSON

CLASS 455   BREL YORK

Inner suburban units. During 2016–17 the South Western Railway fleet was fitted with new AC traction motors by Vossloh Kiepe. During 2022 the whole Southern fleet of Class 455/8 units was withdrawn and scrapped.

Formation: DTS–MS–TS–DTS.
Construction: Steel. Class 455/7 TS have a steel underframe and an aluminium alloy body and roof.
Traction Motors: Four TSA010163 AC motors of 240 kW.
Wheel Arrangement: 2-2 + Bo-Bo + 2-2 + 2-2.
Braking: Disc and regenerative).   **Dimensions:** 19.92/19.83 x 2.82 m.
Bogies: P7 (motor) and T3 (455/8 & 455/9) BX1 (455/7) trailer.
Gangways: Within unit + end doors.
Couplers: Tightlock.   **Maximum Speed:** 75 mph.
Control System: IGBT Inverter.
Doors: Sliding.   **Heating & Ventilation:** Various.

Seating Layout: 2+2 high-back unidirectional/facing seating.
Multiple Working: Within class.

Class 455/7. Second series with TSs originally in Class 508s. Pressure heating & ventilation.

DTS. Lot No. 30976 1984–85. –/50(+4) 1W. 30.8t.
MS. Lot No. 30975 1984–85. –/68. 45.7t.
TS. Lot No. 30944 1979–80. –/68. 26.1t.

5701	**SS**	P	*SW*	WD	77727	62783	71545	77728
5702	**SS**	P	*SW*	WD	77729	62784	71547	77730
5703	**SS**	P	*SW*	WD	77731	62785	71540	77732
5705	**SS**	P	*SW*	WD	77735	62787	71565	77736
5706	**SS**	P	*SW*	WD	77737	62788	71534	77738
5707	**SS**	P	*SW*	WD	77739	62789	71536	77740
5708	**SS**	P	*SW*	WD	77741	62790	71560	77742
5709	**SS**	P	*SW*	WD	77743	62791	71532	77744
5710	**SS**	P	*SW*	WD	77745	62792	71566	77746
5711	**SS**	P	*SW*	WD	77747	62793	71542	77748
5712	**SS**	P	*SW*	WD	77749	62794	71550	77750
5713	**SS**	P	*SW*	WD	77751	62795	71567	77752
5714	**SS**	P	*SW*	WD	77753	62796	71539	77754
5715	**SS**	P	*SW*	WD	77755	62797	71535	77756
5716	**SS**	P	*SW*	WD	77757	62798	71564	77758
5717	**SS**	P	*SW*	WD	77759	62799	71528	77760
5718	**SS**	P	*SW*	WD	77761	62800	71557	77762
5719	**SS**	P	*SW*	WD	77763	62801	71558	77764
5720	**SS**	P	*SW*	WD	77765	62802	71568	77766
5721	**SS**	P	*SW*	WD	77767	62803	71553	77768
5722	**SS**	P	*SW*	WD	77769	62804	71533	77770
5723	**SS**	P	*SW*	WD	77771	62805	71526	77772
5724	**SS**	P	*SW*	WD	77773	62806	71561	77774
5725	**SS**	P	*SW*	WD	77775	62807	71541	77776
5727	**SS**	P	*SW*	WD	77779	62809	71562	77780
5728	**SS**	P	*SW*	WD	77781	62810	71527	77782
5729	**SS**	P	*SW*	WD	77783	62811	71550	77784
5730	**SS**	P	*SW*	WD	77785	62812	71551	77786
5731	**SS**	P	*SW*	WD	77787	62813	71553	77788
5732	**SS**	P	*SW*	WD	77789	62814	71552	77790
5733	**SS**	P	*SW*	WD	77791	62815	71549	77792
5734	**SS**	P	*SW*	WD	77793	62816	71531	77794
5735	**SS**	P	*SW*	WD	77795	62817	71563	77796
5737	**SS**	P	*SW*	WD	77799	62819	71544	77800
5738	**SS**	P	*SW*	WD	77801	62820	71529	77802
5739	**SS**	P	*SW*	WD	77803	62821	71537	77804
5741	**SS**	P	*SW*	WD	77807	62823	71559	77808
5742	**SS**	P	*SW*	WD	77809	62824	71543	77810
5750	**SS**	P	*SW*	WD	77811	62825	71538	77812

Class 455/8. First series. Pressure heating & ventilation.

DTS. Lot No. 30972 York 1982–84. –50(+4) 1W. 29.5 t.
MS. Lot No. 30973 York 1982–84. –/68. 45.6 t.
TS. Lot No. 30974 York 1982–84. –/68. 27.1 t.

5848	**SS**	P	*SW*	WD	77673	62756	71684	77674
5849	**SS**	P	*SW*	WD	77675	62757	71685	77676
5850	**SS**	P	*SW*	WD	77677	62758	71686	77678
5851	**SS**	P	*SW*	WD	77679	62759	71687	77680
5852	**SS**	P	*SW*	WD	77681	62760	71688	77682
5853	**SS**	P	*SW*	WD	77683	62761	71689	77684
5854	**SS**	P	*SW*	WD	77685	62762	71690	77686
5856	**SS**	P	*SW*	WD	77689	62764	71692	77690
5857	**SS**	P	*SW*	WD	77691	62765	71693	77692
5858	**SS**	P	*SW*	WD	77693	62766	71694	77694
5859	**SS**	P	*SW*	WD	77695	62767	71695	77696
5860	**SS**	P	*SW*	WD	77697	62768	71696	77698
5861	**SS**	P	*SW*	WD	77699	62769	71697	77700
5862	**SS**	P	*SW*	WD	77701	62770	71698	77702
5863	**SS**	P		WD	77703	62771	71699	77704
5864	**SS**	P	*SW*	WD	77705	62772	71700	77706
5865	**SS**	P	*SW*	WD	77707	62773	71701	77708
5866	**SS**	P	*SW*	WD	77709	62774	71702	77710
5867	**SS**	P	*SW*	WD	77711	62775	71703	77712
5868	**SS**	P	*SW*	WD	77713	62776	71704	77714
5869	**SS**	P	*SW*	WD	77715	62777	71705	77716
5870	**SS**	P	*SW*	WD	77717	62778	71706	77718
5871	**SS**	P	*SW*	WD	77719	62779	71707	77720
5872	**SS**	P	*SW*	WD	77721	62780	71708	77722
5873	**SS**	P	*SW*	WD	77723	62781	71709	77724
5874	**SS**	P	*SW*	WD	77725	62782	71710	77726

Class 455/9. Third series. Convection heating.
Dimensions: 19.96/20.18 x 2.82 m.

67301 and 67400 were converted from Class 210 DEMU vehicles to replace accident damaged cars.

DTS. Lot No. 30991 York 1985. –/50(+4) 1W. 30.7 t.
MS. Lot No. 30992 York 1985. –/68. 46.3 t.
MS 67301. Lot No. 30932 Derby 1981. –/68.   t.
TS. Lot No. 30993 York 1985. –/68. 28.3 t.
TS 67400. Lot No. 30932 Derby 1981. –/68. 28.3 t.

5901	**SS**	P	*SW*	WD	77813	62826	71714	77814
5902	**SS**	P	*SW*	WD	77815	62827	71715	77816
5903	**SS**	P	*SW*	WD	77817	62828	71716	77818
5904	**SS**	P	*SW*	WD	77819	62829	71717	77820
5905	**SS**	P	*SW*	WD	77821	62830	71725	77822
5906	**SS**	P	*SW*	WD	77823	62831	71719	77824
5908	**SS**	P	*SW*	WD	77827	62833	71721	77828
5909	**SS**	P	*SW*	WD	77829	62834	71722	77830
5910	**SS**	P	*SW*	WD	77831	62835	71723	77832

5911	**SS**	P	*SW*	WD	77833	62836	71724	77834
5912	**SS**	P	*SW*	WD	77835	62837	67400	77836
5913	**SS**	P	*SW*	WD	77837	67301	71726	77838
5914	**SS**	P	*SW*	WD	77839	62839	71727	77840
5915	**SS**	P	*SW*	WD	77841	62840	71728	77842
5916	**SS**	P	*SW*	WD	77843	62841	71729	77844
5917	**SS**	P	*SW*	WD	77845	62842	71730	77846
5919	**SS**	P	*SW*	WD	77849	62844	71718	77850
5920	**SS**	P	*SW*	WD	77851	62845	71733	77852

CLASS 458   JUNIPER   ALSTOM BIRMINGHAM

Outer suburban units. In 2013–16 the fleet of 30 4-car Class 458 units and the former Gatwick Express eight 8-car Class 460 units was combined to form a fleet of 36 5-car Standard Class only Class 458/5s. Former Class 460 driving cars 67901/903/907/908 were not included in this programme and were scrapped. After lengthening each unit was renumbered into the 458 5xx series. All individual vehicles retained their original numbers.

In the longer-term South Western Railway intends to retain 28 units (458501–528) which are currently being reformed back as 4-car sets numbered 458401–428. The work to refurbish these units is being carried out at Alstom, Widnes and also includes a change in maximum speed to 100 mph for longer-distance work.

Formation: See class sub-headings.
Construction: Steel.   **Dimensions:** 21.16 or 21.06 x 2.80 m.
Traction Motors: Two Alstom ONIX 800 asynchronous of 270 kW.
Wheel Arrangement: 2-Bo(+ 2-2) + 2-2 + Bo-2 + Bo-2.
Braking: Disc & regenerative.   **Control System:** IGBT Inverter.
Bogies: ACR.   **Doors:** Sliding plug.
Gangways: Throughout.   **Couplers:** Voith 136.
Maximum Speed: 75 mph (Class 458/4: 100 mph).
Heating & Ventilation: Air conditioning. **Multiple Working:** Within class.
Seating Layout: 2+2 facing/unidirectional.

Class 458/4. 4-car units. Following refurbishment these units are being returned to their original formation for longer-distance duties. Full details awaited. **Formation:** DMC–TS–MS–DMC.

DMC(A). Alstom 1998–2000. 12/52.
TS. Alstom 1998–2000. –/42 1TD 2W.
MS. Alstom 1998–2000. –/64 1T.
DMC(B). Alstom 1998–2000. 12/52.

458401								
458402								
458403								
458404								
458405	**SW**	P		BM	67605	74005	74105	67705
458406								
458407	**SW**	P	*SW*	BM	67607	74007	74107	67707

458408					
458409					
458410					
458411					
458412					
458413					
458414					
458415					
458416	SW	P		WI	67616 74016 74116 67716
458417	SW	P	SW	BM	67617 74017 74117 67717
458418					
458419					
458420					
458421					
458422					
458423	SW	P		BM	67623 74023 74123 67723
458424					
458425	SW	P		BM	67625 74025 74125 67725
458426					
458427					
458428	SW	P		WI	67628 74028 74128 67728

Class 458/5. 5-car units. **Formation:** DMS–TS*–TS–MS–DMS (* ex-Class 460 in 458501–530).

DMS(A). Alstom 1998–2000. –/60. 45.7 t.
TS. Alstom 1998–2000. 458 501–530 –/56; 458 531–536 –/52 1T. 34.4 t.
TS. Alstom 1998–2000. –/42 1TD 2W. 34.1 t.
MS. Alstom 1998–2000. 458 501–530 –56 1T; 458 531–536 –/56. 40.1 t.
DMS(B). Alstom 1998–2000. –/60. 44.9 t.

458501	SD	P	SW	WD	67601 74431 74001 74101 67701
458502	SD	P	SW	WD	67602 74421 74002 74102 67702
458503	SD	P	SW	WD	67603 74441 74003 74103 67703
458504	SD	P	SW	WD	67604 74451 74004 74104 67704
458506	SD	P	SW	WD	67606 74436 74006 74106 67706
458508	SD	P	SW	WD	67608 74433 74008 74108 67708
458509	SD	P	SW	WD	67609 74452 74009 74109 67709
458510	SD	P	SW	WD	67610 74405 74010 74110 67710
458511	SD	P	SW	WD	67611 74435 74011 74111 67711
458512	SD	P	SW	WD	67612 74427 74012 74112 67712
458513	SD	P	SW	WD	67613 74437 74013 74113 67713
458514	SD	P	SW	WD	67614 74407 74014 74114 67714
458515	SD	P	SW	WD	67615 74404 74015 74115 67715
458518	SD	P	SW	WD	67618 74432 74018 74118 67718
458519	SD	P	SW	WD	67619 74403 74019 74119 67719
458520	SD	P	SW	WD	67620 74401 74020 74120 67720
458521	SD	P	SW	WD	67621 74438 74021 74121 67721
458522	SD	P	SW	WD	67622 74424 74022 74122 67722
458524	SD	P	SW	WD	67624 74402 74024 74124 67724
458526	SD	P	SW	WD	67626 74442 74026 74126 67726
458527	SD	P	SW	WD	67627 74412 74027 74127 67727

458529	**SD**	P	*SW*	WD	67629 74423 74029 74129 67729
458530	**SD**	P	*SW*	WD	67630 74411 74030 74130 67730
Spares	**SD**	P		LM	74422 74425 74426 74428 74434
Spares	**SD**	P		WI	74406 74408

The following units were converted entirely from Class 460s.

458531	**SD**	P	*SW*	WD	67913 74418 74446 74458 67912
458532	**SD**	P	*SW*	WD	67904 74417 74447 74457 67905
458533	**SD**	P	*SW*	WD	67917 74413 74443 74453 67916
458534	**SD**	P	*SW*	WD	67914 74414 74444 74454 67918
458535	**SD**	P	*SW*	WD	67915 74415 74445 74455 67911
458536	**SD**	P	*SW*	WD	67906 74416 74448 74456 67902

CLASS 465   NETWORKER

Inner and outer suburban units.

Formation: DMS–TS–TS–DMS.
Construction: Welded aluminium alloy.
Traction Motors: Four Hitachi asynchronous of 280 kW (Classes 465/0 and 465/1) or Four GEC-Alsthom G352BY of 280 kW (Classes 465/2 and 465/9).
Wheel Arrangement: Bo-Bo + 2-2 + 2-2 + Bo-Bo.
Braking: Disc & rheostatic and regenerative (Classes 465/0 and 465/1 only).
Bogies: BREL P3/T3 (465/0 and 465/1), SRP BP62/BT52 (465/2 and 465/9).
Dimensions: 20.89/20.06 x 2.81 m.
Control System: IGBT Inverter (465/0 and 465/1) or 1992-type GTO Inverter.
Gangways: Within unit.   **Couplers**: Tightlock.
Doors: Sliding plug.   **Maximum Speed**: 75 mph.
Seating Layout: 3+2 facing/unidirectional.
Multiple Working: Within class and with Class 466.

64759–808. DMS(A). Lot No. 31100 BREL York 1991–93. –/86. 39.2 t.
64809–858. DMS(B). Lot No. 31100 BREL York 1991–93. –/86. 39.2 t.
65734–749. DMS(A). Lot No. 31103 Metro-Cammell 1991–93. –/86. 39.2 t.
65784–799. DMS(B). Lot No. 31103 Metro-Cammell 1991–93. –/86. 39.2 t.
65800–846. DMS(A). Lot No. 31130 ABB York 1993–94. –/86. 39.2 t.
65847–893. DMS(B). Lot No. 31130 ABB York 1993–94. –/86. 39.2 t.
72028–126 (even nos.) TS. Lot No. 31102 BREL York 1991–93. –/90. 27.2 t.
72029–127 (odd nos.) TS. Lot No. 31101 BREL York 1991–93. –/65(+7) 1TD 2W. 29.6 t.
72787–817 (odd nos.) TS. Lot No. 31104 Metro-Cammell 1991–92. –/65(+7) 1TD 2W. 30.2 t.
72788–818 (even nos.) TS. Lot No. 31105 Metro-Cammell 1991–92. –/90. 29.4 t.
72900–992 (even nos.) TS. Lot No. 31102 ABB York 1993–94. –/90. 27.2 t.
72901–993 (odd nos.) TS. Lot No. 31101 ABB York 1993–94. –/65(+7) 1TD 2W. 29.6 t.

Class 465/0. Built by BREL/ABB.

465001	**SE**	E	*SE*	SG	64759 72028 72029 64809
465002	**SE**	E	*SE*	SG	64760 72030 72031 64810
465003	**SE**	E	*SE*	SG	64761 72032 72033 64811
465004	**SE**	E	*SE*	SG	64762 72034 72035 64812
465005	**SE**	E	*SE*	SG	64763 72036 72037 64813

465 006	**SE**	E	*SE*	SG	64764	72038	72039	64814
465 007	**SE**	E	*SE*	SG	64765	72040	72041	64815
465 008	**SE**	E	*SE*	SG	64766	72042	72043	64816
465 009	**SE**	E	*SE*	SG	64767	72044	72045	64817
465 010	**SE**	E	*SE*	SG	64768	72046	72047	64818
465 011	**SE**	E	*SE*	SG	64769	72048	72049	64819
465 012	**SE**	E	*SE*	SG	64770	72050	72051	64820
465 013	**SE**	E	*SE*	SG	64771	72052	72053	64821
465 014	**SE**	E	*SE*	SG	64772	72054	72055	64822
465 015	**SE**	E	*SE*	SG	64773	72056	72057	64823
465 016	**SE**	E	*SE*	SG	64774	72058	72059	64824
465 017	**SE**	E	*SE*	SG	64775	72060	72061	64825
465 018	**SE**	E	*SE*	SG	64776	72062	72063	64826
465 019	**SE**	E	*SE*	SG	64777	72064	72065	64827
465 020	**SE**	E	*SE*	SG	64778	72066	72067	64828
465 021	**SE**	E	*SE*	SG	64779	72068	72069	64829
465 022	**SE**	E	*SE*	SG	64780	72070	72071	64830
465 023	**SE**	E	*SE*	SG	64781	72072	72073	64831
465 024	**SE**	E	*SE*	SG	64782	72074	72075	64832
465 025	**SE**	E	*SE*	SG	64783	72076	72077	64833
465 026	**SE**	E	*SE*	SG	64784	72078	72079	64834
465 027	**SE**	E	*SE*	SG	64785	72080	72081	64835
465 028	**SE**	E	*SE*	SG	64786	72082	72083	64836
465 029	**SE**	E	*SE*	SG	64787	72084	72085	64837
465 030	**SE**	E	*SE*	SG	64788	72086	72087	64838
465 031	**SE**	E	*SE*	SG	64789	72088	72089	64839
465 032	**SE**	E	*SE*	SG	64790	72090	72091	64840
465 033	**SE**	E	*SE*	SG	64791	72092	72093	64841
465 034	**SE**	E	*SE*	SG	64792	72094	72095	64842
465 035	**SE**	E	*SE*	SG	64793	72096	72097	64843
465 036	**SE**	E	*SE*	SG	64794	72098	72099	64844
465 037	**SE**	E	*SE*	SG	64795	72100	72101	64845
465 038	**SE**	E	*SE*	SG	64796	72102	72103	64846
465 039	**SE**	E	*SE*	SG	64797	72104	72105	64847
465 040	**SE**	E	*SE*	SG	64798	72106	72107	64848
465 041	**SE**	E	*SE*	SG	64799	72108	72109	64849
465 042	**SE**	E	*SE*	SG	64800	72110	72111	64850
465 043	**SE**	E	*SE*	SG	64801	72112	72113	64851
465 044	**SE**	E	*SE*	SG	64802	72114	72115	64852
465 045	**SE**	E	*SE*	SG	64803	72116	72117	64853
465 046	**SE**	E	*SE*	SG	64804	72118	72119	64854
465 047	**SE**	E	*SE*	SG	64805	72120	72121	64855
465 048	**SE**	E	*SE*	SG	64806	72122	72123	64856
465 049	**SE**	E	*SE*	SG	64807	72124	72125	64857
465 050	**SE**	E	*SE*	SG	64808	72126	72127	64858

Class 465/1. Built by BREL/ABB. Similar to Class 465/0 but with detail differences.

465 151	**SE**	E	*SE*	SG	65800	72900	72901	65847
465 152	**SE**	E	*SE*	SG	65801	72902	72903	65848
465 153	**SE**	E	*SE*	SG	65802	72904	72905	65849
465 154	**SE**	E	*SE*	SG	65803	72906	72907	65850

465 155	**SE**	E	*SE*	SG	65804	72908	72909	65851
465 156	**SE**	E	*SE*	SG	65805	72910	72911	65852
465 157	**SE**	E	*SE*	SG	65806	72912	72913	65853
465 158	**SE**	E	*SE*	SG	65807	72914	72915	65854
465 159	**SE**	E	*SE*	SG	65808	72916	72917	65855
465 160	**SE**	E	*SE*	SG	65809	72918	72919	65856
465 161	**SE**	E	*SE*	SG	65810	72920	72921	65857
465 162	**SE**	E	*SE*	SG	65811	72922	72923	65858
465 163	**SE**	E	*SE*	SG	65812	72924	72925	65859
465 164	**SE**	E	*SE*	SG	65813	72926	72927	65860
465 165	**SE**	E	*SE*	SG	65814	72928	72929	65861
465 166	**SE**	E	*SE*	SG	65815	72930	72931	65862
465 167	**SE**	E	*SE*	SG	65816	72932	72933	65863
465 168	**SE**	E	*SE*	SG	65817	72934	72935	65864
465 169	**SE**	E	*SE*	SG	65818	72936	72937	65865
465 170	**SE**	E	*SE*	SG	65819	72938	72939	65866
465 171	**SE**	E	*SE*	SG	65820	72940	72941	65867
465 172	**SE**	E	*SE*	SG	65821	72942	72943	65868
465 173	**SE**	E	*SE*	SG	65822	72944	72945	65869
465 174	**SE**	E	*SE*	SG	65823	72946	72947	65870
465 175	**SE**	E	*SE*	SG	65824	72948	72949	65871
465 176	**SE**	E	*SE*	SG	65825	72950	72951	65872
465 177	**SE**	E	*SE*	SG	65826	72952	72953	65873
465 178	**SE**	E	*SE*	SG	65827	72954	72955	65874
465 179	**SE**	E	*SE*	SG	65828	72956	72957	65875
465 180	**SE**	E	*SE*	SG	65829	72958	72959	65876
465 181	**SE**	E	*SE*	SG	65830	72960	72961	65877
465 182	**SE**	E	*SE*	SG	65831	72962	72963	65878
465 183	**SE**	E	*SE*	SG	65832	72964	72965	65879
465 184	**SE**	E	*SE*	SG	65833	72966	72967	65880
465 185	**SE**	E	*SE*	SG	65834	72968	72969	65881
465 186	**SE**	E	*SE*	SG	65835	72970	72971	65882
465 187	**SE**	E	*SE*	SG	65836	72972	72973	65883
465 188	**SE**	E	*SE*	SG	65837	72974	72975	65884
465 189	**SE**	E	*SE*	SG	65838	72976	72977	65885
465 190	**SE**	E	*SE*	SG	65839	72978	72979	65886
465 191	**SE**	E	*SE*	SG	65840	72980	72981	65887
465 192	**SE**	E	*SE*	SG	65841	72982	72983	65888
465 193	**SE**	E	*SE*	SG	65842	72984	72985	65889
465 194	**SE**	E	*SE*	SG	65843	72986	72987	65890
465 195	**SE**	E	*SE*	SG	65844	72988	72989	65891
465 196	**SE**	E	*SE*	SG	65845	72990	72991	65892
465 197	**SE**	E	*SE*	SG	65846	72992	72993	65893

Class 465/2. Built by Metro-Cammell. **Dimensions**: 20.80/20.15 x 2.81 m.

465 235	**SE**	A		ZB	65734	72787	72788	65784
465 236	**SE**	A		EP	65735	72789	72790	65785
465 237	**SE**	A		EP	65736	72791	72792	65786
465 238	**SE**	A		EP	65737	72793	72794	65787
465 239	**SE**	A		EP	65738	72795	72796	65788
465 240	**SE**	A		EP	65739	72797	72798	65789

465 241	**SE**	A	WS	65740	72799	72800	65790
465 242	**SE**	A	WS	65741	72801	72802	65791
465 243	**SE**	A	EP	65742	72803	72804	65792
465 244	**SE**	A	EP	65743	72805	72806	65793
465 245	**SE**	A	EP	65744	72807	72808	65794
465 246	**SE**	A	EP	65745	72809	72810	65795
465 247	**SE**	A	WS	65746	72811	72812	65796
465 248	**SE**	A	EP	65747	72813	72814	65797
465 249	**SE**	A	EP	65748	72815	72816	65798
465 250	**SE**	A	EP	65749	72817	72818	65799

Class 465/9. Built by Metro-Cammell. Refurbished 2005 for longer distance services, with the addition of First Class (now declassified). Details as Class 465/0 unless stated.

Formation: DMC–TS–TS–DMC.
Seating Layout: 1: 2+2 facing/unidirectional, 2: 3+2 facing/unidirectional.

65700–733. DMC(A). Lot No. 31103 Metro-Cammell 1991–93. –/80. 39.2t.
72719–785 (odd nos.) TS(A). Lot No. 31104 Metro-Cammell 1991–92. –/65(+7) 1TD 2W. 30.3t.
72720–786 (even nos.) TS(B). Lot No. 31105 Metro-Cammell 1991–92. –/90. 29.5t.
65750–783. DMC(B). Lot No. 31103 Metro-Cammell 1991–93. –/80. 39.2t.

465 901	(465 201)	**SE**	A	*SE*	SG	65700	72719	72720	65750
465 902	(465 202)	**SE**	A	*SE*	SG	65701	72721	72722	65751
465 903	(465 203)	**SE**	A	*SE*	SG	65702	72723	72724	65752
465 904	(465 204)	**SE**	A	*SE*	SG	65703	72725	72726	65753
465 905	(465 205)	**SE**	A		WS	65704	72727	72728	65754
465 906	(465 206)	**SE**	A	*SE*	SG	65705	72729	72730	65755
465 907	(465 207)	**SE**	A	*SE*	SG	65706	72731	72732	65756
465 908	(465 208)	**SE**	A	*SE*	SG	65707	72733	72734	65757
465 909	(465 209)	**SE**	A	*SE*	SG	65708	72735	72736	65758
465 910	(465 210)	**SE**	A	*SE*	SG	65709	72737	72738	65759
465 911	(465 211)	**SE**	A	*SE*	SG	65710	72739	72740	65760
465 912	(465 212)	**SE**	A	*SE*	SG	65711	72741	72742	65761
465 913	(465 213)	**SE**	A	*SE*	SG	65712	72743	72744	65762
465 914	(465 214)	**SE**	A	*SE*	SG	65713	72745	72746	65763
465 915	(465 215)	**SE**	A	*SE*	SG	65714	72747	72748	65764
465 916	(465 216)	**SE**	A	*SE*	SG	65715	72749	72750	65765
465 917	(465 217)	**SE**	A	*SE*	SG	65716	72751	72752	65766
465 918	(465 218)	**SE**	A		WS	65717	72753	72754	65767
465 919	(465 219)	**SE**	A	*SE*	SG	65718	72755	72756	65768
465 920	(465 220)	**SE**	A		WS	65719	72757	72758	65769
465 921	(465 221)	**SE**	A		WS	65720	72759	72760	65770
465 922	(465 222)	**SE**	A	*SE*	SG	65721	72761	72762	65771
465 923	(465 223)	**SE**	A	*SE*	SG	65722	72763	72764	65772
465 924	(465 224)	**SE**	A	*SE*	SG	65723	72765	72766	65773
465 925	(465 225)	**SE**	A	*SE*	SG	65724	72767	72768	65774
465 926	(465 226)	**SE**	A	*SE*	SG	65725	72769	72770	65775
465 927	(465 227)	**SE**	A	*SE*	SG	65726	72771	72772	65776
465 928	(465 228)	**SE**	A	*SE*	SG	65727	72773	72774	65777
465 929	(465 229)	**SE**	A	*SE*	SG	65728	72775	72776	65778

465930	(465230)	**SE**	A	*SE*	SG	65729 72777 72778 65779
465931	(465231)	**SE**	A		WS	65730 72779 72780 65780
465932	(465232)	**SE**	A	*SE*	SG	65731 72781 72782 65781
465933	(465233)	**SE**	A		WS	65732 72783 72784 65782
465934	(465234)	**SE**	A		WS	65733 72785 72786 65783

CLASS 466   NETWORKER   GEC-ALSTHOM

Inner and outer suburban units.

Formation: DMS–DTS.
Construction: Welded aluminium alloy.
Traction Motors: Two GEC-Alsthom G352AY asynchronous of 280 kW.
Wheel Arrangement: Bo-Bo + 2-2.   **Couplers:** Tightlock.
Braking: Disc, rheostatic & regen.   **Control System:** 1992-type GTO Inverter.
Dimensions: 20.80 x 2.80 m.   **Maximum Speed:** 75 mph.
Bogies: BREL P3/T3.   **Doors:** Sliding plug.
Gangways: Within unit.
Seating Layout: 3+2 facing/unidirectional.
Multiple Working: Within class and with Class 465.

DMS. Lot No. 31128 Birmingham 1993–94. –/86. 40.6 t.
DTS. Lot No. 31129 Birmingham 1993–94. –/82 1T. 31.4 t.

466001	**SE**	A		WS	64860 78312
466002	**SE**	A	*SE*	SG	64861 78313
466003	**SE**	A	*SE*	SG	64862 78314
466004	**SE**	A	*SE*	SG	64863 78315
466005	**SE**	A		WS	64864 78316
466006	**SE**	A	*SE*	SG	64865 78317
466007	**SE**	A	*SE*	SG	64866 78318
466008	**SE**	A	*SE*	SG	64867 78319
466009	**SE**	A		WS	64868 78320
466010	**SE**	A		WS	64869 78321
466011	**SE**	A	*SE*	SG	64870 78322
466012	**SE**	A	*SE*	SG	64871 78323
466013	**SE**	A		WS	64872 78324
466014	**SE**	A	*SE*	SG	64873 78325
466015	**SE**	A	*SE*	SG	64874 78326
466016	**SE**	A		ZB	64875 78327
466017	**SE**	A		WS	64876 78328
466018	**SE**	A	*SE*	SG	64877 78329
466019	**SE**	A	*SE*	SG	64878 78330
466020	**SE**	A	*SE*	SG	64879 78331
466021	**SE**	A	*SE*	SG	64880 78332
466022	**SE**	A	*SE*	SG	64881 78333
466023	**SE**	A	*SE*	SG	64882 78334
466024	**SE**	A		WS	64883 78335
466025	**SE**	A	*SE*	SG	64884 78336
466026	**SE**	A	*SE*	SG	64885 78337
466027	**SE**	A		WS	64886 78338
466028	**SE**	A	*SE*	SG	64887 78339

466 029	**SE**	A	*SE*	SG	64888	78340
466 030	**SE**	A		WS	64889	78341
466 031	**SE**	A	*SE*	SG	64890	78342
466 032	**SE**	A	*SE*	SG	64891	78343
466 033	**SE**	A		WS	64892	78344
466 034	**SE**	A	*SE*	SG	64893	78345
466 035	**SE**	A	*SE*	SG	64894	78346
466 036	**SE**	A	*SE*	SG	64895	78347
466 037	**SE**	A	*SE*	SG	64896	78348
466 038	**SE**	A	*SE*	SG	64897	78349
466 039	**SE**	A	*SE*	SG	64898	78350
466 040	**SE**	A	*SE*	SG	64899	78351
466 041	**SE**	A	*SE*	SG	64900	78352
466 042	**SE**	A	*SE*	SG	64901	78353
466 043	**SE**	A		WS	64902	78354

CLASS 484   D-TRAIN   METRO-CAMMELL/VIVARAIL

Rebuilt from former London Underground D78 stock for use by South Western Railway on the Isle of Wight "Island Line". Similar to the converted Class 230 DMUs or diesel-battery units, the Class 484s are straight third-rail EMUs.

Formation: DMS–DMS.
Construction: Aluminium.
Traction motors: TSA AC motors.
Braking: Rheostatic & Dynamic.
Bogies: Bombardier FLEXX1000 flexible-frame.
Gangways: Within unit only.
Doors: Sliding.
Seating Layout: Longitudinal or 2+2 facing.
Multiple Working: Within class.

System: 750 V DC third rail.
Wheel Arrangement:
Couplers: LUL automatic wedgelock.
Dimensions: 18.37 x 2.84 m.
Control System: IGBT Inverter.
Maximum Speed: 60 mph.

DMS(A). Metro-Cammell Birmingham 1979–83. –/40(+2). 32.5 t.
DMS(B). Metro-Cammell Birmingham 1979–83. –/40(+2). 30.4 t.

484 001	**SW**	LF	*SW*	RY	131	(7086)	231	(7011)
484 002	**SW**	LF	*SW*	RY	132	(7068)	232	(7002)
484 003	**SW**	LF	*SW*	RY	133	(7059)	233	(7083)
484 004	**SW**	LF	*SW*	RY	134	(7074)	234	(7111)
484 005	**SW**	LF	*SW*	RY	135	(7124)	235	(7093)

CLASS 507   BREL YORK

Formation: BDMS–TS–DMS.
Construction: Steel underframe, aluminium alloy body and roof.
Traction Motors: Four GEC G310AZ of 82.125 kW.
Wheel Arrangement: Bo-Bo + 2-2 + Bo-Bo.
Braking: Disc & rheostatic.
Bogies: BX1.
Gangways: Within unit + end doors.
Doors: Sliding.

Dimensions: 20.18 x 2.82 m.
Couplers: Tightlock.
Control System: Camshaft.
Maximum Speed: 75 mph.

Seating Layout: All refurbished with 2+2 high-back facing seating.
Multiple Working: Within class and with Class 508.

Fitted with tripcocks for operating on the Merseyrail Wirral Lines.

Advertising livery: 507 002 Liverpool Hope University (white).

BDMS. Lot No. 30906 1978–80. –/56(+3) 1W. 37.0 t.
TS. Lot No. 30907 1978–80. –/74. 25.5 t.
DMS. Lot No. 30908 1978–80. –/56(+3) 1W. 35.5 t.

507001	**MY**	A	*ME*	BD	64367	71342	64405
507002	**AL**	A	*ME*	BD	64368	71343	64406
507003	**MY**	A	*ME*	BD	64369	71344	64407
507004	**MY**	A	*ME*	BD	64388	71345	64408
507007	**MY**	A	*ME*	BD	64373	71348	64411
507010	**MY**	A	*ME*	BD	64376	71351	64414
507011	**MY**	A	*ME*	BD	64377	71352	64415
507013	**MY**	A	*ME*	BD	64379	71354	64417
507014	**MY**	A	*ME*	BD	64380	71355	64418
507015	**MY**	A	*ME*	BD	64381	71356	64419
507016	**MY**	A	*ME*	BD	64382	71357	64420
507017	**MY**	A	*ME*	BD	64383	71358	64421
507018	**MY**	A	*ME*	BD	64384	71359	64422
507020	**MY**	A	*ME*	BD	64386	71361	64424
507021	**MY**	A	*ME*	BD	64387	71362	64425
507023	**MY**	A	*ME*	BD	64389	71364	64427
507028	**MY**	A	*ME*	BD	64394	71369	64432
507029	**MY**	A	*ME*	BD	64395	71370	64433
507030	**MY**	A	*ME*	BD	64396	71371	64434
507031	**MY**	A	*ME*	BD	64397	71372	64435
507032	**MY**	A	*ME*	BD	64398	71373	64436
507033	**MY**	A	*ME*	BD	64399	71374	64437

Names:

507004	Bob Paisley	507021	Red Rum
507016	Merseyrail – celebrating the first ten years 2003–2013	507023	Operations Inspector Stuart Mason
507020	John Peel	507033	Councillor Jack Spriggs

CLASS 508   BREL YORK

Formation: DMS–TS–BDMS.
Construction: Steel underframe, aluminium alloy body and roof.
Traction Motors: Four GEC G310AZ of 82.125 kW.
Wheel Arrangement: Bo-Bo + 2-2 + Bo-Bo.
Braking: Disc & rheostatic.   **Dimensions:** 20.18 x 2.82 m.
Bogies: BX1.   **Couplers:** Tightlock.
Gangways: Within unit + end doors. **Control System:** Camshaft.
Doors: Sliding.   **Maximum Speed:** 75 mph.
Seating Layout: All refurbished with 2+2 high-back facing seating.
Multiple Working: Within class and with Class 507.

Fitted with tripcocks for operating on the Merseyrail Wirral Lines.

DMS. Lot No. 30979 1979–80. –/56(+3) 1W. 36.0 t.
TS. Lot No. 30980 1979–80. –/74. 26.5 t.
BDMS. Lot No. 30981 1979–80. –/56(+3) 1W. 36.5 t.

508 103	**MY**	A	*ME*	BD	64651	71485	64694
508 104	**MY**	A	*ME*	BD	64652	71486	64695
508 108	**MY**	A	*ME*	BD	64656	71490	64699
508 112	**MY**	A	*ME*	BD	64660	71494	64703
508 114	**MY**	A	*ME*	BD	64662	71496	64705
508 120	**MY**	A	*ME*	BD	64668	71502	64711
508 131	**MY**	A	*ME*	BD	64679	71513	64722
508 136	**MY**	A	*ME*	BD	64684	71518	64727
508 137	**MY**	A	*ME*	BD	64685	71519	64728
508 139	**MY**	A	*ME*	BD	64687	71521	64730
508 141	**MY**	A	*ME*	BD	64689	71523	64732

Name: 508 136 Wilfred Owen MC

CLASS 555   STADLER

This fleet of articulated 5-car units was ordered from Stadler in 2020 by Nexus for the Tyne & Wear Metro, which shares Network Rail tracks between Heworth and Sunderland. They will replace the original Tyne & Wear Metro light rail stock which dates from 1975–81. The first of the new units were delivered in spring 2023, and the fleet is due to enter service from early 2024. The trains are also fitted with batteries for use in an emergency situation. Full details awaited.

Formation: DMS–MS–MS–MS–DMS.
System: 1500 V DC overhead + batteries.
Construction: Aluminium.
Traction Motors: Eight TSA air-cooled TMF 41-17-4 of 120 kW (161 hp).
Wheel Arrangement: 2-Bo-Bo-Bo-Bo-2.
Dimensions: 59.90 x 2.65 m (full unit).
Braking: Disc, regenerative & magnetic track brakes.
Couplers: Dellner.
Bogies: Jacobs.   **Control System:** IGBT Inverter.
Gangways: Within unit.   **Maximum Speed:** 50 mph.
Doors: Sliding plug.   **Heating & ventilation:** Air conditioning.
Seating Layout: Longitudinal.
Multiple Working: Within class.

DMS(A). Stadler Szolnok/St Margrethen 2021–24.
MS(A). Stadler Szolnok/St Margrethen 2021–24.
MS(B). Stadler Szolnok/St Margrethen 2021–24.
MS(C). Stadler Szolnok/St Margrethen 2021–24.
DMS(B). Stadler Szolnok/St Margrethen 2021–24.

555 001	**TY**	990101	990201	990301	990401	990501
555 002	**TY**	990102	990202	990302	990402	990502
555 003	**TY**	990103	990203	990303	990403	990503
555 004	**TY**	990104	990204	990304	990404	990504
555 005	**TY**	990105	990205	990305	990405	990505
555 006	**TY**	990106	990206	990306	990406	990506
555 007	**TY**	990107	990207	990307	990407	990507
555 008	**TY**	990108	990208	990308	990408	990508
555 009	**TY**	990109	990209	990309	990409	990509
555 010	**TY**	990110	990210	990310	990410	990510
555 011	**TY**	990111	990211	990311	990411	990511
555 012	**TY**	990112	990212	990312	990412	990512
555 013	**TY**	990113	990213	990313	990413	990513
555 014	**TY**	990114	990214	990314	990414	990514
555 015	**TY**	990115	990215	990315	990415	990515
555 016	**TY**	990116	990216	990316	990416	990516
555 017	**TY**	990117	990217	990317	990417	990517
555 018	**TY**	990118	990218	990318	990418	990518
555 019	**TY**	990119	990219	990319	990419	990519
555 020	**TY**	990120	990220	990320	990420	990520
555 021	**TY**	990121	990221	990321	990421	990521
555 022	**TY**	990122	990222	990322	990422	990522
555 023	**TY**	990123	990223	990323	990423	990523
555 024	**TY**	990124	990224	990324	990424	990524
555 025	**TY**	990125	990225	990325	990425	990525
555 026	**TY**	990126	990226	990326	990426	990526
555 027	**TY**	990127	990227	990327	990427	990527
555 028	**TY**	990128	990228	990328	990428	990528
555 029	**TY**	990129	990229	990329	990429	990529
555 030	**TY**	990130	990230	990330	990430	990530
555 031	**TY**	990131	990231	990331	990431	990531
555 032	**TY**	990132	990232	990332	990432	990532
555 033	**TY**	990133	990233	990333	990433	990533
555 034	**TY**	990134	990234	990334	990434	990534
555 035	**TY**	990135	990235	990335	990435	990535
555 036	**TY**	990136	990236	990336	990436	990536
555 037	**TY**	990137	990237	990337	990437	990537
555 038	**TY**	990138	990238	990338	990438	990538
555 039	**TY**	990139	990239	990339	990439	990539
555 040	**TY**	990140	990240	990340	990440	990540
555 041	**TY**	990141	990241	990341	990441	990541
555 042	**TY**	990142	990242	990342	990442	990542
555 043	**TY**	990143	990243	990343	990443	990543
555 044	**TY**	990144	990244	990344	990444	990544
555 045	**TY**	990145	990245	990345	990445	990545
555 046	**TY**	990146	990246	990346	990446	990546

3. PROTOTYPE HYDROGEN UNIT

During 2021–22 Arcola Energy converted the sole remaining former ScotRail Class 314 EMU into a testbed hydrogen train at Bo'ness on the Bo'ness & Kinneil Railway, as part of the Scottish Hydrogen Train Project sponsored by the Scottish Government to demonstrate how existing trains can be converted to operate using hydrogen power. To reflect its new identity the unit has been renumbered in the Class 614 series. It has been tested on the Bo'ness & Kinneil Railway.

All hydrogen equipment has been fitted to the vehicle underframes rather than taking up room in the passenger areas. A fuel cell raft is located in each driving car, comprising a 70 kW Ballard fuel cell and hydrogen cylinders. The DC traction motors have be replaced by magnet motors powered by three-phase AC. The centre car houses Toshiba lithium-titanate batteries. The interior of the centre car has also been refurbished, using former Pendolino seats.

CLASS 614   BREL YORK

Formation: DMS–PTS–DMS.
Construction: Steel underframe, aluminium alloy body and roof.
Traction Motors: Dana AC traction motors.
Wheel Arrangement: Bo-Bo + 2-2 + Bo-Bo.
Braking: Disc & rheostatic.   **Dimensions:** 20.33/20.18 x 2.82 m.
Bogies: BX1.   **Couplers:** Tightlock.
Gangways: Within unit + end doors.   **Control System:**
Doors: Sliding.   **Maximum Speed:** 70 mph.
Seating Layout: Originally 3+2 low-back facing, PTS reseated as 2+2 facing.
Multiple Working: Within class.

DMS. Lot No. 30912 1979.
PTS. Lot No. 30913 1979.
DMS. Lot No. 30912 1979.

614 209	(314 209)	**SR**	SR	BO	64599	71458	64600

4. DUAL VOLTAGE OR 25 kV AC OVERHEAD UNITS

The Class 7xx series is being used for some new-build EMUs built from 2014 onwards as freight wagons take up many of the remaining potential Class 3xx series'. Rebuilt Class 319s as either Class 768, 769 or 799 also take up this number series.

CLASS 700   DESIRO CITY   SIEMENS

The Class 700s are the large new fleet of EMUs for Govia Thameslink, entering service between 2016 and 2018. The units are financed by Cross London Trains (a consortium of Siemens Project Ventures, Innisfree Ltd and 3i Infrastructure Ltd).

Formation (8-car): DMC–PTS–MS–TS–TS–MS–PTS–DMC or
(12-car): DMC–PTS–MS–MS–TS–TS–TS–TS–MS–MS–PTS–DMC.
Systems: 25 kV AC overhead/750 V DC third rail.
Construction: Aluminium.
Traction Motors: Four Siemens asynchronous of 200 kW.
Wheel Arrangement (8-car): Bo-Bo + 2-2 + Bo-Bo + 2-2 + 2-2 + Bo-Bo + 2-2 + Bo-Bo. **(12-car):** Bo-Bo + 2-2 + Bo-Bo + Bo-Bo + 2-2 + 2-2 + 2-2 + 2-2 + Bo-Bo + Bo-Bo + 2-2 + Bo-Bo.
Braking: Disc, tread & regenerative.   **Dimensions:** 20.52/20.16 m x 2.80 m.
Bogies: Siemens SF7000 inside-frame. **Couplers:** Dellner 12.
Gangways: Within unit.   **Control System:** IGBT Inverter.
Doors: Sliding plug.   **Maximum Speed:** 100 mph.
Heating & ventilation: Air conditioning.
Seating Layout: 2+2 facing/unidirectional.
Multiple Working: Within class and with Classes 707 and 717.

Class 700/0. 8-car units.

DMC(A). Siemens Krefeld 2014–18. 26/16(+3). 38.5 t.
PTS. Siemens Krefeld 2014–18. –/54 1T. 33.1 t.
MS. Siemens Krefeld 2014–18. –/64. 36.2 t.
TS. Siemens Krefeld 2014–18. –/56(+3). 28.7 t.
TS(W). Siemens Krefeld 2014–18. –/40(+8) 1TD 2W. 29.1 t.
MS. Siemens Krefeld 2014–18. –/64. 36.2 t.
PTS. Siemens Krefeld 2014–18. –/54 1T. 33.2 t.
DMC(B). Siemens Krefeld 2014–18. 26/16(+3). 38.5 t.

700001	**TL**	CT	*TL*	TB	401001	402001	403001	406001
					407001	410001	411001	412001
700002	**TL**	CT	*TL*	TB	401002	402002	403002	406002
					407002	410002	411002	412002
700003	**TL**	CT	*TL*	TB	401003	402003	403003	406003
					407003	410003	411003	412003
700004	**TL**	CT	*TL*	TB	401004	402004	403004	406004
					407004	410004	411004	412004

700 005	**TL**	CT	*TL*	TB	401005	402005	403005	406005
					407005	410005	411005	412005
700 006	**TL**	CT	*TL*	TB	401006	402006	403006	406006
					407006	410006	411006	412006
700 007	**TL**	CT	*TL*	TB	401007	402007	403007	406007
					407007	410007	411007	412007
700 008	**TL**	CT	*TL*	TB	401008	402008	403008	406008
					407008	410008	411008	412008
700 009	**TL**	CT	*TL*	TB	401009	402009	403009	406009
					407009	410009	411009	412009
700 010	**TL**	CT	*TL*	TB	401010	402010	403010	406010
					407010	410010	411010	412010
700 011	**TL**	CT	*TL*	TB	401011	402011	403011	406011
					407011	410011	411011	412011
700 012	**TL**	CT	*TL*	TB	401012	402012	403012	406012
					407012	410012	411012	412012
700 013	**TL**	CT	*TL*	TB	401013	402013	403013	406013
					407013	410013	411013	412013
700 014	**TL**	CT	*TL*	TB	401014	402014	403014	406014
					407014	410014	411014	412014
700 015	**TL**	CT	*TL*	TB	401015	402015	403015	406015
					407015	410015	411015	412015
700 016	**TL**	CT	*TL*	TB	401016	402016	403016	406016
					407016	410016	411016	412016
700 017	**TL**	CT	*TL*	TB	401017	402017	403017	406017
					407017	410017	411017	412017
700 018	**TL**	CT	*TL*	TB	401018	402018	403018	406018
					407018	410018	411018	412018
700 019	**TL**	CT	*TL*	TB	401019	402019	403019	406019
					407019	410019	411019	412019
700 020	**TL**	CT	*TL*	TB	401020	402020	403020	406020
					407020	410020	411020	412020
700 021	**TL**	CT	*TL*	TB	401021	402021	403021	406021
					407021	410021	411021	412021
700 022	**TL**	CT	*TL*	TB	401022	402022	403022	406022
					407022	410022	411022	412022
700 023	**TL**	CT	*TL*	TB	401023	402023	403023	406023
					407023	410023	411023	412023
700 024	**TL**	CT	*TL*	TB	401024	402024	403024	406024
					407024	410024	411024	412024
700 025	**TL**	CT	*TL*	TB	401025	402025	403025	406025
					407025	410025	411025	412025
700 026	**TL**	CT	*TL*	TB	401026	402026	403026	406026
					407026	410026	411026	412026
700 027	**TL**	CT	*TL*	TB	401027	402027	403027	406027
					407027	410027	411027	412027
700 028	**TL**	CT	*TL*	TB	401028	402028	403028	406028
					407028	410028	411028	412028
700 029	**TL**	CT	*TL*	TB	401029	402029	403029	406029
					407029	410029	411029	412029

700030	**TL**	CT	*TL*	TB	401030	402030	403030	406030
					407030	410030	411030	412030
700031	**TL**	CT	*TL*	TB	401031	402031	403031	406031
					407031	410031	411031	412031
700032	**TL**	CT	*TL*	TB	401032	402032	403032	406032
					407032	410032	411032	412032
700033	**TL**	CT	*TL*	TB	401033	402033	403033	406033
					407033	410033	411033	412033
700034	**TL**	CT	*TL*	TB	401034	402034	403034	406034
					407034	410034	411034	412034
700035	**TL**	CT	*TL*	TB	401035	402035	403035	406035
					407035	410035	411035	412035
700036	**TL**	CT	*TL*	TB	401036	402036	403036	406036
					407036	410036	411036	412036
700037	**TL**	CT	*TL*	TB	401037	402037	403037	406037
					407037	410037	411037	412037
700038	**TL**	CT	*TL*	TB	401038	402038	403038	406038
					407038	410038	411038	412038
700039	**TL**	CT	*TL*	TB	401039	402039	403039	406039
					407039	410039	411039	412039
700040	**TL**	CT	*TL*	TB	401040	402040	403040	406040
					407040	410040	411040	412040
700041	**TL**	CT	*TL*	TB	401041	402041	403041	406041
					407041	410041	411041	412041
700042	**TL**	CT	*TL*	TB	401042	402042	403042	406042
					407042	410042	411042	412042
700043	**TL**	CT	*TL*	TB	401043	402043	403043	406043
					407043	410043	411043	412043
700044	**TL**	CT	*TL*	TB	401044	402044	403044	406044
					407044	410044	411044	412044
700045	**TL**	CT	*TL*	TB	401045	402045	403045	406045
					407045	410045	411045	412045
700046	**TL**	CT	*TL*	TB	401046	402046	403046	406046
					407046	410046	411046	412046
700047	**TL**	CT	*TL*	TB	401047	402047	403047	406047
					407047	410047	411047	412047
700048	**TL**	CT	*TL*	TB	401048	402048	403048	406048
					407048	410048	411048	412048
700049	**TL**	CT	*TL*	TB	401049	402049	403049	406049
					407049	410049	411049	412049
700050	**TL**	CT	*TL*	TB	401050	402050	403050	406050
					407050	410050	411050	412050
700051	**TL**	CT	*TL*	TB	401051	402051	403051	406051
					407051	410051	411051	412051
700052	**TL**	CT	*TL*	TB	401052	402052	403052	406052
					407052	410052	411052	412052
700053	**TL**	CT	*TL*	TB	401053	402053	403053	406053
					407053	410053	411053	412053
700054	**TL**	CT	*TL*	TB	401054	402054	403054	406054
					407054	410054	411054	412054

700 055	**TL** CT *TL* TB	401055 402055 403055 406055
		407055 410055 411055 412055
700 056	**TL** CT *TL* TB	401056 402056 403056 406056
		407056 410056 411056 412056
700 057	**TL** CT *TL* TB	401057 402057 403057 406057
		407057 410057 411057 412057
700 058	**TL** CT *TL* TB	401058 402058 403058 406058
		407058 410058 411058 412058
700 059	**TL** CT *TL* TB	401059 402059 403059 406059
		407059 410059 411059 412059
700 060	**TL** CT *TL* TB	401060 402060 403060 406060
		407060 410060 411060 412060

Class 700/1. 12-car units.

Additions to the standard livery: 700 155 Pride stripes on driving cars.

DMC(A). Siemens Krefeld 2013–18. 26/20. 38.2 t.
PTS. Siemens Krefeld 2013–18. –/54 1T. 34.4 t.
MS. Siemens Krefeld 2013–18. –/60(+3). 36.0 t.
MS. Siemens Krefeld 2013–18. –/56 1T. 35.8 t.
TS. Siemens Krefeld 2013–18. –/64. 26.8 t.
TS. Siemens Krefeld 2013–18. –/56(+3). 28.3 t.
TS(W). Siemens Krefeld 2013–18. –/38(+9) 1TD 2W. 28.7 t.
TS. Siemens Krefeld 2013–18. –/64. 27.9 t.
MS. Siemens Krefeld 2013–18. –/56 1T. 35.6 t.
MS. Siemens Krefeld 2013–18. –/60(+3). 35.3 t.
PTS. Siemens Krefeld 2013–18. –/54 1T. 34.4 t.
DMC(B). Siemens Krefeld 2013–18. 26/20. 38.2 t.

700 101	**TL** CT *TL* TB	401101 402101 403101 404101 405101 406101
		407101 408101 409101 410101 411101 412101
700 102	**TL** CT *TL* TB	401102 402102 403102 404102 405102 406102
		407102 408102 409102 410102 411102 412102
700 103	**TL** CT *TL* TB	401103 402103 403103 404103 405103 406103
		407103 408103 409103 410103 411103 412103
700 104	**TL** CT *TL* TB	401104 402104 403104 404104 405104 406104
		407104 408104 409104 410104 411104 412104
700 105	**TL** CT *TL* TB	401105 402105 403105 404105 405105 406105
		407105 408105 409105 410105 411105 412105
700 106	**TL** CT *TL* TB	401106 402106 403106 404106 405106 406106
		407106 408106 409106 410106 411106 412106
700 107	**TL** CT *TL* TB	401107 402107 403107 404107 405107 406107
		407107 408107 409107 410107 411107 412107
700 108	**TL** CT *TL* TB	401108 402108 403108 404108 405108 406108
		407108 408108 409108 410108 411108 412108
700 109	**TL** CT *TL* TB	401109 402109 403109 404109 405109 406109
		407109 408109 409109 410109 411109 412109
700 110	**TL** CT *TL* TB	401110 402110 403110 404110 405110 406110
		407110 408110 409110 410110 411110 412110
700 111	**TL** CT *TL* TB	401111 402111 403111 404111 405111 406111
		407111 408111 409111 410111 411111 412111

700 112	**TL** CT *TL*	TB	401112	402112	403112	404112	405112	406112			
			407112	408112	409112	410112	411112	412112			
700 113	**TL** CT *TL*	TB	401113	402113	403113	404113	405113	406113			
			407113	408113	409113	410113	411113	412113			
700 114	**TL** CT *TL*	TB	401114	402114	403114	404114	405114	406114			
			407114	408114	409114	410114	411114	412114			
700 115	**TL** CT *TL*	TB	401115	402115	403115	404115	405115	406115			
			407115	408115	409115	410115	411115	412115			
700 116	**TL** CT *TL*	TB	401116	402116	403116	404116	405116	406116			
			407116	408116	409116	410116	411116	412116			
700 117	**TL** CT *TL*	TB	401117	402117	403117	404117	405117	406117			
			407117	408117	409117	410117	411117	412117			
700 118	**TL** CT *TL*	TB	401118	402118	403118	404118	405118	406118			
			407118	408118	409118	410118	411118	412118			
700 119	**TL** CT *TL*	TB	401119	402119	403119	404119	405119	406119			
			407119	408119	409119	410119	411119	412119			
700 120	**TL** CT *TL*	TB	401120	402120	403120	404120	405120	406120			
			407120	408120	409120	410120	411120	412120			
700 121	**TL** CT *TL*	TB	401121	402121	403121	404121	405121	406121			
			407121	408121	409121	410121	411121	412121			
700 122	**TL** CT *TL*	TB	401122	402122	403122	404122	405122	406122			
			407122	408122	409122	410122	411122	412122			
700 123	**TL** CT *TL*	TB	401123	402123	403123	404123	405123	406123			
			407123	408123	409123	410123	411123	412123			
700 124	**TL** CT *TL*	TB	401124	402124	403124	404124	405124	406124			
			407124	408124	409124	410124	411124	412124			
700 125	**TL** CT *TL*	TB	401125	402125	403125	404125	405125	406125			
			407125	408125	409125	410125	411125	412125			
700 126	**TL** CT *TL*	TB	401126	402126	403126	404126	405126	406126			
			407126	408126	409126	410126	411126	412126			
700 127	**TL** CT *TL*	TB	401127	402127	403127	404127	405127	406127			
			407127	408127	409127	410127	411127	412127			
700 128	**TL** CT *TL*	TB	401128	402128	403128	404128	405128	406128			
			407128	408128	409128	410128	411128	412128			
700 129	**TL** CT *TL*	TB	401129	402129	403129	404129	405129	406129			
			407129	408129	409129	410129	411129	412129			
700 130	**TL** CT *TL*	TB	401130	402130	403130	404130	405130	406130			
			407130	408130	409130	410130	411130	412130			
700 131	**TL** CT *TL*	TB	401131	402131	403131	404131	405131	406131			
			407131	408131	409131	410131	411131	412131			
700 132	**TL** CT *TL*	TB	401132	402132	403132	404132	405132	406132			
			407132	408132	409132	410132	411132	412132			
700 133	**TL** CT *TL*	TB	401133	402133	403133	404133	405133	406133			
			407133	408133	409133	410133	411133	412133			
700 134	**TL** CT *TL*	TB	401134	402134	403134	404134	405134	406134			
			407134	408134	409134	410134	411134	412134			
700 135	**TL** CT *TL*	TB	401135	402135	403135	404135	405135	406135			
			407135	408135	409135	410135	411135	412135			
700 136	**TL** CT *TL*	TB	401136	402136	403136	404136	405136	406136			
			407136	408136	409136	410136	411136	412136			

700 137	**TL** CT *TL*	TB	401137 402137 403137 404137 405137 406137
			407137 408137 409137 410137 411137 412137
700 138	**TL** CT *TL*	TB	401138 402138 403138 404138 405138 406138
			407138 408138 409138 410138 411138 412138
700 139	**TL** CT *TL*	TB	401139 402139 403139 404139 405139 406139
			407139 408139 409139 410139 411139 412139
700 140	**TL** CT *TL*	TB	401140 402140 403140 404140 405140 406140
			407140 408140 409140 410140 411140 412140
700 141	**TL** CT *TL*	TB	401141 402141 403141 404141 405141 406141
			407141 408141 409141 410141 411141 412141
700 142	**TL** CT *TL*	TB	401142 402142 403142 404142 405142 406142
			407142 408142 409142 410142 411142 412142
700 143	**TL** CT *TL*	TB	401143 402143 403143 404143 405143 406143
			407143 408143 409143 410143 411143 412143
700 144	**TL** CT *TL*	TB	401144 402144 403144 404144 405144 406144
			407144 408144 409144 410144 411144 412144
700 145	**TL** CT *TL*	TB	401145 402145 403145 404145 405145 406145
			407145 408145 409145 410145 411145 412145
700 146	**TL** CT *TL*	TB	401146 402146 403146 404146 405146 406146
			407146 408146 409146 410146 411146 412146
700 147	**TL** CT *TL*	TB	401147 402147 403147 404147 405147 406147
			407147 408147 409147 410147 411147 412147
700 148	**TL** CT *TL*	TB	401148 402148 403148 404148 405148 406148
			407148 408148 409148 410148 411148 412148
700 149	**TL** CT *TL*	TB	401149 402149 403149 404149 405149 406149
			407149 408149 409149 410149 411149 412149
700 150	**TL** CT *TL*	TB	401150 402150 403150 404150 405150 406150
			407150 408150 409150 410150 411150 412150
700 151	**TL** CT *TL*	TB	401151 402151 403151 404151 405151 406151
			407151 408151 409151 410151 411151 412151
700 152	**TL** CT *TL*	TB	401152 402152 403152 404152 405152 406152
			407152 408152 409152 410152 411152 412152
700 153	**TL** CT *TL*	TB	401153 402153 403153 404153 405153 406153
			407153 408153 409153 410153 411153 412153
700 154	**TL** CT *TL*	TB	401154 402154 403154 404154 405154 406154
			407154 408154 409154 410154 411154 412154
700 155	**TL** CT *TL*	TB	401155 402155 403155 404155 405155 406155
			407155 408155 409155 410155 411155 412155

CLASS 701 AVENTRA BOMBARDIER/ALSTOM DERBY

South Western Railway has 60 10-car and 30 5-car Aventra EMUs on order from Alstom (previously Bombardier), financed by Rock Rail. The first units have been delivered for testing but a number of design problems has delayed service introduction which is is expected from late 2023. The units have been branded "Arterio" by SWR and will be used on inner and outer suburban duties.

Formation (10-car): DMS–MS–TS–MS–MS–MS–MS–TS–MS–DMS or
(5-car): DMS–MS–TS–MS–DMS.
Systems: 750 V DC third rail.
Construction: Aluminium.
Traction Motors: Two Bombardier asynchronous of 250 kW.
Wheel Arrangement (10-car): 2-Bo + Bo-2 + 2-2 + 2-Bo + Bo-2 + 2-Bo + Bo-2 + 2-2 + 2-Bo + Bo-2 or (5-car): 2-Bo + Bo-2 + 2-2 + 2-Bo + Bo-2.
Braking: Disc, rheostatic & regenerative.
Dimensions: 20.88/19.90 m x 2.78 m.
Bogies: FLEXX B5000 inside-frame.   **Couplers:** Dellner 12.
Gangways: Within unit.   **Control System:** IGBT Inverter.
Doors: Sliding plug.   **Maximum Speed:** 100 mph.
Heating & ventilation: Air conditioning.
Seating Layout: 2+2 unidirectional/facing.
Multiple Working: Within class.

Class 701/0. 10-car units.

DMS(A). Alstom Derby 2020–22. –/56.   t.
MS. Alstom Derby 2020–22. –/60.   t.
TS. Alstom Derby 2020–22. –/34(+10) 1TD 2W.   t.
MS. Alstom Derby 2020–22. –/60.   t.
MS. Alstom Derby 2020–22. –/60.   t.
MS. Alstom Derby 2020–22. –/60.   t.
MS. Alstom Derby 2020–22. –/60.   t.
TS. Alstom Derby 2020–22. –/34(+10) 1TD 2W.   t.
MS. Alstom Derby 2020–22. –/60.   t.
DMS(B). Alstom Derby 2020–22. –/56.   t.

701 001	**SW**	RR	480001	481001	482001	483001	484001
			485001	486001	487001	488001	489001
701 002	**SW**	RR	480002	481002	482002	483002	484002
			485002	486002	487002	488002	489002
701 003	**SW**	RR	480003	481003	482003	483003	484003
			485003	486003	487003	488003	489003
701 004	**SW**	RR	480004	481004	482004	483004	484004
			485004	486004	487004	488004	489004
701 005	**SW**	RR	480005	481005	482005	483005	484005
			485005	486005	487005	488005	489005
701 006	**SW**	RR	480006	481006	482006	483006	484006
			485006	486006	487006	488006	489006
701 007	**SW**	RR	480007	481007	482007	483007	484007
			485007	486007	487007	488007	489007

701 008	**SW** RR	480008	481008	482008	483008	484008
		485008	486008	487008	488008	489008
701 009	**SW** RR	480009	481009	482009	483009	484009
		485009	486009	487009	488009	489009
701 010	**SW** RR	480010	481010	482010	483010	484010
		485010	486010	487010	488010	489010
701 011	**SW** RR	480011	481011	482011	483011	484011
		485011	486011	487011	488011	489011
701 012	**SW** RR	480012	481012	482012	483012	484012
		485012	486012	487012	488012	489012
701 013	**SW** RR	480013	481013	482013	483013	484013
		485013	486013	487013	488013	489013
701 014	**SW** RR	480014	481014	482014	483014	484014
		485014	486014	487014	488014	489014
701 015	**SW** RR	480015	481015	482015	483015	484015
		485015	486015	487015	488015	489015
701 016	**SW** RR	480016	481016	482016	483016	484016
		485016	486016	487016	488016	489016
701 017	**SW** RR	480017	481017	482017	483017	484017
		485017	486017	487017	488017	489017
701 018	**SW** RR	480018	481018	482018	483018	484018
		485018	486018	487018	488018	489018
701 019	**SW** RR	480019	481019	482019	483019	484019
		485019	486019	487019	488019	489019
701 020	**SW** RR	480020	481020	482020	483020	484020
		485020	486020	487020	488020	489020
701 021	**SW** RR	480021	481021	482021	483021	484021
		485021	486021	487021	488021	489021
701 022	**SW** RR	480022	481022	482022	483022	484022
		485022	486022	487022	488022	489022
701 023	**SW** RR	480023	481023	482023	483023	484023
		485023	486023	487023	488023	489023
701 024	**SW** RR	480024	481024	482024	483024	484024
		485024	486024	487024	488024	489024
701 025	**SW** RR	480025	481025	482025	483025	484025
		485025	486025	487025	488025	489025
701 026	**SW** RR	480026	481026	482026	483026	484026
		485026	486026	487026	488026	489026
701 027	**SW** RR	480027	481027	482027	483027	484027
		485027	486027	487027	488027	489027
701 028	**SW** RR	480028	481028	482028	483028	484028
		485028	486028	487028	488028	489028
701 029	**SW** RR	480029	481029	482029	483029	484029
		485029	486029	487029	488029	489029
701 030	**SW** RR	480030	481030	482030	483030	484030
		485030	486030	487030	488030	489030
701 031	**SW** RR	480031	481031	482031	483031	484031
		485031	486031	487031	488031	489031
701 032	**SW** RR	480032	481032	482032	483032	484032
		485032	486032	487032	488032	489032

701033	**SW** RR	480033	481033	482033	483033	484033
		485033	486033	487033	488033	489033
701034	**SW** RR	480034	481034	482034	483034	484034
		485034	486034	487034	488034	489034
701035	**SW** RR	480035	481035	482035	483035	484035
		485035	486035	487035	488035	489035
701036	**SW** RR	480036	481036	482036	483036	484036
		485036	486036	487036	488036	489036
701037	**SW** RR	480037	481037	482037	483037	484037
		485037	486037	487037	488037	489037
701038	**SW** RR	480038	481038	482038	483038	484038
		485038	486038	487038	488038	489038
701039	**SW** RR	480039	481039	482039	483039	484039
		485039	486039	487039	488039	489039
701040	**SW** RR	480040	481040	482040	483040	484040
		485040	486040	487040	488040	489040
701041	**SW** RR	480041	481041	482041	483041	484041
		485041	486041	487041	488041	489041
701042	**SW** RR	480042	481042	482042	483042	484042
		485042	486042	487042	488042	489042
701043	**SW** RR	480043	481043	482043	483043	484043
		485043	486043	487043	488043	489043
701044	**SW** RR	480044	481044	482044	483044	484044
		485044	486044	487044	488044	489044
701045	**SW** RR	480045	481045	482045	483045	484045
		485045	486045	487045	488045	489045
701046	**SW** RR	480046	481046	482046	483046	484046
		485046	486046	487046	488046	489046
701047	**SW** RR	480047	481047	482047	483047	484047
		485047	486047	487047	488047	489047
701048	**SW** RR	480048	481048	482048	483048	484048
		485048	486048	487048	488048	489048
701049	**SW** RR	480049	481049	482049	483049	484049
		485049	486049	487049	488049	489049
701050	**SW** RR	480050	481050	482050	483050	484050
		485050	486050	487050	488050	489050
701051	**SW** RR	480051	481051	482051	483051	484051
		485051	486051	487051	488051	489051
701052	**SW** RR	480052	481052	482052	483052	484052
		485052	486052	487052	488052	489052
701053	**SW** RR	480053	481053	482053	483053	484053
		485053	486053	487053	488053	489053
701054	**SW** RR	480054	481054	482054	483054	484054
		485054	486054	487054	488054	489054
701055	**SW** RR	480055	481055	482055	483055	484055
		485055	486055	487055	488055	489055
701056	**SW** RR	480056	481056	482056	483056	484056
		485056	486056	487056	488056	489056
701057	**SW** RR	480057	481057	482057	483057	484057
		485057	486057	487057	488057	489057

701058	**SW** RR		480058	481058	482058	483058	484058
			485058	486058	487058	488058	489058
701059	**SW** RR		480059	481059	482059	483059	484059
			485059	486059	487059	488059	489059
701060	**SW** RR		480060	481060	482060	483060	484060
			485060	486060	487060	488060	489060

Class 701/5. 5-car units.

DMS(A). Alstom Derby 2019–23. –/56.   t.
MS. Alstom Derby 2019–23. –/60.   t.
TS. Alstom Derby 2019–23. –/34(+10) 1TD 2W.   t.
MS. Alstom Derby 2019–23. –/60.   t.
DMS(B). Alstom Derby 2019–23. –/56.   t.

701501	**SW** RR	480101	481101	482101	483101	484101
701502	**SW** RR	480102	481102	482102	483102	484102
701503	**SW** RR	480103	481103	482103	483103	484103
701504	**SW** RR	480104	481104	482104	483104	484104
701505	**SW** RR	480105	481105	482105	483105	484105
701506	**SW** RR	480106	481106	482106	483106	484106
701507	**SW** RR	480107	481107	482107	483107	484107
701508	**SW** RR	480108	481108	482108	483108	484108
701509	**SW** RR	480109	481109	482109	483109	484109
701510	**SW** RR	480110	481110	482110	483110	484110
701511	**SW** RR	480111	481111	482111	483111	484111
701512	**SW** RR	480112	481112	482112	483112	484112
701513	**SW** RR	480113	481113	482113	483113	484113
701514	**SW** RR	480114	481114	482114	483114	484114
701515	**SW** RR	480115	481115	482115	483115	484115
701516	**SW** RR	480116	481116	482116	483116	484116
701517	**SW** RR	480117	481117	482117	483117	484117
701518	**SW** RR	480118	481118	482118	483118	484118
701519	**SW** RR	480119	481119	482119	483119	484119
701520	**SW** RR	480120	481120	482120	483120	484120
701521	**SW** RR	480121	481121	482121	483121	484121
701522	**SW** RR	480122	481122	482122	483122	484122
701523	**SW** RR	480123	481123	482123	483123	484123
701524	**SW** RR	480124	481124	482124	483124	484124
701525	**SW** RR	480125	481125	482125	483125	484125
701526	**SW** RR	480126	481126	482126	483126	484126
701527	**SW** RR	480127	481127	482127	483127	484127
701528	**SW** RR	480128	481128	482128	483128	484128
701529	**SW** RR	480129	481129	482129	483129	484129
701530	**SW** RR	480130	481130	482130	483130	484130

CLASS 707   DESIRO CITY   SIEMENS

Suburban units. Built with the capability to be easily converted to dual-voltage units. Operated by South West Trains/South Western Railway until 2021–23 when they transferred to Southeastern. Southeastern markets the units as "City Beam" units.

Formation: DMS–TS–TS–TS–DMS.
Systems: 750 V DC third rail but with 25 kV AC overhead capability.
Construction: Aluminium.
Traction Motors: Four Siemens asynchronous of 200 kW.
Wheel Arrangement: Bo-Bo + 2-2 + 2-2 + 2-2 + Bo-Bo.
Braking: Disc, tread & regenerative. **Dimensions:** 20.00/20.16 m x 2.80 m.
Bogies: Siemens SF7000 inside-frame. **Couplers:** Dellner 12.
Gangways: Within unit.   **Control System:** IGBT Inverter.
Doors: Sliding plug.   **Maximum Speed:** 100 mph.
Heating & ventilation: Air conditioning.
Seating Layout: 2+2/2+1 facing/unidirectional.
Multiple Working: Within class and with Classes 700 and 717.

DMS(A). Siemens Krefeld 2015–17. –/46. 37.9 t.
TS. Siemens Krefeld 2015–17. –/64. 28.3 t.
TS. Siemens Krefeld 2015–17. –/53(+4) 2W. 28.5 t.
TS. Siemens Krefeld 2015–17. –/62. 27.7 t.
DMS(B). Siemens Krefeld 2015–17. –/46. 37.9 t.

707 001	**SB**	A	*SE*	SG	421001	422001	423001	424001	425001
707 002	**SB**	A	*SE*	SG	421002	422002	423002	424002	425002
707 003	**SB**	A	*SE*	SG	421003	422003	423003	424003	425003
707 004	**SB**	A	*SE*	SG	421004	422004	423004	424004	425004
707 005	**SB**	A	*SE*	SG	421005	422005	423005	424005	425005
707 006	**SB**	A	*SE*	SG	421006	422006	423006	424006	425006
707 007	**SB**	A	*SE*	SG	421007	422007	423007	424007	425007
707 008	**SB**	A	*SE*	SG	421008	422008	423008	424008	425008
707 009	**SB**	A	*SE*	SG	421009	422009	423009	424009	425009
707 010	**SB**	A	*SE*	SG	421010	422010	423010	424010	425010
707 011	**SB**	A	*SE*	SG	421011	422011	423011	424011	425011
707 012	**SB**	A	*SE*	SG	421012	422012	423012	424012	425012
707 013	**SB**	A	*SE*	SG	421013	422013	423013	424013	425013
707 014	**SB**	A	*SE*	SG	421014	422014	423014	424014	425014
707 015	**SB**	A	*SE*	SG	421015	422015	423015	424015	425015
707 016	**SB**	A	*SE*	SG	421016	422016	423016	424016	425016
707 017	**SB**	A	*SE*	SG	421017	422017	423017	424017	425017
707 018	**SB**	A	*SE*	SG	421018	422018	423018	424018	425018
707 019	**SB**	A	*SE*	SG	421019	422019	423019	424019	425019
707 020	**SB**	A	*SE*	SG	421020	422020	423020	424020	425020
707 021	**SB**	A	*SE*	SG	421021	422021	423021	424021	425021
707 022	**SB**	A	*SE*	SG	421022	422022	423022	424022	425022
707 023	**SB**	A	*SE*	SG	421023	422023	423023	424023	425023
707 024	**SB**	A	*SE*	SG	421024	422024	423024	424024	425024
707 025	**SB**	A	*SE*	SG	421025	422025	423025	424025	425025
707 026	**SB**	A	*SE*	SG	421026	422026	423026	424026	425026

707027	**SB**	A	*SE*	SG	421027	422027	423027	424027	425027
707028	**SB**	A	*SE*	SG	421028	422028	423028	424028	425028
707029	**SB**	A	*SE*	SG	421029	422029	423029	424029	425029
707030	**SB**	A	*SE*	SG	421030	422030	423030	424030	425030

Names:

707001 Spirit of Ukraine
707005 Rt Hon James Brokenshire MP Old Bexley and Sidcup

CLASS 710 AVENTRA BOMBARDIER/ALSTOM DERBY

These suburban 4-car Aventras are used by London Overground on Gospel Oak–Barking, London Euston–Watford Junction and Liverpool Street local services. There are a mix of AC only and dual-voltage units.

Originally 45 4-car units were ordered. In 2018 an extra three 4-cars and six 5-cars were ordered.

Formation: DMS–MS–PMS–DMS or DMS–MS–PMS–MS–DMS.
Systems: Class 710/1 25 kV AC overhead only. Class 710/2 and 710/3 25 kV AC overhead and 750 V DC third rail.
Construction: Aluminium.
Traction Motors: Two Bombardier asynchronous of 265 kW.
Wheel Arrangement: Bo-2 + 2-Bo + Bo-2 (+ 2-Bo) + 2-Bo.
Braking: Disc & regenerative.   **Dimensions:** 21.45/19.99 m x 2.78 m.
Bogies: FLEXX B5000 inside-frame. **Couplers:** Dellner 12.
Gangways: Within unit.   **Control System:** IGBT Inverter.
Doors: Sliding plug.   **Maximum Speed:** 75 mph.
Heating & ventilation: Air conditioning.
Seating Layout: Longitudinal ("tube style") low density.
Multiple Working: Within class.

Class 710/1. 25 kV AC only 4-car units.

DMS(A). Alstom Derby 2017–19. –/40(+6). 41.1 t.
MS. Alstom Derby 2017–19. –/52. 32.2 t.
PMS. Alstom Derby 2017–19. –/45(+6) 2W. 38.5 t.
DMS(B). Alstom Derby 2017–19. –/40(+6). 41.1 t.

710101	**LD**	RF	*LO*	WN	431101	431201	431301	431501
710102	**LD**	RF	*LO*	WN	431102	431202	431302	431502
710103	**LD**	RF	*LO*	WN	431103	431203	431303	431503
710104	**LD**	RF	*LO*	WN	431104	431204	431304	431504
710105	**LD**	RF	*LO*	WN	431105	431205	431305	431505
710106	**LD**	RF	*LO*	WN	431106	431206	431306	431506
710107	**LD**	RF	*LO*	WN	431107	431207	431307	431507
710108	**LD**	RF	*LO*	WN	431108	431208	431308	431508
710109	**LD**	RF	*LO*	WN	431109	431209	431309	431509
710110	**LD**	RF	*LO*	WN	431110	431210	431310	431510
710111	**LD**	RF	*LO*	WN	431111	431211	431311	431511
710112	**LD**	RF	*LO*	WN	431112	431212	431312	431512
710113	**LD**	RF	*LO*	WN	431113	431213	431313	431513
710114	**LD**	RF	*LO*	WN	431114	431214	431314	431514

710115	**LD**	RF	*LO*	WN	431115	431215	431315	431515
710116	**LD**	RF	*LO*	WN	431116	431216	431316	431516
710117	**LD**	RF	*LO*	WN	431117	431217	431317	431517
710118	**LD**	RF	*LO*	WN	431118	431218	431318	431518
710119	**LD**	RF	*LO*	WN	431119	431219	431319	431519
710120	**LD**	RF	*LO*	WN	431120	431220	431320	431520
710121	**LD**	RF	*LO*	WN	431121	431221	431321	431521
710122	**LD**	RF	*LO*	WN	431122	431222	431322	431522
710123	**LD**	RF	*LO*	WN	431123	431223	431323	431523
710124	**LD**	RF	*LO*	WN	431124	431224	431324	431524
710125	**LD**	RF	*LO*	WN	431125	431225	431325	431525
710126	**LD**	RF	*LO*	WN	431126	431226	431326	431526
710127	**LD**	RF	*LO*	WN	431127	431227	431327	431527
710128	**LD**	RF	*LO*	WN	431128	431228	431328	431528
710129	**LD**	RF	*LO*	WN	431129	431229	431329	431529
710130	**LD**	RF	*LO*	WN	431130	431230	431330	431530

Class 710/2. 25 kV AC/750 V DC 4-car unit.

DMS(A). Alstom Derby 2017–19. –/40(+6). 43.5 t.
MS. Alstom Derby 2017–19. –/52. 32.3 t.
PMS. Alstom Derby 2017–19. –/45(+6) 2W. 38.5 t.
DMS(B). Alstom Derby 2017–19. –/40(+6).43.5 t.

710256	**LD**	RF	*LO*	WN	432156	432256	432356	432556
710257	**LD**	RF	*LO*	WN	432157	432257	432357	432557
710258	**LD**	RF	*LO*	WN	432158	432258	432358	432558
710259	**LD**	RF	*LO*	WN	432159	432259	432359	432559
710260	**LD**	RF	*LO*	WN	432160	432260	432360	432560
710261	**LD**	RF	*LO*	WN	432161	432261	432361	432561
710262	**LD**	RF	*LO*	WN	432162	432262	432362	432562
710263	**LD**	RF	*LO*	WN	432163	432263	432363	432563
710264	**LD**	RF	*LO*	WN	432164	432264	432364	432564
710265	**LD**	RF	*LO*	WN	432165	432265	432365	432565
710266	**LD**	RF	*LO*	WN	432166	432266	432366	432566
710267	**LD**	RF	*LO*	WN	432167	432267	432367	432567
710268	**LD**	RF	*LO*	WN	432168	432268	432368	432568
710269	**LD**	RF	*LO*	WN	432169	432269	432369	432569
710270	**LD**	RF			432170	432270	432370	432570
710271	**LD**	RF	*LO*	WN	432171	432271	432371	432571
710272	**LD**	RF	*LO*	WN	432172	432272	432372	432572
710273	**LD**	RF	*LO*	WN	432173	432273	432373	432573

Class 710/3. 25 kV AC/750 V DC 5-car units. Originally numbered 710274–279 as-built, but renumbered in the 7103xx series before entering service.

DMS(A). Alstom Derby 2019–20. –/40(+6). 43.5 t.
MS. Alstom Derby 2019–20. –/52. 32.3 t.
PMS. Alstom Derby 2019–20. –/45(+6) 2W. 38.5 t.
MS. Alstom Derby 2019–20. –/52. 33.1 t.
DMS(B). Alstom Derby 2019–20. –/40(+6). 43.5 t.

710374	**LD**	RF			432174	432274	432374	432474	432574
710375	**LD**	RF			432175	432275	432375	432475	432575

710376	**LD**	RF	*LO*	WN	432176	432276	432376	432476	432576
710377	**LD**	RF	*LO*	WN	432177	432277	432377	432477	432577
710378	**LD**	RF	*LO*	WN	432178	432278	432378	432478	432578
710379	**LD**	RF	*LO*	WN	432179	432279	432379	432479	432579

CLASS 717   DESIRO CITY   SIEMENS

Dual-voltage 6-car units used on Great Northern services from London Moorgate. The design is based on Classes 700/707, but has emergency end doors for tunnel operation.

Formation: DMS–TS–TS–MS–PTS–DMS.
Systems: 25 kV AC overhead and 750 V DC third rail.
Construction: Aluminium.
Traction Motors: Four Siemens asynchronous of 200 kW.
Wheel Arrangement: Bo-Bo + 2-2 + 2-2 + Bo-Bo + 2-2 + Bo-Bo.
Braking: Disc, tread & regenerative.   **Dimensions:** 20.00 x 2.80 m.
Bogies: Siemens SF7000 inside-frame. **Couplers:** Dellner 12.
Gangways: Within unit + end doors. **Control System:** IGBT Inverter.
Doors: Sliding plug.   **Maximum Speed:** 85 mph.
Heating & ventilation: Air conditioning.
Seating Layout: 2+2 facing/unidirectional.
Multiple Working: Within class and with Classes 700 and 707.

DMS(A). Siemens Krefeld 2017–18. –/52(+4). 38.8 t.
TS. Siemens Krefeld 2017–18. –/68. 28.8 t.
TS. Siemens Krefeld 2017–18. –/61(+4) 2W. 28.7 t.
MS. Siemens Krefeld 2017–18. –/68. 35.5 t.
PTS. Siemens Krefeld 2017–18. –/61(+3). 33.9 t.
DMS(B). Siemens Krefeld 2017–18. –/52(+4). 38.8 t.

717001	**TL**	RR	*GN*	HE	451001	452001	453001	454001	455001	456001
717002	**TL**	RR	*GN*	HE	451002	452002	453002	454002	455002	456002
717003	**TL**	RR	*GN*	HE	451003	452003	453003	454003	455003	456003
717004	**TL**	RR	*GN*	HE	451004	452004	453004	454004	455004	456004
717005	**TL**	RR	*GN*	HE	451005	452005	453005	454005	455005	456005
717006	**TL**	RR	*GN*	HE	451006	452006	453006	454006	455006	456006
717007	**TL**	RR	*GN*	HE	451007	452007	453007	454007	455007	456007
717008	**TL**	RR	*GN*	HE	451008	452008	453008	454008	455008	456008
717009	**TL**	RR	*GN*	HE	451009	452009	453009	454009	455009	456009
717010	**TL**	RR	*GN*	HE	451010	452010	453010	454010	455010	456010
717011	**TL**	RR	*GN*	HE	451011	452011	453011	454011	455011	456011
717012	**TL**	RR	*GN*	HE	451012	452012	453012	454012	455012	456012
717013	**TL**	RR	*GN*	HE	451013	452013	453013	454013	455013	456013
717014	**TL**	RR	*GN*	HE	451014	452014	453014	454014	455014	456014
717015	**TL**	RR	*GN*	HE	451015	452015	453015	454015	455015	456015
717016	**TL**	RR	*GN*	HE	451016	452016	453016	454016	455016	456016
717017	**TL**	RR	*GN*	HE	451017	452017	453017	454017	455017	456017
717018	**TL**	RR	*GN*	HE	451018	452018	453018	454018	455018	456018
717019	**TL**	RR	*GN*	HE	451019	452019	453019	454019	455019	456019
717020	**TL**	RR	*GN*	HE	451020	452020	453020	454020	455020	456020
717021	**TL**	RR	*GN*	HE	451021	452021	453021	454021	455021	456021

717022	**TL**	RR	*GN*	HE	451022 452022 453022 454022 455022 456022
717023	**TL**	RR	*GN*	HE	451023 452023 453023 454023 455023 456023
717024	**TL**	RR	*GN*	HE	451024 452024 453024 454024 455024 456024
717025	**TL**	RR	*GN*	HE	451025 452025 453025 454025 455025 456025

CLASS 720 AVENTRA BOMBARDIER/ALSTOM DERBY

This large fleet of Standard Class only Aventra EMUs was ordered by Greater Anglia in 2016 to replace its entire Class 317, 321, 360 and 379 fleets on outer suburban and medium-distance services. In 2020 the order was amended – originally it was to be for 89 5-car units and 22 10-car units, but it was changed so that the whole order consists of 5-car units (133 5-cars in total). The additional 5-car units are still numbered in the 720/1 series.

After many delays the units were finally introduced in autumn 2020.

The Class 720/6 units are 5-car sets on order for c2c (originally these were also to be formed as six 10-car units but the order was later amended to 12 5-car units).

Formation: DMS–PMS–MS–MS–DTS.
Systems: 25 kV AC overhead.
Construction: Aluminium.
Traction Motors: Two Bombardier asynchronous of 265 kW.
Wheel Arrangement:
Braking: Disc & regenerative   **Dimensions**: 24.54/24.21 x 2.77 m.
Bogies: FLEXX B5000 inside-frame.   **Couplers**: Dellner 12.
Gangways: Within unit.   **Control System**: IGBT Inverter.
Doors: Sliding plug.   **Maximum Speed**: 100 mph.
Heating & ventilation: Air conditioning.
Seating Layout: 3+2 facing/unidirectional.
Multiple Working: Within class.

Class 720/1. Greater Anglia units.

Additions to the standard livery: 720506 Pride stripes on driving cars.

DMS. Alstom Derby 2018–23. –/91(+4). 42.5 t.
PMS. Alstom Derby 2018–23. –/93(+8) 1T. 39.8 t.
MS(A). Alstom Derby 2018–23. –/109(+4). 39.6 t.
MS(B). Alstom Derby 2018–23. –/109(+4). 34.1 t.
DTS. Alstom Derby 2018–23. –/59(+9) 1TD 2W. 37.7 t.

720101	**GR**	A				450101	451101	452101	453101	459101
720102	**GR**	A			450102	451102	452102	453102	459102
720103	**GR**	A	*GA*	IL	450103	451103	452103	453103	459103
720104	**GR**	A			450104	451104	452104	453104	459104
720105	**GR**	A	*GA*	IL	450105	451105	452105	453105	459105
720106	**GR**	A	*GA*	IL	450106	451106	452106	453106	459106
720107	**GR**	A	*GA*	IL	450107	451107	452107	453107	459107
720108	**GR**	A	*GA*	IL	450108	451108	452108	453108	459108
720109	**GR**	A	*GA*	IL	450109	451109	452109	453109	459109
720110	**GR**	A	*GA*	IL	450110	451110	452110	453110	459110
720111	**GR**	A	*GA*	IL	450111	451111	452111	453111	459111

720 112	**GR**	A	*GA*	IL	450112	451112	452112	453112	459112
720 113	**GR**	A	*GA*	IL	450113	451113	452113	453113	459113
720 114	**GR**	A	*GA*	IL	450114	451114	452114	453114	459114
720 115	**GR**	A	*GA*	IL	450115	451115	452115	453115	459115
720 116	**GR**	A	*GA*	IL	450116	451116	452116	453116	459116
720 117	**GR**	A	*GA*	IL	450117	451117	452117	453117	459117
720 118	**GR**	A	*GA*	IL	450118	451118	452118	453118	459118
720 119	**GR**	A	*GA*	IL	450119	451119	452119	453119	459119
720 120	**GR**	A	*GA*	IL	450120	451120	452120	453120	459120
720 121	**GR**	A	*GA*	IL	450121	451121	452121	453121	459121
720 122	**GR**	A	*GA*	IL	450122	451122	452122	453122	459122
720 123	**GR**	A	*GA*	IL	450123	451123	452123	453123	459123
720 124	**GR**	A	*GA*	IL	450124	451124	452124	453124	459124
720 125	**GR**	A	*GA*	IL	450125	451125	452125	453125	459125
720 126	**GR**	A	*GA*	IL	450126	451126	452126	453126	459126
720 127	**GR**	A	*GA*	IL	450127	451127	452127	453127	459127
720 128	**GR**	A			450128	451128	452128	453128	459128
720 129	**GR**	A	*GA*	IL	450129	451129	452129	453129	459129
720 130	**GR**	A	*GA*	IL	450130	451130	452130	453130	459130
720 131	**GR**	A	*GA*	IL	450131	451131	452131	453131	459131
720 132	**GR**	A	*GA*	IL	450132	451132	452132	453132	459132
720 133	**GR**	A	*GA*	IL	450133	451133	452133	453133	459133
720 134	**GR**	A	*GA*	IL	450134	451134	452134	453134	459134
720 135	**GR**	A	*GA*	IL	450135	451135	452135	453135	459135
720 136	**GR**	A	*GA*	IL	450136	451136	452136	453136	459136
720 137	**GR**	A			450137	451137	452137	453137	459137
720 138	**GR**	A			450138	451138	452138	453138	459138
720 139	**GR**	A			450139	451139	452139	453139	459139
720 140	**GR**	A			450140	451140	452140	453140	459140
720 141	**GR**	A			450141	451141	452141	453141	459141
720 142	**GR**	A			450142	451142	452142	453142	459142
720 143	**GR**	A			450143	451143	452143	453143	459143
720 144	**GR**	A			450144	451144	452144	453144	459144
720 501	**GR**	A	*GA*	IL	450501	451501	452501	453501	459501
720 502	**GR**	A			450502	451502	452502	453502	459502
720 503	**GR**	A			450503	451503	452503	453503	459503
720 504	**GR**	A			450504	451504	452504	453504	459504
720 505	**GR**	A			450505	451505	452505	453505	459505
720 506	**GR**	A	*GA*	IL	450506	451506	452506	453506	459506
720 507	**GR**	A	*GA*	IL	450507	451507	452507	453507	459507
720 508	**GR**	A	*GA*	IL	450508	451508	452508	453508	459508
720 509	**GR**	A			450509	451509	452509	453509	459509
720 510	**GR**	A			450510	451510	452510	453510	459510
720 511	**GR**	A	*GA*	IL	450511	451511	452511	453511	459511
720 512	**GR**	A	*GA*	IL	450512	451512	452512	453512	459512
720 513	**GR**	A	*GA*	IL	450513	451513	452513	453513	459513
720 514	**GR**	A	*GA*	IL	450514	451514	452514	453514	459514
720 515	**GR**	A	*GA*	IL	450515	451515	452515	453515	459515
720 516	**GR**	A			450516	451516	452516	453516	459516
720 517	**GR**	A	*GA*	IL	450517	451517	452517	453517	459517

720518	GR	A	GA	IL	450518	451518	452518	453518	459518
720519	GR	A			450519	451519	452519	453519	459519
720520	GR	A	GA	IL	450520	451520	452520	453520	459520
720521	GR	A	GA	IL	450521	451521	452521	453521	459521
720522	GR	A	GA	IL	450522	451522	452522	453522	459522
720523	GR	A	GA	IL	450523	451523	452523	453523	459523
720524	GR	A	GA	IL	450524	451524	452524	453524	459524
720525	GR	A	GA	IL	450525	451525	452525	453525	459525
720526	GR	A	GA	IL	450526	451526	452526	453526	459526
720527	GR	A	GA	IL	450527	451527	452527	453527	459527
720528	GR	A	GA	IL	450528	451528	452528	453528	459528
720529	GR	A	GA	IL	450529	451529	452529	453529	459529
720530	GR	A	GA	IL	450530	451530	452530	453530	459530
720531	GR	A	GA	IL	450531	451531	452531	453531	459531
720532	GR	A	GA	IL	450532	451532	452532	453532	459532
720533	GR	A	GA	IL	450533	451533	452533	453533	459533
720534	GR	A			450534	451534	452534	453534	459534
720535	GR	A	GA	IL	450535	451535	452535	453535	459535
720536	GR	A	GA	IL	450536	451536	452536	453536	459536
720537	GR	A	GA	IL	450537	451537	452537	453537	459537
720538	GR	A	GA	IL	450538	451538	452538	453538	459538
720539	GR	A	GA	IL	450539	451539	452539	453539	459539
720540	GR	A	GA	IL	450540	451540	452540	453540	459540
720541	GR	A	GA	IL	450541	451541	452541	453541	459541
720542	GR	A	GA	IL	450542	451542	452542	453542	459542
720543	GR	A	GA	IL	450543	451543	452543	453543	459543
720544	GR	A	GA	IL	450544	451544	452544	453544	459544
720545	GR	A	GA	IL	450545	451545	452545	453545	459545
720546	GR	A	GA	IL	450546	451546	452546	453546	459546
720547	GR	A	GA	IL	450547	451547	452547	453547	459547
720548	GR	A	GA	IL	450548	451548	452548	453548	459548
720549	GR	A	GA	IL	450549	451549	452549	453549	459549
720550	GR	A	GA	IL	450550	451550	452550	453550	459550
720551	GR	A	GA	IL	450551	451551	452551	453551	459551
720552	GR	A	GA	IL	450552	451552	452552	453552	459552
720553	GR	A	GA	IL	450553	451553	452553	453553	459553
720554	GR	A	GA	IL	450554	451554	452554	453554	459554
720555	GR	A	GA	IL	450555	451555	452555	453555	459555
720556	GR	A	GA	IL	450556	451556	452556	453556	459556
720557	GR	A	GA	IL	450557	451557	452557	453557	459557
720558	GR	A	GA	IL	450558	451558	452558	453558	459558
720559	GR	A	GA	IL	450559	451559	452559	453559	459559
720560	GR	A	GA	IL	450560	451560	452560	453560	459560
720561	GR	A	GA	IL	450561	451561	452561	453561	459561
720562	GR	A	GA	IL	450562	451562	452562	453562	459562
720563	GR	A	GA	IL	450563	451563	452563	453563	459563
720564	GR	A	GA	IL	450564	451564	452564	453564	459564
720565	GR	A	GA	IL	450565	451565	452565	453565	459565
720566	GR	A	GA	IL	450566	451566	452566	453566	459566
720567	GR	A	GA	IL	450567	451567	452567	453567	459567
720568	GR	A	GA	IL	450568	451568	452568	453568	459568

720569	**GR**	A	*GA*	IL	450569	451569	452569	453569	459569
720570	**GR**	A	*GA*	IL	450570	451570	452570	453570	459570
720571	**GR**	A	*GA*	IL	450571	451571	452571	453571	459571
720572	**GR**	A	*GA*	IL	450572	451572	452572	453572	459572
720573	**GR**	A	*GA*	IL	450573	451573	452573	453573	459573
720574	**GR**	A	*GA*	IL	450574	451574	452574	453574	459574
720575	**GR**	A	*GA*	IL	450575	451575	452575	453575	459575
720576	**GR**	A	*GA*	IL	450576	451576	452576	453576	459576
720577	**GR**	A	*GA*	IL	450577	451577	452577	453577	459577
720578	**GR**	A	*GA*	IL	450578	451578	452578	453578	459578
720579	**GR**	A	*GA*	IL	450579	451579	452579	453579	459579
720580	**GR**	A	*GA*	IL	450580	451580	452580	453580	459580
720581	**GR**	A	*GA*	IL	450581	451581	452581	453581	459581
720582	**GR**	A	*GA*	IL	450582	451582	452582	453582	459582
720583	**GR**	A	*GA*	IL	450583	451583	452583	453583	459583
720584	**GR**	A	*GA*	IL	450584	451584	452584	453584	459584
720585	**GR**	A	*GA*	IL	450585	451585	452585	453585	459585
720586	**GR**	A	*GA*	IL	450586	451586	452586	453586	459586
720587	**GR**	A	*GA*	IL	450587	451587	452587	453587	459587
720588	**GR**	A	*GA*	IL	450588	451588	452588	453588	459588
720589	**GR**	A	*GA*	IL	450589	451589	452589	453589	459589

Class 720/6. c2c units. Full details awaited.

DMS. Alstom Derby 2021–22.
PMS. Alstom Derby 2021–22.
MS(A). Alstom Derby 2021–22.
MS(B). Alstom Derby 2021–22.
DTS. Alstom Derby 2021–22.

720601	**C2C**	P	*C2*	EM	450601	451601	452601	453601	459601
720602	**C2C**	P	*C2*	EM	450602	451602	452602	453602	459602
720603	**C2C**	P			450603	451603	452603	453603	459603
720604	**C2C**	P	*C2*	EM	450604	451604	452604	453604	459604
720605	**C2C**	P	*C2*	EM	450605	451605	452605	453605	459605
720606	**C2C**	P			450606	451606	452606	453606	459606
720607	**C2C**	P			450607	451607	452607	453607	459607
720608	**C2C**	P			450608	451608	452608	453608	459608
720609	**C2C**	P	*C2*	EM	450609	451609	452609	453609	459609
720610	**C2C**	P	*C2*	EM	450610	451610	452610	453610	459610
720611	**C2C**	P			450611	451611	452611	453611	459611
720612	**C2C**	P			450612	451612	452612	453612	459612

Name: 720601 Julian Drury c2c Managing Director 2008–2020

CLASS 730 AVENTRA BOMBARDIER/ALSTOM DERBY

West Midlands Trains has a mixed fleet of 3- and 5-car Aventra EMUs on order from Alstom (previously Bombardier). The 3-car units will be used on suburban services around Birmingham, mainly on the Cross City line, while the 5-car units will be used on outer suburban and inter urban services from London Euston and in the West Midlands. The 3-car units are due to enter service initially on selected services from London Euston from late 2023.

The order was amended in 2022, originally it was for 36 x 3-cars and 45 x 5-cars split into Class 730/1 and 730/2 but this was changed to 48 x 3-cars and 36 x 5-cars each with the same interior specification.

Formation: DMS–PMS–DMS or DMS–MS–PMS–MS–DMS.
Systems: 25 kV AC overhead.
Construction: Aluminium.
Traction Motors: Two Bombardier asynchronous of 250 kW.
Wheel Arrangement:
Braking: Disc & regenerative.   **Dimensions:** 23.91/24.21 x 2.77 m.
Bogies: FLEXX B5000 inside-frame.   **Couplers:** Dellner 12.
Gangways: End gangways.   **Control System:** IGBT Inverter.
Doors: Sliding plug.
Maximum Speed: 730/0: 90 mph; 730/2: 110 mph.
Heating & ventilation: Air conditioning.
Seating Layout: 2+2 facing/unidirectional.
Multiple Working: Within class.

Class 730/0. 3-car units. Principally for West Midlands area suburban services.

DMS(A). Alstom Derby 2020–23. –/67. 41.7t.
PMS. Alstom Derby 2020–23. –/57(+12) 1TD 2W. 39.8t.
DMS(B). Alstom Derby 2020–23. –/67. 41.7t.

730001	**WM** CO	490001	492001	494001
730002	**WM** CO	490002	492002	494002
730003	**WM** CO	490003	492003	494003
730004	**WM** CO	490004	492004	494004
730005	**WM** CO	490005	492005	494005
730006	**WM** CO	490006	492006	494006
730007	**WM** CO	490007	492007	494007
730008	**WM** CO	490008	492008	494008
730009	**WM** CO	490009	492009	494009
730010	**WM** CO	490010	492010	494010
730011	**WM** CO	490011	492011	494011
730012	**WM** CO	490012	492012	494012
730013	**WM** CO	490013	492013	494013
730014	**WM** CO	490014	492014	494014
730015	**WM** CO	490015	492015	494015
730016	**WM** CO	490016	492016	494016
730017	**WM** CO	490017	492017	494017
730018	**WM** CO	490018	492018	494018
730019	**WM** CO	490019	492019	494019

730020	**WM** CO		490020	492020	494020
730021	**WM** CO		490021	492021	494021
730022	**WM** CO		490022	492022	494022
730023	**WM** CO		490023	492023	494023
730024	**WM** CO		490024	492024	494024
730025	**WM** CO		490025	492025	494025
730026	**WM** CO		490026	492026	494026
730027	**WM** CO		490027	492027	494027
730028	**WM** CO		490028	492028	494028
730029	**WM** CO		490029	492029	494029
730030	**WM** CO		490030	492030	494030
730031	**WM** CO		490031	492031	494031
730032	**WM** CO		490032	492032	494032
730033	**WM** CO		490033	492033	494033
730034	**WM** CO		490034	492034	494034
730035	**WM** CO		490035	492035	494035
730036	**WM** CO		490036	492036	494036
730037	**WM** CO		490037	492037	494037
730038	**WM** CO		490038	492038	494038
730039	**WM** CO		490039	492039	494039
730040	**WM** CO		490040	492040	494040
730041	**WM** CO		490041	492041	494041
730042	**WM** CO		490042	492042	494042
730043	**WM** CO		490043	492043	494043
730044	**WM** CO		490044	492044	494044
730045	**WM** CO		490045	492045	494045
730046	**WM** CO		490046	492046	494046
730047	**WM** CO		490047	492047	494047
730048	**WM** CO		490048	492048	494048

Class 730/2. 5-car units. Pre-series units 730201–203 were originally built as 730101–103. Full details awaited.

DMS(A). Alstom Derby 2020–23.   t.
MS(A). Alstom Derby 2020–23.   t.
PMS. Alstom Derby 2020–23.   t.
MS(B). Alstom Derby 2020–23.   t.
DMS(B). Alstom Derby 2020–23.   t.

730201	**LN** CO	490201	491201	492201	493201	494201
730202	**LN** CO	490202	491202	492202	493202	494202
730203	**LN** CO	490203	491203	492203	493203	494203
730204	**LN** CO	490204	491204	492204	493204	494204
730205	**LN** CO	490205	491205	492205	493205	494205
730206	**LN** CO	490206	491206	492206	493206	494206
730207	**LN** CO	490207	491207	492207	493207	494207
730208	**LN** CO	490208	491208	492208	493208	494208
730209	**LN** CO	490209	491209	492209	493209	494209
730210	**LN** CO	490210	491210	492210	493210	494210
730211	**LN** CO	490211	491211	492211	493211	494211
730212	**LN** CO	490212	491212	492212	493212	494212
730213	**LN** CO	490213	491213	492213	493213	494213

730 214	LN	CO	490214	491214	492214	493214	494214
730 215	LN	CO	490215	491215	492215	493215	494215
730 216	LN	CO	490216	491216	492216	493216	494216
730 217	LN	CO	490217	491217	492217	493217	494217
730 218	LN	CO	490218	491218	492218	493218	494218
730 219	LN	CO	490219	491219	492219	493219	494219
730 220	LN	CO	490220	491220	492220	493220	494220
730 221	LN	CO	490221	491221	492221	493221	494221
730 222	LN	CO	490222	491222	492222	493222	494222
730 223	LN	CO	490223	491223	492223	493223	494223
730 224	LN	CO	490224	491224	492224	493224	494224
730 225	LN	CO	490225	491225	492225	493225	494225
730 226	LN	CO	490226	491226	492226	493226	494226
730 227	LN	CO	490227	491227	492227	493227	494227
730 228	LN	CO	490228	491228	492228	493228	494228
730 229	LN	CO	490229	491229	492229	493229	494229
730 230	LN	CO	490230	491230	492230	493230	494230
730 231	LN	CO	490231	491231	492231	493231	494231
730 232	LN	CO	490232	491232	492232	493232	494232
730 233	LN	CO	490233	491233	492233	493233	494233
730 234	LN	CO	490234	491234	492234	493234	494234
730 235	LN	CO	490235	491235	492235	493235	494235
730 236	LN	CO	490236	491236	492236	493236	494236

CLASS 745   FLIRT ELECTRIC   STADLER

These 20 12-car articulated Stadler EMUs were ordered by Greater Anglia in 2016 to replace its locomotive-hauled sets on Liverpool Street–Norwich services and Class 379s on the Stansted Express services. The 12-car units are formed of two 6-car half units formed of three coupled articulated pairs.

Formations (745/0): DMF–PTF–TS–TS–TS–MS–MS–TS–TS–TS–PTS–DMS.
or **(745/1):** DMS–PTS–TS–TS–TS–MS–MS–TS–TS–TS–PTS–DMS.
Systems: 25 kV AC overhead.
Construction: Aluminium.
Traction Motors: Four TSA of 325 kW.
Wheel Arrangement: Bo-2-2 + 2-2-2 + 2-2-Bo + Bo-2-2 + Bo-2-2 + 2-2-2 + 2-2-Bo.
Braking: Disc & regenerative   **Dimensions:** 21.05/19.45 x 2.72 m.
Bogies: Stadler/Jacobs.   **Couplers:** Dellner 10.
Gangways: Within unit.   **Control System:** IGBT Inverter.
Doors: Sliding plug (one per vehicle). **Maximum Speed:** 100 mph.
Heating & ventilation: Air conditioning.
Seating Layout: 1: 2+1 facing/unidirectional, 2: 2+2 unidirectional/facing.
Multiple Working: Within class.

Class 745/0. Fitted with First Class and café bar and built for use on the London Liverpool Street–Norwich route.

DMF. Stadler Bussnang/Szolnok 2018–19. 36/–. 41.3 t.
PTF. Stadler Bussnang/Szolnok 2018–19. 44/– 1T. 28.4 t.
TSMB. Stadler Bussnang/Szolnok 2018–19. –/26(+9) 1TD 2W. 26.8 t.

TS. Stadler Bussnang/Szolnok 2018–19. –/66(+12). 26.7 t.
TS. Stadler Bussnang/Szolnok 2018–19. –/70(+4) 1T. 28.0 t.
MS. Stadler Bussnang/Szolnok 2018–19. –/58(+4). 37.4 t.
MS. Stadler Bussnang/Szolnok 2018–19. –/58(+4). 37.4 t.
TS. Stadler Bussnang/Szolnok 2018–19. –/70(+4) 1T. 28.0 t.
TS. Stadler Bussnang/Szolnok 2018–19. –/74(+4). 25.9 t.
TS. Stadler Bussnang/Szolnok 2018–19. –/74(+4). 25.9 t.
PTS. Stadler Bussnang/Szolnok 2018–19. –/70(+4) 1T. 28.7 t.
DMS. Stadler Bussnang/Szolnok 2018–19. –/58(+4). 41.3 t.

745001	**GR**	RR	*GA*	NC	413001 426001 332001 343001 341001 301001
					302001 342001 344001 346001 322001 312001
745002	**GR**	RR	*GA*	NC	413002 426002 332002 343002 341002 301002
					302002 342002 344002 346002 322002 312002
745003	**GR**	RR	*GA*	NC	413003 426003 332003 343003 341003 301003
					302003 342003 344003 346003 322003 312003
745004	**GR**	RR	*GA*	NC	413004 426004 332004 343004 341004 301004
					302004 342004 344004 346004 322004 312004
745005	**GR**	RR	*GA*	NC	413005 426005 332005 343005 341005 301005
					302005 342005 344005 346005 322005 312005
745006	**GR**	RR	*GA*	NC	413006 426006 332006 343006 341006 301006
					302006 342006 344006 346006 322006 312006
745007	**GR**	RR	*GA*	NC	413007 426007 332007 343007 341007 301007
					302007 342007 344007 346007 322007 312007
745008	**GR**	RR	*GA*	NC	413008 426008 332008 343008 341008 301008
					302008 342008 344008 346008 322008 312008
745009	**GR**	RR	*GA*	NC	413009 426009 332009 343009 341009 301009
					302009 342009 344009 346009 322009 312009
745010	**GR**	RR	*GA*	NC	413010 426010 332010 343010 341010 301010
					302010 342010 344010 346010 322010 312010

Class 745/1. Standard Class only units mainly for use between London Liverpool Street and Stansted Airport and for selected services to/from Norwich for maintenance purposes.

DMS. Stadler Bussnang/Szolnok 2018–19. –/48(+6). 41.3 t.
PTS. Stadler Bussnang/Szolnok 2018–19. –/68 1T. 28.4 t.
TS(A). Stadler Bussnang/Szolnok 2018–19. –/50(+9) 1TD 2W. 26.8 t.
TS(B). Stadler Bussnang/Szolnok 2018–19. –/64(+8). 26.7 t.
TS(C). Stadler Bussnang/Szolnok 2018–19. –/68 1T. 28.0 t.
MS(A). Stadler Bussnang/Szolnok 2018–19. –/56. 37.4 t.
MS(B). Stadler Bussnang/Szolnok 2018–19. –/56. 37.4 t.
TS(D). Stadler Bussnang/Szolnok 2018–19. –/68 1T. 28.0 t.
TS(E). Stadler Bussnang/Szolnok 2018–19. –/64(+8). 25.9 t.
TS(F). Stadler Bussnang/Szolnok 2018–19. –/64(+8). 25.9 t.
PTS. Stadler Bussnang/Szolnok 2018–19. –/68 1T. 28.7 t.
DMS. Stadler Bussnang/Szolnok 2018–19. –/48(+6). 41.3 t.

745101	**GR**	RR	*GA*	NC	313101 326101 332101 343101 341101 301101
					302101 342101 344101 346101 322101 312101
745102	**GR**	RR	*GA*	NC	313102 326102 332102 343102 341102 301102
					302102 342102 344102 346102 322102 312102

745 103	**GR**	RR	*GA*	NC	313103 326103 332103 343103 341103 301103
					302103 342103 344103 346103 322103 312103
745 104	**GR**	RR	*GA*	NC	313104 326104 332104 343104 341104 301104
					302104 342104 344104 346104 322104 312104
745 105	**GR**	RR	*GA*	NC	313105 326105 332105 343105 341105 301105
					302105 342105 344105 346105 322105 312105
745 106	**GR**	RR	*GA*	NC	313106 326106 332106 343106 341106 301106
					302106 342106 344106 346106 322106 312106
745 107	**GR**	RR	*GA*	NC	313107 326107 332107 343107 341107 301107
					302107 342107 344107 346107 322107 312107
745 108	**GR**	RR	*GA*	NC	313108 326108 332108 343108 341108 301108
					302108 342108 344108 346108 322108 312108
745 109	**GR**	RR	*GA*	NC	313109 326109 332109 343109 341109 301109
					302109 342109 344109 346109 322109 312109
745 110	**GR**	RR	*GA*	NC	313110 326110 332110 343110 341110 301110
					302110 342110 344110 346110 322110 312110

CLASS 755   FLIRT BI-MODE   STADLER

This fleet of 3- and 4-car articulated Stadler bi-mode units was ordered by Greater Anglia in 2016 to replace all of its older DMU fleets. The first units entered service in summer 2019. The design features a "power pack" in the middle that houses two diesel engines for the 3-car units and four diesel engines for the 4-car units. This has been given its own number, effectively making the units 4- and 5-car, although there is no passenger accommodation in the power pack car.

Formation: DMS–PP–PTS–DMS or DMS–PTS–PP–PTS–DMS.
Systems: Diesel/25 kV AC overhead.
Construction: Aluminium.
Engines: (4-car): Four Deutz V8 of 480 kW (645 hp), (3-car): Two Four Deutz V8 of 480 kW (645 hp).
Traction Motors: 4 x TSA of 325 kW.
Wheel Arrangement: Bo-2-2-2-Bo or Bo-2-2-2-2-Bo.
Braking: Disc & regenerative.
Dimensions: 20.81/15.22/6.69 (PP) m x 2.72/2.82 (PP) m.
Bogies: Stadler/Jacobs.   **Couplers:** Dellner 10.
Gangways: Within unit.   **Control System:** IGBT Inverter.
Doors: Sliding plug (one per vehicle). **Maximum Speed:** 100 mph.
Heating & ventilation: Air conditioning.
Seating Layout: 2+2 unidirectional/facing.
Multiple Working: Within class.

Class 755/3. 3-car (plus power pack) units.

DMS(A). Stadler Szolnok/Siedlce/Bussnang/Valencia 2018–19. –/60(+4). 43.4 t.
PP. Stadler Bussnang/Valencia 2018–19. 25.4 t.
PTS. Stadler Szolnok/Siedlce/Bussnang/Valencia 2018–19. –/32(+7) 1TD 1T 2W. 24.2 t.
DMS(B). Stadler Szolnok/Siedlce/Bussnang/Valencia 2018–19.–/52(+12).42.1t.

755 325	**GR**	RR *GA*	NC	911325	971325	981325	912325
755 326	**GR**	RR *GA*	NC	911326	971326	981326	912326
755 327	**GR**	RR *GA*	NC	911327	971327	981327	912327
755 328	**GR**	RR *GA*	NC	911328	971328	981328	912328
755 329	**GR**	RR *GA*	NC	911329	971329	981329	912329
755 330	**GR**	RR *GA*	NC	911330	971330	981330	912330
755 331	**GR**	RR *GA*	NC	911331	971331	981331	912331
755 332	**GR**	RR *GA*	NC	911332	971332	981332	912332
755 333	**GR**	RR *GA*	NC	911333	971333	981333	912333
755 334	**GR**	RR *GA*	NC	911334	971334	981334	912334
755 335	**GR**	RR *GA*	NC	911335	971335	981335	912335
755 336	**GR**	RR *GA*	NC	911336	971336	981336	912336
755 337	**GR**	RR *GA*	NC	911337	971337	981337	912337
755 338	**GR**	RR *GA*	NC	911338	971338	981338	912338

Class 755/4. 4-car (plus power pack) units.

DMS(A). Stadler Szolnok/Siedlce/Bussnang/Valencia 2018–19. –/60(+4). 41.4 t.
PTS(A). Stadler Szolnok/Siedlce/Bussnang/Valencia 2018–19. –/58(+4). 25.0 t.
PP. Stadler Bussnang/Valencia 2018–19. 28.5 t.
PTS(B). Stadler Szolnok/Siedlce/Bussnang/Valencia 2018–19. –/32(+7). 1TD 1T 2W. 26.4 t.
DMS(B). Stadler Szolnok/Siedlce/Bussnang/Valencia 2018–19. –/52(+12). 42.2 t.

755 401	**GR**	RR *GA*	NC	911401	961401	971401	981401	912401
755 402	**GR**	RR *GA*	NC	911402	961402	971402	981402	912402
755 403	**GR**	RR *GA*	NC	911403	961403	971403	981403	912403
755 404	**GR**	RR *GA*	NC	911404	961404	971404	981404	912404
755 405	**GR**	RR *GA*	NC	911405	961405	971405	981405	912405
755 406	**GR**	RR *GA*	NC	911406	961406	971406	981406	912406
755 407	**GR**	RR *GA*	NC	911407	961407	971407	981407	912407
755 408	**GR**	RR *GA*	NC	911408	961408	971408	981408	912408
755 409	**GR**	RR *GA*	NC	911409	961409	971409	981409	912409
755 410	**GR**	RR *GA*	NC	911410	961410	971410	981410	912410
755 411	**GR**	RR *GA*	NC	911411	961411	971411	981411	912411
755 412	**GR**	RR *GA*	NC	911412	961412	971412	981412	912412
755 413	**GR**	RR *GA*	NC	911413	961413	971413	981413	912413
755 414	**GR**	RR *GA*	NC	911414	961414	971414	981414	912414
755 415	**GR**	RR *GA*	NC	911415	961415	971415	981415	912415
755 416	**GR**	RR *GA*	NC	911416	961416	971416	981416	912416
755 417	**GR**	RR *GA*	NC	911417	961417	971417	981417	912417
755 418	**GR**	RR *GA*	NC	911418	961418	971418	981418	912418
755 419	**GR**	RR *GA*	NC	911419	961419	971419	981419	912419
755 420	**GR**	RR *GA*	NC	911420	961420	971420	981420	912420
755 421	**GR**	RR *GA*	NC	911421	961421	971421	981421	912421
755 422	**GR**	RR *GA*	NC	911422	961422	971422	981422	912422
755 423	**GR**	RR *GA*	NC	911423	961423	971423	981423	912423
755 424	**GR**	RR *GA*	NC	911424	961424	971424	981424	912424

CLASS 756   FLIRT TRI-MODE   STADLER

This fleet of articulated FLIRT tri-mode diesel/electric/battery units is on order for Transport for Wales for use on the Cardiff Valley Lines (Rhymney, Coryton, Vale of Glamorgan, Penarth and Barry Island) from 2024/25. The units look similar to Greater Anglia's Class 755s.

Formation: DMS–PP–PTS–DMS or DMS–PTS–PP–PTS–DMS.
Systems: Diesel/25 kV AC overhead/battery.
Construction: Aluminium.
Engines: Deutz V8 of 480 kW (645 hp) + three battery modules.
Traction Motors: 4 x TSA of 325 kW.
Battery: 1300 kW.
Wheel Arrangement: Bo-2-2-2-Bo or Bo-2-2-2-2-Bo.
Braking: Disc & regenerative.
Dimensions: 21.05/15.70/7.20 (PP) m x 2.72/2.82 (PP) m.
Bogies: Stadler/Jacobs.   **Couplers:** Dellner 10.
Gangways: Within unit.   **Control System:** IGBT Inverter.
Doors: Sliding plug.   **Maximum Speed:** 75 mph.
Heating & ventilation: Air conditioning.
Seating Layout: 2+2 unidirectional/facing.
Multiple Working: Within class.

Class 756/0. 3-car (plus power pack) units. Full details awaited.

DMS(A). Stadler Bussnang 2021–23. –/40(+12).
PP. Stadler Bussnang 2021–23.
PTS. Stadler Bussnang 2021–23. –/38(+5) 1TD 2W.
DMS(B). Stadler Bussnang 2021–23. –/40(+12).

756 001	**TW**	SM	911001	971001	981001	912001
756 002	**TW**	SM	911002	971002	981002	912002
756 003	**TW**	SM	911003	971003	981003	912003
756 004	**TW**	SM	911004	971004	981004	912004
756 005	**TW**	SM	911005	971005	981005	912005
756 006	**TW**	SM	911006	971006	981006	912006
756 007	**TW**	SM	911007	971007	981007	912007

Class 756/1. 4-car (plus power pack) units.

DMS(A). Stadler Bussnang 2021–23. –/40(+12). 42.3 t.
PTS(A). Stadler Bussnang 2021–23. –/40(+8). 25.9 t.
PP. Stadler Bussnang 2021–23. 28.7 t.
PTS(B). Stadler Bussnang 2021–23. –/38(+5) 1TD 2W. 26.6 t.
DMS(B). Stadler Bussnang 2021–23. –/40(+12). 42.7 t.

756 101	**TW**	SM	911101	961101	971101	981101	912101
756 102	**TW**	SM	911102	961102	971102	981102	912102
756 103	**TW**	SM	911103	961103	971103	981103	912103
756 104	**TW**	SM	911104	961104	971104	981104	912104
756 105	**TW**	SM	911105	961105	971105	981105	912105
756 106	**TW**	SM	911106	961106	971106	981106	912106
756 107	**TW**	SM	911107	961107	971107	981107	912107
756 108	**TW**	SM	911108	961108	971108	981108	912108

756 109	**TW**	SM	911109	961109	971109	981109	912109
756 110	**TW**	SM	911110	961110	971110	981110	912110
756 111	**TW**	SM	911111	961111	971111	981111	912111
756 112	**TW**	SM	911112	961112	971112	981112	912112
756 113	**TW**	SM	911113	961113	971113	981113	912113
756 114	**TW**	SM	911114	961114	971114	981114	912114
756 115	**TW**	SM	911115	961115	971115	981115	912115
756 116	**TW**	SM	911116	961116	971116	981116	912116
756 117	**TW**	SM	911117	961117	971117	981117	912117

CLASS 768   FLEX   BREL YORK/BRUSH

Two Class 319/0 and 319/4 units were converted for Rail Operations Group's subsidiary Orion as bi-mode parcels/freight units and renumbered in the Class 768 series.

Formation: DTV–PMV–TV–DTV.
Systems: Diesel/25 kV AC overhead/750 V DC third rail.
Construction: Steel.
Engines: Two MAN D2876 of 390 kW (523 hp).
Traction Motors: Four GEC G315BZ of 268 kW.
Wheel Arrangement: 2-2 + Bo-Bo + 2-2 + 2-2.
Braking: Disc.   **Dimensions:** 20.17/20.16 x 2.82 m.
Bogies: P7-4 (MS), T3-7 (others).   **Couplers:** Tightlock.
Gangways: Within unit + end doors. **Control System:** GTO chopper.
Doors: Sliding.
Maximum Speed: 100 mph (electric); 85 mph (diesel).
Seating Layout: No seats (removed to allow space for parcels and freight).
Multiple Working: Within class & with Classes 319 and 769.

DTV. Lot No. 31022 (odd nos.) 1987–88.
PMV. Lot No. 31023 1987–88.
TV. Lot No. 31024 1987–88.
DTV. Lot No. 31025 (even nos.) 1987–88.

768 001	(319010)	**ON**	P	CN	77309	62900	71781	77308
768 002	(319009)	**ON**	P	CN	77307	62899	71780	77306

CLASS 769   FLEX   BREL YORK/BRUSH

In 2016 it was announced that Porterbrook would be converting eight Class 319s into bi-mode "Flex" units for Northern, with two new diesel engines being fitted (one under each of the driving trailer cars) to drive ABB alternators. After a series of problems and delays the units finally entered service with Northern in 2021. Subsequently orders were placed by Transport for Wales for nine units (later reduced to eight, which entered service in 2020–21) and Great Western Railway for 19 units. The units for GWR were "tri-mode", with both AC overhead and DC third rail capability. Unfortunately, owing to continued unreliability of the units on test and changing passenger growth forecasts, in 2022 GWR decided that it would not be leasing its Class 769/9s and the units would be returned to

Porterbrook Leasing. The Transport for Wales units were withdrawn from service in 2022–23.

Work on the conversions took place at Brush Loughborough. All conversions were from Class 319/0 or 319/4 Phase 1 units.

Formation: DTC–MS–TS–DTS.
Systems: Diesel/25 kV AC overhead/750 V DC third rail (GWR units only).
Construction: Steel.
Engines: Two MAN D2876 of 390 kW (523 hp).
Traction Motors: Four GEC G315BZ of 268 kW.
Wheel Arrangement: 2-2 + Bo-Bo + 2-2 + 2-2.
Braking: Disc.   **Dimensions**: 20.17/20.16 x 2.82 m.
Bogies: P7-4 (MS), T3-7 (others).   **Couplers**: Tightlock.
Gangways: Within unit + end doors. **Control System**: GTO chopper.
Doors: Sliding.
Maximum Speed: 100 mph (electric); 85 mph (diesel).
Seating Layout: 1: 2+1 facing (declassified); 2: 2+2/3+2 facing.
Multiple Working: Within class and with Classes 319, 326 and 768.

Class 769/0. Former Transport for Wales bi-mode units converted from Class 319/0.

DTS(A). Lot No. 31022 (odd nos.) 1987–88.–/79. 37.5 t.
MS. Lot No. 31023 1987–88. –/79. 51.0 t.
TS. Lot No. 31024 1987–88. –/64 1TD 2W. 34.0 t.
DTS(B). Lot No. 31025 (even nos.) 1987–88. –/79. 37.2 t.

769002	(319002)	**TW**	P		LM	77293	62892	71773	77292
769003	(319003)	**TW**	P		LM	77295	62893	71774	77294
769006	(319006)	**TW**	P		LM	77301	62896	71777	77300
769007	(319007)	**TW**	P		LM	77303	62897	71778	77302
769008	(319008)	**TW**	P		LM	77305	62898	71779	77304

Class 769/4. Northern and former Transport for Wales bi-mode units converted from Class 319/4.

77331–381. DTC. Lot No. 31022 (odd nos.) 1987–88. 12/50. 37.3 t.
77431–457. DTC. Lot No. 31038 (odd nos.) 1988. 12/50. 37.3 t.
62911–936. MS. Lot No. 31023 1987–88. –/75. 51.0 t.
62961–974. MS. Lot No. 31039 1988. –/75. 51.0 t.
71792–817. TS. Lot No. 31024 1987–88. –/58 1TD 2W. 34.0 t.
71866–879. TS. Lot No. 31040 1988. –/58 1TD 2W. 34.0 t.
77330–380. DTS. Lot No. 31025 (even nos.) 1987–88. –/73. 37.2 t.
77430–456. DTS. Lot No. 31041 (even nos.) 1988. –/73. 37.2 t.

769421	(319421)	**TW**	P		LM	77331	62911	71792	77330
769424	(319424)	**NR**	P	*NO*	AN	77337	62914	71795	77336
769431	(319431)	**NR**	P	*NO*	AN	77351	62921	71802	77350
769434	(319434)	**NR**	P	*NO*	AN	77357	62924	71805	77356
769442	(319442)	**NR**	P	*NO*	AN	77373	62932	71813	77372
769445	(319445)	**TW**	P		LM	77379	62935	71816	77378
769448	(319448)	**NR**	P	*NO*	AN	77433	62962	71867	77432
769450	(319450)	**NR**	P	*NO*	AN	77437	62964	71869	77436
769452	(319452)	**TW**	P		LM	77441	62966	71871	77440

769 456	(319 456)	**NR**	P	*NO*	AN	77449	62970	71875	77448
769 458	(319 458)	**NR**	P	*NO*	AN	77453	62972	71877	77452

Class 769/9. Units rebuilt for Great Western Railway as tri-mode units converted from Class 319/4. Now stored awaiting a decision on their future.

77331–381. DTC. Lot No. 31022 (odd nos.) 1987–88. 12/52.
77431–457. DTC. Lot No. 31038 (odd nos.) 1988. 12/52.
62911–936. MS. Lot No. 31023 1987–88. –/77.
62961–974. MS. Lot No. 31039 1988. –/77.
71792–817. TS. Lot No. 31024 1987–88. –/60 1TD 2W.
71866–879. TS. Lot No. 31040 1988. –/60 1TD 2W.
77330–380. DTS. Lot No. 31025 (even nos.) 1987–88. –/75.
77430–456. DTS. Lot No. 31041 (even nos.) 1988. –/75.

769 922	(319 422)	**GW**	P		ZK	77333	62912	71793	77332
769 923	(319 423)	**GW**	P		LM	77335	62913	71794	77334
769 925	(319 425)	**GW**	P		LM	77339	62915	71796	77338
769 927	(319 427)	**GW**	P		LM	77343	62917	71798	77342
769 928	(319 428)	**GW**	P		LM	77345	62918	71799	77344
769 930	(319 430)	**GW**	P		LM	77349	62920	71801	77348
769 932	(319 432)	**GW**	P		LM	77353	62922	71803	77352
769 935	(319 435)	**GW**	P		LM	77359	62925	71806	77358
769 936	(319 436)	**GW**	P		LM	77361	62926	71807	77360
769 937	(319 437)	**GW**	P		LM	77363	62927	71808	77362
769 938	(319 438)	**GW**	P		LM	77365	62928	71809	77364
769 939	(319 439)	**GW**	P		LM	77367	62929	71810	77366
769 940	(319 440)	**GW**	P		LM	77369	62930	71811	77368
769 943	(319 443)	**GW**	P		LM	77375	62933	71814	77374
769 944	(319 444)	**GW**	P		LM	77377	62934	71815	77376
769 946	(319 446)	**GW**	P		LM	77381	62936	71817	77380
769 947	(319 447)	**GW**	P		LM	77431	62961	71866	77430
769 949	(319 449)	**GW**	P		LM	77435	62963	71868	77434
769 959	(319 459)	**GW**	P		ZK	77455	62973	71878	77454

CLASS 777   STADLER

This fleet of articulated 4-car units was ordered from Stadler in 2017 by Merseytravel for the DC third rail Merseyrail suburban network. An option exists for up to a further 59 units. Seven units at the end of the build are fitted with batteries and numbered in the Class 777/1 series.

Formation: DMS–MS–MS–DMS.
System: 750 V DC third rail.
Construction: Aluminium.
Traction Motors: Six TSA of 350 kW (470 hp) per unit.
Wheel Arrangement: 2-Bo-Bo-Bo-2. **Dimensions:** 18.10/14.40 x 2.82 m.
Braking: Tread & regenerative. **Couplers:** Dellner 12.
Bogies: Jacobs. **Control System:** IGBT Inverter.
Gangways: Within unit. **Maximum Speed:** 75 mph.
Doors: Sliding plug. **Heating & ventilation:** Air conditioning.
Seating Layout: 2+2 facing/unidirectional.
Multiple Working: Within class.

Class 777/0. Original series, third rail 750 V DC only.

Advertising livery: 777 013 Eurovision (various colours).

DMS(A). Stadler Szolnok/Siedlce/Altenrhein 2018–22. –/53.　　　t.
MS(A). Stadler Szolnok/Siedlce/Altenrhein 2018–22. –/38(+1) 1W.　　t.
MS(B). Stadler Szolnok/Siedlce/Altenrhein 2018–22. –/38(+1) 1W.　　t.
DMS(B). Stadler Szolnok/Siedlce/Altenrhein 2018–22. –/53.　　　t.

777 001	**ME**	MT	*ME*	KK	427 001	428 001	429 001	430 001
777 002	**ME**	MT	*ME*	KK	427 002	428 002	429 002	430 002
777 003	**ME**	MT	*ME*	KK	427 003	428 003	429 003	430 003
777 004	**ME**	MT	*ME*	KK	427 004	428 004	429 004	430 004
777 005	**ME**	MT	*ME*	KK	427 005	428 005	429 005	430 005
777 006	**ME**	MT	*ME*	KK	427 006	428 006	429 006	430 006
777 007	**ME**	MT	*ME*	KK	427 007	428 007	429 007	430 007
777 008	**ME**	MT	*ME*	KK	427 008	428 008	429 008	430 008
777 009	**ME**	MT	*ME*	KK	427 009	428 009	429 009	430 009
777 010	**ME**	MT	*ME*	KK	427 010	428 010	429 010	430 010
777 011	**ME**	MT	*ME*	KK	427 011	428 011	429 011	430 011
777 012	**ME**	MT	*ME*	KK	427 012	428 012	429 012	430 012
777 013	**AL**	MT	*ME*	KK	427 013	428 013	429 013	430 013
777 014	**ME**	MT	*ME*	KK	427 014	428 014	429 014	430 014
777 015	**ME**	MT	*ME*	KK	427 015	428 015	429 015	430 015
777 016	**ME**	MT	*ME*	KK	427 016	428 016	429 016	430 016
777 017	**ME**	MT			427 017	428 017	429 017	430 017
777 018	**ME**	MT	*ME*	KK	427 018	428 018	429 018	430 018
777 019	**ME**	MT			427 019	428 019	429 019	430 019
777 020	**ME**	MT			427 020	428 020	429 020	430 020
777 021	**ME**	MT			427 021	428 021	429 021	430 021
777 022	**ME**	MT			427 022	428 022	429 022	430 022
777 023	**ME**	MT			427 023	428 023	429 023	430 023
777 024	**ME**	MT			427 024	428 024	429 024	430 024
777 025	**ME**	MT			427 025	428 025	429 025	430 025
777 026	**ME**	MT			427 026	428 026	429 026	430 026
777 027	**ME**	MT			427 027	428 027	429 027	430 027
777 028	**ME**	MT			427 028	428 028	429 028	430 028
777 029	**ME**	MT			427 029	428 029	429 029	430 029
777 030	**ME**	MT			427 030	428 030	429 030	430 030
777 031	**ME**	MT			427 031	428 031	429 031	430 031
777 032	**ME**	MT			427 032	428 032	429 032	430 032
777 033	**ME**	MT			427 033	428 033	429 033	430 033
777 034	**ME**	MT			427 034	428 034	429 034	430 034
777 035	**ME**	MT			427 035	428 035	429 035	430 035
777 036	**ME**	MT			427 036	428 036	429 036	430 036
777 037	**ME**	MT			427 037	428 037	429 037	430 037
777 038	**ME**	MT			427 038	428 038	429 038	430 038
777 039	**ME**	MT			427 039	428 039	429 039	430 039
777 041	**ME**	MT			427 041	428 041	429 041	430 041
777 043	**ME**	MT			427 043	428 043	429 043	430 043
777 045	**ME**	MT			427 045	428 045	429 045	430 045
777 047	**ME**	MT			427 047	428 047	429 047	430 047

777049	**ME**	MT	*ME*	KK	427049	428049	429049	430049
777051	**ME**	MT			427051	428051	429051	430051
777053	**ME**	MT			427053	428053	429053	430053

Class 777/1. Fitted with 360kWh Lithium Titanate Oxide traction batteries for operation away from the 750 V DC third rail network, initially from Kirkby to Headbolt Lane.

777140	**ME**	MT			427140	428140	429140	430140
777142	**ME**	MT	*ME*	KK	427142	428142	429142	430142
777144	**ME**	MT			427144	428144	429144	430144
777146	**ME**	MT	*ME*	KK	427146	428146	429146	430146
777148	**ME**	MT	*ME*	KK	427148	428148	429148	430148
777150	**ME**	MT			427150	428150	429150	430150
777152	**ME**	MT			427152	428152	429152	430152

CLASS 799   HYDROFLEX   BREL YORK/BRUSH

Porterbrook rebuilt two Class 319s as hydrogen demonstrator units, although the first conversion in 2019 (799001) has now been scrapped. In 2021 a second demonstrator was converted. One of the driving cars was converted to a hydrogen chamber housing 36 high pressure 150kg aluminium tanks to store hydrogen. The chamber feeds a 400kW fuel cell system supported by a lithium-ion battery.

Formation: DMC–MS–TS–DMS.
Systems: Hydrogen/25 kV AC overhead/750 V DC third rail.
Construction: Steel.
Traction Motors: Four GEC G315BZ of 268 kW.
Wheel Arrangement: 2-2 + Bo-Bo + 2-2 + 2-2.
Braking: Disc.   **Dimensions:** 20.17/20.16 x 2.82 m.
Bogies: P7-4 (MS), T3-7 (others).   **Couplers:** Tightlock.
Gangways: Within unit + end doors. **Doors:** Sliding.
Maximum Speed: 75 mph.
Seating Layout: 1: 2+1 facing (declassified); 2: 2+2/3+2 facing unless stated.

Class 799/2. Second Prototype unit converted 2021. Currently used only for testing or demonstation purposes.

Non-standard livery: HydroFlex (dark blue & green).

77975. DMC. Lot No. 31063. 1990. No seats (hydrogen chamber). 49.2 t.
63094. MS. Lot No. 31064. 1990. –/57. 50.6 t.
71980. TS. Lot No. 31065. 1990. Converted to boardroom. –/26 1TD 2W. 31.0 t.
77976. DMS. Lot No. 31066. 1990. –/79. 29.7 t.

| 799201 | (319382) | **0** | P | | LM | 77975 | 63094 | 71980 | 77976 |

5. HITACHI IEP UNITS

CLASS 800 INTERCITY EXPRESS PROGRAMME
BI-MODE   HITACHI

In 2012 Agility Trains, a consortium of Hitachi and John Laing, signed a deal with the DfT to design, build, finance and maintain the next generation of InterCity rolling stock for the Great Western and East Coast Main Lines, principally to replace ageing High Speed Trains on these routes. A follow-on order in 2013 was placed for 30 9-car trains to replace the Class 91 and Mark 4 carriages on the ECML. This brought the total number of vehicles ordered to 866. Both GWR and LNER were originally planned to have a mix of 5-car and 9-car units which will be bi-mode and straight electric trains (although the EMUs also have one diesel engine fitted to each set). However, owing to delays with electrification works on the GWML, in 2016 it was announced that the 21 9-car electric Class 801 units for GWR would be built as 21 9-car bi-mode units, numbered instead in the Class 800/3 series.

The initial units were broadly based on the Southeastern Class 395s, but have 25–25.35 m length bodyshells. These are numbered in the Class 800 (bi-mode) and Class 801 (EMU) number series'. 12 trains (76 vehicles) were fully manufactured at Kasado in Japan before the new Hitachi factory at Newton Aycliffe, County Durham was up and running. The remaining trains were assembled at either Newton Aycliffe or Kasado. New maintenance depots for the trains have been built at Stoke Gifford (Bristol), Swansea and North Pole (London, the former Eurostar depot) for the GWR sets and at Doncaster for the LNER units.

The first trains arrived for testing in 2015. 5-car units entered service on the Great Western Main Line in autumn 2017 and the fleet of Class 800s and 801s entered service on the East Coast Main Line in 2019–20.

In 2015 GWR ordered a further similar 22 5-car and seven 9-car IEPs, designated Class 802/0 (5-car) and Class 802/1 (9-car). These are mainly used on Paddington–West of England services.

In 2016 GWR ordered a further seven 9-car Class 802s, TransPennine Express ordered 19 5-car Class 802s and Hull Trains ordered five 5-car Class 802s, for delivery 2019–20. The majority of the Class 802s were constructed at Pistoia in Italy, with some at Kasado.

Subsequent orders for similar derivatives of this type of train have come from First Group for its ECML open access service (Lumo – the electric-only Class 803), Avanti West Coast (Classes 805 and 807) and East Midlands Railway (Class 810).

Formation: Various, see class headings for details.
Systems: Diesel/25 kV AC overhead electric.
Construction: Aluminium.
Diesel engines: In the 5-car sets diesel engines are located in cars 2, 3 and 4. In the 9-car sets diesel engines are located in cars 2, 3, 5, 7 and 8.

Engines: MTU 12V 1600 R80L of 700 kW (940 hp).
Traction Motors: Four Hitachi asynchronous of 226 kW.
Wheel Arrangement: 2-2 + Bo-Bo + Bo-Bo + Bo-Bo + 2-2 or
2-2 + Bo-Bo + Bo-Bo + 2-2 + Bo-Bo + 2-2 + Bo-Bo + Bo-Bo + 2-2.
Braking: Disc & regenerative.   **Dimensions:** 25.35/25.00 m x 2.74 m.
Bogies: Hitachi.   **Couplers:** Dellner 10.
Gangways: Within unit.   **Control System:** IGBT Inverter.
Doors: Single-leaf sliding.   **Maximum Speed:** 125 mph.
Heating & ventilation: Air conditioning.
Seating Layout: 1: 2+1 facing/unidirectional; 2+2 facing/unidirectional.
Multiple Working: Within class and with all Classes 8xx.

Class 800/0. 5-car Great Western Railway units.
Formation: PDTS–MS–MS–MC–PDTRBF.

Additions to the standard livery: 800008 Pride stripes on driving cars.

PDTS. Hitachi Newton Aycliffe/Kasado 2013–17. –/56 1TD. 47.8 t.
MS. Hitachi Newton Aycliffe/Kasado 2013–17. –/88. 50.1 t.
MS. Hitachi Newton Aycliffe/Kasado 2013–17. –/88 2T. 50.3 t.
MC. Hitachi Newton Aycliffe/Kasado 2013–17. 18/58 1T. 50.6 t.
PDTRBF. Hitachi Newton Aycliffe/Kasado 2013–17. 18/– 1TD 2W. 51.7 t.

800001	**GW**	AT	*GW*	NP	811001	812001	813001	814001	815001
800002	**GW**	AT	*GW*	NP	811002	812002	813002	814002	815002
800003	**GW**	AT	*GW*	NP	811003	812003	813003	814003	815003
800004	**GW**	AT	*GW*	NP	811004	812004	813004	814004	815004
800005	**GW**	AT	*GW*	NP	811005	812005	813005	814005	815005
800006	**GW**	AT	*GW*	NP	811006	812006	813006	814006	815006
800007	**GW**	AT	*GW*	NP	811007	812007	813007	814007	815007
800008	**GW**	AT	*GW*	NP	811008	812008	813008	814008	815008
800009	**GW**	AT	*GW*	NP	811009	812009	813009	814009	815009
800010	**GW**	AT	*GW*	NP	811010	812010	813010	814010	815010
800011	**GW**	AT	*GW*	NP	811011	812011	813011	814011	815011
800012	**GW**	AT	*GW*	NP	811012	812012	813012	814012	815012
800013	**GW**	AT	*GW*	NP	811013	812013	813013	814013	815013
800014	**GW**	AT	*GW*	NP	811014	812014	813014	814014	815014
800015	**GW**	AT	*GW*	NP	811015	812015	813015	814015	815015
800016	**GW**	AT	*GW*	NP	811016	812016	813016	814016	815016
800017	**GW**	AT	*GW*	NP	811017	812017	813017	814017	815017
800018	**GW**	AT	*GW*	NP	811018	812018	813018	814018	815018
800019	**GW**	AT	*GW*	NP	811019	812019	813019	814019	815019
800020	**GW**	AT	*GW*	NP	811020	812020	813020	814020	815020
800021	**GW**	AT	*GW*	NP	811021	812021	813021	814021	815021
800022	**GW**	AT	*GW*	NP	811022	812022	813022	814022	815022
800023	**GW**	AT	*GW*	NP	811023	812023	813023	814023	815023
800024	**GW**	AT	*GW*	NP	811024	812024	813024	814024	815024
800025	**GW**	AT	*GW*	NP	811025	812025	813025	814025	815025
800026	**GW**	AT	*GW*	NP	811026	812026	813026	814026	815026
800027	**GW**	AT	*GW*	NP	811027	812027	813027	814027	815027
800028	**GW**	AT	*GW*	NP	811028	812028	813028	814028	815028
800029	**GW**	AT	*GW*	NP	811029	812029	813029	814029	815029
800030	**GW**	AT	*GW*	NP	811030	812030	813030	814030	815030

800031	**GW**	AT	*GW*	NP	811031	812031	813031	814031	815031
800032	**GW**	AT	*GW*	NP	811032	812032	813032	814032	815032
800033	**GW**	AT	*GW*	NP	811033	812033	813033	814033	815033
800034	**GW**	AT	*GW*	NP	811034	812034	813034	814034	815034
800035	**GW**	AT	*GW*	NP	811035	812035	813035	814035	815035
800036	**GW**	AT	*GW*	NP	811036	812036	813036	814036	815036

Names (one on each driving car unless shown):

800003	Queen Victoria/Queen Elizabeth II
800005	Aneurin Bevan NHS 1948–2023 *(vehicle 815005)*
800008	Alan Turing OBE FRS *(vehicle 815008)*
800009	Sir Gareth Edwards/John Charles
800010	Michael Bond/Paddington Bear
800014	Megan Lloyd George CH/Edith New
800016	WHITE RIBBON *(carried on both driving cars)*
800019	Joy Lofthouse/Johnny Johnson MBE DFM
800020	Bob Woodward/Elizabeth Ralph
800022	Tulbahadur Pun VC *(vehicle 815022)*
800023	Firefighter Fleur Lombard QGM/Kathryn Osmond
800025	Captain Sir Tom Moore *(vehicle 815025)*
800026	Don Cameron *(vehicle 815026)*
800029	Evette Wakely/Christopher Dando
800030	Henry Cleary/Lincoln Callaghan
800031	Charlotte Marsland/Mazen Salmou
800032	Iain Bugler/Sarah Williams-Martin
800033	Emma Hurrell/Martin Heath
800034	Tracy Devlin/Jo Prosser
800035	Naomi Betts/Liz Gallagher
800036	Dr Paul Stephenson OBE *(carried on both driving cars)*

Class 800/1. 9-car LNER units.

Additions to the standard livery:

800104	Scottish Saltire flag on driving car 819104.
800106	"You Belong" branding (green/purple on alternate sides of driving car 819106)

Formation: PDTS–MS–MS–TSRB–MS–TS–MC–MF–PDTRBF.

PDTS. Hitachi Kasado/Newton Aycliffe 2013–18. –/48 1TD 2W. 47.7 t.
MS. Hitachi Kasado/Newton Aycliffe 2013–18. –/84 1T. 50.5 t.
MS. Hitachi Kasado/Newton Aycliffe 2013–18. –/84 2T. 50.3 t.
TSRB. Hitachi Kasado/Newton Aycliffe 2013–18. –/70. 41.0 t.
MS. Hitachi Kasado/Newton Aycliffe 2013–18. –/84 2T. 50.3 t.
TS. Hitachi Kasado/Newton Aycliffe 2013–18. –/84 2T. 38.3 t.
MC. Hitachi Kasado/Newton Aycliffe 2013–18. 30/36. 49.1 t.
MF. Hitachi Kasado/Newton Aycliffe 2013–18. 15/– 1TD 2W. 51.7 t.
PDTRBF. Hitachi Kasado/Newton Aycliffe 2013–18. 15/– 1TD 2W. 51.7 t.

800101	**LZ**	AT	*LN*	DN	811101	812101	813101	814101	815101
					816101	817101	818101	819101	
800102	**LZ**	AT	*LN*	DN	811102	812102	813102	814102	815102
					816102	817102	818102	819102	

800 103	**LZ**	AT	*LN*	DN	811103	812103	813103	814103	815103
					816103	817103	818103	819103	
800 104	**LZ**	AT	*LN*	DN	811104	812104	813104	814104	815104
					816104	817104	818104	819104	
800 105	**LZ**	AT	*LN*	DN	811105	812105	813105	814105	815105
					816105	817105	818105	819105	
800 106	**LZ**	AT	*LN*	DN	811106	812106	813106	814106	815106
					816106	817106	818106	819106	
800 107	**LZ**	AT	*LN*	DN	811107	812107	813107	814107	815107
					816107	817107	818107	819107	
800 108	**LZ**	AT	*LN*	DN	811108	812108	813108	814108	815108
					816108	817108	818108	819108	
800 109	**LZ**	AT	*LN*	DN	811109	812109	813109	814109	815109
					816109	817109	818109	819109	
800 110	**LZ**	AT	*LN*	DN	811110	812110	813110	814110	815110
					816110	817110	818110	819110	
800 111	**LZ**	AT	*LN*	DN	811111	812111	813111	814111	815111
					816111	817111	818111	819111	
800 112	**LZ**	AT	*LN*	DN	811112	812112	813112	814112	815112
					816112	817112	818112	819112	
800 113	**LZ**	AT	*LN*	DN	811113	812113	813113	814113	815113
					816113	817113	818113	819113	

Name (carried on PDTRBF):

800 106   YOU BELONG

Class 800/2. 5-car LNER units.
Formation: PDTS–MSRB–MS–MC–PDTRBF.

PDTS. Hitachi Newton Aycliffe/Kasado 2018–19. –/56 1TD. 47.8 t.
MSRB. Hitachi Newton Aycliffe/Kasado 2018–19. –/72. 50.1 t.
MS. Hitachi Newton Aycliffe/Kasado 2018–19. –/88 2T. 50.3 t.
MC. Hitachi Newton Aycliffe/Kasado 2018–19. 30/38 1T. 50.6 t.
PDTRBF. Hitachi Newton Aycliffe/Kasado 2018–19. 18/– 1TD 2W. 51.7 t.

800 201	**LZ**	AT	*LN*	DN	811201	812201	813201	814201	815201
800 202	**LZ**	AT	*LN*	DN	811202	812202	813202	814202	815202
800 203	**LZ**	AT	*LN*	DN	811203	812203	813203	814203	815203
800 204	**LZ**	AT	*LN*	DN	811204	812204	813204	814204	815204
800 205	**LZ**	AT	*LN*	DN	811205	812205	813205	814205	815205
800 206	**LZ**	AT	*LN*	DN	811206	812206	813206	814206	815206
800 207	**LZ**	AT	*LN*	DN	811207	812207	813207	814207	815207
800 208	**LZ**	AT	*LN*	DN	811208	812208	813208	814208	815208
800 209	**LZ**	AT	*LN*	DN	811209	812209	813209	814209	815209
800 210	**LZ**	AT	*LN*	DN	811210	812210	813210	814210	815210

Class 800/3. 9-car Great Western Railway units. Originally to be built as electric trains and numbered in the Class 801/0 series.
Formation: PDTS–MS–MS–TS–MS–TS–MS–MF–PDTRBF.

PDTS. Hitachi Newton Aycliffe/Kasado 2017–18. –/48 1TD 2W. 47.8 t.
MS. Hitachi Newton Aycliffe/Kasado 2017–18. –/88 1T. 50.1 t.
MS. Hitachi Newton Aycliffe/Kasado 2017–18. –/88 2T. 50.3 t.

TS. Hitachi Newton Aycliffe/Kasado 2017–18. –/88. 41.0 t.
MS. Hitachi Newton Aycliffe/Kasado 2017–18. –/88 2T. 50.3 t.
TS. Hitachi Newton Aycliffe/Kasado 2017–18. –/88 2T. 38.3 t.
MS. Hitachi Newton Aycliffe/Kasado 2017–18. –/88. 49.1 t.
MF. Hitachi Newton Aycliffe/Kasado 2017–18. 56/– 1T. 50.6 t.
PDTRBF. Hitachi Newton Aycliffe/Kasado 2017–18. 15/– 1TD 2W. 51.7 t.

800 301	**GW**	AT *GW* NP	821001	822001	823001	824001	825001
			826001	827001	828001	829001	
800 302	**GW**	AT *GW* NP	821002	822002	823002	824002	825002
			826002	827002	828002	829002	
800 303	**GW**	AT *GW* NP	821003	822003	823003	824003	825003
			826003	827003	828003	829003	
800 304	**GW**	AT *GW* NP	821004	822004	823004	824004	825004
			826004	827004	828004	829004	
800 305	**GW**	AT *GW* NP	821005	822005	823005	824005	825005
			826005	827005	828005	829005	
800 306	**GW**	AT *GW* NP	821006	822006	823006	824006	825006
			826006	827006	828006	829006	
800 307	**GW**	AT *GW* NP	821007	822007	823007	824007	825007
			826007	827007	828007	829007	
800 308	**GW**	AT *GW* NP	821008	822008	823008	824008	825008
			826008	827008	828008	829008	
800 309	**GW**	AT *GW* NP	821009	822009	823009	824009	825009
			826009	827009	828009	829009	
800 310	**GW**	AT *GW* NP	821010	822010	823010	824010	825010
			826010	827010	828010	829010	
800 311	**GW**	AT *GW* NP	821011	822011	823011	824011	825011
			826011	827011	828011	829011	
800 312	**GW**	AT *GW* NP	821012	822012	823012	824012	825012
			826012	827012	828012	829012	
800 313	**GW**	AT *GW* NP	821013	822013	823013	824013	825013
			826013	827013	828013	829013	
800 314	**GW**	AT *GW* NP	821014	822014	823014	824014	825014
			826014	827014	828014	829014	
800 315	**GW**	AT *GW* NP	821015	822015	823015	824015	825015
			826015	827015	828015	829015	
800 316	**GW**	AT *GW* NP	821016	822016	823016	824016	825016
			826016	827016	828016	829016	
800 317	**GW**	AT *GW* NP	821017	822017	823017	824017	825017
			826017	827017	828017	829017	
800 318	**GW**	AT *GW* NP	821018	822018	823018	824018	825018
			826018	827018	828018	829018	
800 319	**GW**	AT *GW* NP	821019	822019	823019	824019	825019
			826019	827019	828019	829019	
800 320	**GW**	AT *GW* NP	821020	822020	823020	824020	825020
			826020	827020	828020	829020	
800 321	**GW**	AT *GW* NP	821021	822021	823021	824021	825021
			826021	827021	828021	829021	

Names (one on each driving car unless shown):

800306 Allan Leonard Lewis VC/Harold Day DSC
800310 Wing Commander Ken Rees *(vehicle 821010)*
800314 Odette Hallowes GC MBE LdH *(vehicle 829014)*
800317 Freya Bevan *(vehicle 829017)*

CLASS 801 INTERCITY EXPRESS PROGRAMME
ELECTRIC   HITACHI

The Class 801s are electric units, but still have one diesel engine fitted per unit for emergency use or for use on diversionary routes when coupled to a Class 800.

Formation: Various, see class headings for details.
Systems: 25 kV AC overhead electric, plus one diesel engine per set.
Construction: Aluminium.
Diesel engines: In the 5-car sets the single diesel engine is located in car 2 and in the 9-car sets the diesel engine is located in car 8.
Engines: MTU 12V 1600 R80L of 700 kW (940 hp).
Traction Motors: Four Hitachi asynchronous of 226 kW.
Wheel Arrangement: 2-2 + Bo-Bo + Bo-Bo + Bo-Bo + 2-2 or
2-2 + Bo-Bo + Bo-Bo + 2-2 + Bo-Bo + 2-2 + Bo-Bo + Bo-Bo + 2-2.
Braking: Disc & regenerative.   **Dimensions:** 25.35/25.00 m x 2.74 m.
Bogies: Hitachi.   **Couplers:** Dellner 10.
Gangways: Within unit.   **Control System:** IGBT Inverter.
Doors: Single-leaf sliding.   **Maximum Speed:** 125 mph.
Heating & ventilation: Air conditioning.
Seating Layout: 1: 2+1 facing/unidirectional; 2+2 facing/unidirectional.
Multiple Working: Within class and with all Classes 8xx.

Class 801/1. 5-car LNER units.
Formation: PDTS–MSRB–MS–MC–PDTRBF.

PDTS. Hitachi Newton Aycliffe/Kasado 2016–19. –/56 1TD. 47.8 t.
MSRB. Hitachi Newton Aycliffe/Kasado 2016–19. –/72. 52.1 t.
MS. Hitachi Newton Aycliffe/Kasado 2016–19. –/88 2T. 43.5 t.
MC. Hitachi Newton Aycliffe/Kasado 2016–19. 30/38 1T. 44.1 t.
PDTRBF. Hitachi Newton Aycliffe/Kasado 2016–19. 18/– 1TD 2W. 51.2 t.

801 101	LZ	AT	LN	DN	821101	822101	823101	824101	825101
801 102	LZ	AT	LN	DN	821102	822102	823102	824102	825102
801 103	LZ	AT	LN	DN	821103	822103	823103	824103	825103
801 104	LZ	AT	LN	DN	821104	822104	823104	824104	825104
801 105	LZ	AT	LN	DN	821105	822105	823105	824105	825105
801 106	LZ	AT	LN	DN	821106	822106	823106	824106	825106
801 107	LZ	AT	LN	DN	821107	822107	823107	824107	825107
801 108	LZ	AT	LN	DN	821108	822108	823108	824108	825108
801 109	LZ	AT	LN	DN	821109	822109	823109	824109	825109
801 110	LZ	AT	LN	DN	821110	822110	823110	824110	825110
801 111	LZ	AT	LN	DN	821111	822111	823111	824111	825111
801 112	LZ	AT	LN	DN	821112	822112	823112	824112	825112

Class 801/2. 9-car LNER units.

Additions to the standard livery:

801 226   Pride celebration colours around the windows.

Formation: PDTS–MS–MS–TSRB–MS–TS–MC–MF–PDTRBF.

PDTS. Hitachi Newton Aycliffe/Kasado 2018–20. –/48 1TD 2W. 47.7 t.
MS. Hitachi Newton Aycliffe/Kasado 2018–20. –/84 1T. 50.5 t.
MS. Hitachi Newton Aycliffe/Kasado 2018–20. –/84 2T. 43.5 t.
TSRB. Hitachi Newton Aycliffe/Kasado 2018–20. –/70. 43.0 t.
MS. Hitachi Newton Aycliffe/Kasado 2018–20. –/84 2T. 43.5 t.
TS. Hitachi Newton Aycliffe/Kasado 2018–20. –/84 2T. 38.3 t.
MC. Hitachi Newton Aycliffe/Kasado 2018–20. 30/36. 42.6 t.
MF. Hitachi Newton Aycliffe/Kasado 2018–20. 55/– 1T. 43.8 t.
PDTRBF. Hitachi Newton Aycliffe/Kasado 2018–20. 15/– 1TD 2W. 51.7 t.

801 201	**LZ**	AT	*LN*	BN	821201	822201	823201	824201	825201
					826201	827201	828201	829201	
801 202	**LZ**	AT	*LN*	BN	821202	822202	823202	824202	825202
					826202	827202	828202	829202	
801 203	**LZ**	AT	*LN*	BN	821203	822203	823203	824203	825203
					826203	827203	828203	829203	
801 204	**LZ**	AT	*LN*	BN	821204	822204	823204	824204	825204
					826204	827204	828204	829204	
801 205	**LZ**	AT	*LN*	BN	821205	822205	823205	824205	825205
					826205	827205	828205	829205	
801 206	**LZ**	AT	*LN*	BN	821206	822206	823206	824206	825206
					826206	827206	828206	829206	
801 207	**LZ**	AT	*LN*	BN	821207	822207	823207	824207	825207
					826207	827207	828207	829207	
801 208	**LZ**	AT	*LN*	BN	821208	822208	823208	824208	825208
					826208	827208	828208	829208	
801 209	**LZ**	AT	*LN*	BN	821209	822209	823209	824209	825209
					826209	827209	828209	829209	
801 210	**LZ**	AT	*LN*	BN	821210	822210	823210	824210	825210
					826210	827210	828210	829210	
801 211	**LZ**	AT	*LN*	BN	821211	822211	823211	824211	825211
					826211	827211	828211	829211	
801 212	**LZ**	AT	*LN*	BN	821212	822212	823212	824212	825212
					826212	827212	828212	829212	
801 213	**LZ**	AT	*LN*	BN	821213	822213	823213	824213	825213
					826213	827213	828213	829213	
801 214	**LZ**	AT	*LN*	BN	821214	822214	823214	824214	825214
					826214	827214	828214	829214	
801 215	**LZ**	AT	*LN*	BN	821215	822215	823215	824215	825215
					826215	827215	828215	829215	
801 216	**LZ**	AT	*LN*	BN	821216	822216	823216	824216	825216
					826216	827216	828216	829216	
801 217	**LZ**	AT	*LN*	BN	821217	822217	823217	824217	825217
					826217	827217	828217	829217	
801 218	**LZ**	AT	*LN*	BN	821218	822218	823218	824218	825218
					826218	827218	828218	829218	

801 219	**LZ**	AT	*LN*	BN	821219 826219	822219 827219	823219 828219	824219 829219	825219
801 220	**LZ**	AT	*LN*	BN	821220 826220	822220 827220	823220 828220	824220 829220	825220
801 221	**LZ**	AT	*LN*	BN	821221 826221	822221 827221	823221 828221	824221 829221	825221
801 222	**LZ**	AT	*LN*	BN	821222 826222	822222 827222	823222 828222	824222 829222	825222
801 223	**LZ**	AT	*LN*	BN	821223 826223	822223 827223	823223 828223	824223 829223	825223
801 224	**LZ**	AT	*LN*	BN	821224 826224	822224 827224	823224 828224	824224 829224	825224
801 225	**LZ**	AT	*LN*	BN	821225 826225	822225 827225	823225 828225	824225 829225	825225
801 226	**LZ**	AT	*LN*	BN	821226 826226	822226 827226	823226 828226	824226 829226	825226
801 227	**LZ**	AT	*LN*	BN	821227 826227	822227 827227	823227 828227	824227 829227	825227
801 228	**LZ**	AT	*LN*	BN	821228 826228	822228 827228	823228 828228	824228 829228	825228
801 229	**LZ**	AT	*LN*	BN	821229 826229	822229 827229	823229 828229	824229 829229	825229
801 230	**LZ**	AT	*LN*	BN	821230 826230	822230 827230	823230 828230	824230 829230	825230

Names (carried on PDTRBF):

801 226   TOGETHER
801 228   CENTURY

CLASS 802   AT300   HITACHI

These units are technically very similar to the Class 800s. The GWR units have modifications to the roof-mounted brake resistors for frequent operation along the Dawlish seawall.

Formation: Various, full details awaited.
Systems: Diesel/25 kV AC overhead electric.
Construction: Aluminium.
Diesel engines: In the 5-car sets diesel engines are located in cars 2, 3 and 4. In the 9-car sets diesel engines are located in cars 2, 3, 5, 7 and 8.
Engines: MTU 12V 1600 R80L of 700 kW (940 hp).
Traction Motors: Four Hitachi asynchronous of 226 kW.
Wheel Arrangement: 2-2 + Bo-Bo + Bo-Bo + Bo-Bo + 2-2 or
2-2 + Bo-Bo + Bo-Bo + 2-2 + Bo-Bo + 2-2 + Bo-Bo + Bo-Bo + 2-2.
Braking: Disc & regenerative.   **Dimensions:** 25.35/25.00 m x 2.74 m.
Bogies: Hitachi.   **Couplers:** Dellner 10.
Gangways: Within unit.   **Control System:** IGBT Inverter.
Doors: Single-leaf sliding.   **Maximum Speed:** 125 mph.
Heating & ventilation: Air conditioning.
Seating Layout: 1: 2+1 facing/unidirectional; 2+2 facing/unidirectional.
Multiple Working: Within class and with all Classes 8xx.

Class 802/0. 5-car Great Western Railway units. Pre-series units 802 001/002 were built at Kasado and the remainder at Pistoia.
Formation: PDTS–MS–MS–MC–PDTRBF.

PDTS. Hitachi Pistoia/Kasado 2017–18. –/56 1TD. 48.0 t.
MS. Hitachi Pistoia/Kasado 2017–18. –/88. 50.9 t.
MS. Hitachi Pistoia/Kasado 2017–18. –/88 2T 51.1 t.
MC. Hitachi Pistoia/Kasado 2017–18. 18/58 1T. 51.5 t.
PDTRBF. Hitachi Pistoia/Kasado 2017–18. 18/ 1TD 2W. 51.3 t.

802 001	**GW**	E	*GW*	NP	831001	832001	833001	834001	835001
802 002	**GW**	E	*GW*	NP	831002	832002	833002	834002	835002
802 003	**GW**	E	*GW*	NP	831003	832003	833003	834003	835003
802 004	**GW**	E	*GW*	NP	831004	832004	833004	834004	835004
802 005	**GW**	E	*GW*	NP	831005	832005	833005	834005	835005
802 006	**GW**	E	*GW*	NP	831006	832006	833006	834006	835006
802 007	**GW**	E	*GW*	NP	831007	832007	833007	834007	835007
802 008	**GW**	E	*GW*	NP	831008	832008	833008	834008	835008
802 009	**GW**	E	*GW*	NP	831009	832009	833009	834009	835009
802 010	**GW**	E	*GW*	NP	831010	832010	833010	834010	835010
802 011	**GW**	E	*GW*	NP	831011	832011	833011	834011	835011
802 012	**GW**	E	*GW*	NP	831012	832012	833012	834012	835012
802 013	**GW**	E	*GW*	NP	831013	832013	833013	834013	835013
802 014	**GW**	E	*GW*	NP	831014	832014	833014	834014	835014
802 015	**GW**	E	*GW*	NP	831015	832015	833015	834015	835015
802 016	**GW**	E	*GW*	NP	831016	832016	833016	834016	835016
802 017	**GW**	E	*GW*	NP	831017	832017	833017	834017	835017
802 018	**GW**	E	*GW*	NP	831018	832018	833018	834018	835018
802 019	**GW**	E	*GW*	NP	831019	832019	833019	834019	835019
802 020	**GW**	E	*GW*	NP	831020	832020	833020	834020	835020
802 021	**GW**	E	*GW*	NP	831021	832021	833021	834021	835021
802 022	**GW**	E	*GW*	NP	831022	832022	833022	834022	835022

Names (one on each driving car unless shown):

802 002	Steve Whiteway *(vehicle 831002)*
802 006	Harry Billinge MBE LdH *(vehicle 835006)*
802 008	Rick Rescorla/RNLB Solomon Browne
802 010	Kieron Griffin/Corporal George Sheard
802 011	Sir Joshua Reynolds PRA/Capt. Robert Falcon Scott RN CVO
802 013	Michael Eavis CBE *(vehicle 835013)*
802 018	Preston de Mendonça/Jeremy Doyle

Class 802/1. 9-car Great Western Railway units. Pre-series unit 802 101 was built at Kasado and the remainder at Pistoia.
Formation: PDTS–MS–MS–TS–MS–TS–MC–MF–PDTRBF.

PDTS. Hitachi Pistoia/Kasado 2017–18. –/48 1TD 2W. 47.7 t.
MS. Hitachi Pistoia/Kasado 2017–18. –/88 1T. 50.1 t.
MS. Hitachi Pistoia/Kasado 2017–18. –/88 2T. 50.3 t.
TS. Hitachi Pistoia/Kasado 2017–18. –/88. 41.0 t.
MS. Hitachi Pistoia/Kasado 2017–18. –/88 2T. 50.3 t.
TS. Hitachi Pistoia/Kasado 2017–18. –/88 2T. 38.3 t.

MS. Hitachi Pistoia/Kasado 2017–18. –/88. 50.3 t.
MF. Hitachi Pistoia/Kasado 2017–18. 56/– 1T. 50.6 t.
PDTRBF. Hitachi Pistoia/Kasado 2017–18. 15/– 1TD 2W. 51.7 t.

802 101	**GW**	E	*GW*	NP	831101	832101	833101	834101	835101
					836101	837101	838101	839101	
802 102	**GW**	E	*GW*	NP	831102	832102	833102	834102	835102
					836102	837102	838102	839102	
802 103	**GW**	E	*GW*	NP	831103	832103	833103	834103	835103
					836103	837103	838103	839103	
802 104	**GW**	E	*GW*	NP	831104	832104	833104	834104	835104
					836104	837104	838104	839104	
802 105	**GW**	E	*GW*	NP	831105	832105	833105	834105	835105
					836105	837105	838105	839105	
802 106	**GW**	E	*GW*	NP	831106	832106	833106	834106	835106
					836106	837106	838106	839106	
802 107	**GW**	E	*GW*	NP	831107	832107	833107	834107	835107
					836107	837107	838107	839107	
802 108	**GW**	E	*GW*	NP	831108	832108	833108	834108	835108
					836108	837108	838108	839108	
802 109	**GW**	E	*GW*	NP	831109	832109	833109	834109	835109
					836109	837109	838109	839109	
802 110	**GW**	E	*GW*	NP	831110	832110	833110	834110	835110
					836110	837110	838110	839110	
802 111	**GW**	E	*GW*	NP	831111	832111	833111	834111	835111
					836111	837111	838111	839111	
802 112	**GW**	E	*GW*	NP	831112	832112	833112	834112	835112
					836112	837112	838112	839112	
802 113	**GW**	E	*GW*	NP	831113	832113	833113	834113	835113
					836113	837113	838113	839113	
802 114	**GW**	E	*GW*	NP	831114	832114	833114	834114	835114
					836114	837114	838114	839114	

Names:

802 101	Nancy Astor CH *(vehicle 839101)*
802 103	FLYING CAROLEAN/Y CAROLEAN HEDEGOG *(alternate sides of vehicle 839103)*
802 110	DAME AGATHA CHRISTIE

Class 802/2. TransPennine Express units.
Formation: PDTS–MS–MS–MS–PDTF.

PDTS. Hitachi Pistoia/Kasado 2018–19. –/56 1TD. 48.0 t.
MS. Hitachi Pistoia/Kasado 2018–19. –/86. 50.9 t.
MS. Hitachi Pistoia/Kasado 2018–19. –/88 2T 51.1 t.
MS. Hitachi Pistoia/Kasado 2018–19. –/88 1T 51.3 t.
PDTRBF. Hitachi Pistoia/Kasado 2018–19. 24/– 1TD 2W. 50.2 t.

802 201	**TP**	A	*TP*	EC	831201	832201	833201	834201	835201
802 202	**TP**	A	*TP*	EC	831202	832202	833202	834202	835202
802 203	**TP**	A	*TP*	EC	831203	832203	833203	834203	835203
802 204	**TP**	A	*TP*	EC	831204	832204	833204	834204	835204

802 205	**TP**	A	*TP*	EC	831205	832205	833205	834205	835205
802 206	**TP**	A	*TP*	EC	831206	832206	833206	834206	835206
802 207	**TP**	A	*TP*	EC	831207	832207	833207	834207	835207
802 208	**TP**	A	*TP*	EC	831208	832208	833208	834208	835208
802 209	**TP**	A	*TP*	EC	831209	832209	833209	834209	835209
802 210	**TP**	A	*TP*	EC	831210	832210	833210	834210	835210
802 211	**TP**	A	*TP*	EC	831211	832211	833211	834211	835211
802 212	**TP**	A	*TP*	EC	831212	832212	833212	834212	835212
802 213	**TP**	A	*TP*	EC	831213	832213	833213	834213	835213
802 214	**TP**	A	*TP*	EC	831214	832214	833214	834214	835214
802 215	**TP**	A	*TP*	EC	831215	832215	833215	834215	835215
802 216	**TP**	A	*TP*	EC	831216	832216	833216	834216	835216
802 217	**TP**	A	*TP*	EC	831217	832217	833217	834217	835217
802 218	**TP**	A	*TP*	EC	831218	832218	833218	834218	835218
802 219	**TP**	A	*TP*	EC	831219	832219	833219	834219	835219

Names (carried on driving cars):

802 208	Diligence Robert Stephenson & Co
802 212	St Abb's Head
802 215	Palace of Holyroodhouse

Class 802/3. Hull Trains units.
Formation: PDTS–MS–MS–MS–PDTF.

PDTS. Hitachi Pistoia 2018–19. –/50 1TD 1W. 48.0 t.
MS. Hitachi Pistoia 2018–19. –/88. 49.6 t.
MS. Hitachi Pistoia 2018–19. –/88 2T 50.4 t.
MC. Hitachi Pistoia 2018–19. 18/58 1T 50.4 t.
PDTRBF. Hitachi Pistoia 2018–19. 25/– 1TD 2W. 49.6 t.

802 301	**HT**	A	*HT*	BN	831301	832301	833301	834301	835301
802 302	**HT**	A	*HT*	BN	831302	832302	833302	834302	835302
802 303	**HT**	A	*HT*	BN	831303	832303	833303	834303	835303
802 304	**HT**	A	*HT*	BN	831304	832304	833304	834304	835304
802 305	**HT**	A	*HT*	BN	831305	832305	833305	834305	835305

Names (carried on driving cars):

802 301	Amy Johnson	802 304	William Wilberforce
802 302	Jean Bishop (The Bee Lady)	802 305	The Humber Bridge
802 303	Land of Green Ginger		

CLASS 803   HITACHI

Five 5-car electric-only, single-class units that entered service in October 2021 with new East Coast Main Line open access operator Lumo, running between London King's Cross and Edinburgh.

Formation: PDTS–MS–MS–MS–PDTS.
Systems: 25 kV AC overhead electric.
Construction: Aluminium.
Traction Motors: Four Hitachi asynchronous of 226 kW.
Wheel Arrangement: 2-2 + Bo-Bo + Bo-Bo + Bo-Bo + 2-2.
Braking: Disc & regenerative.   **Dimensions:** 25.35/25.00 m x 2.74 m.
Bogies: Hitachi.   **Couplers:** Dellner 10.
Gangways: Within unit.   **Control System:** IGBT Inverter.
Doors: Single-leaf sliding.   **Maximum Speed:** 125 mph.
Heating & ventilation: Air conditioning.
Seating Layout: 2+2 mostly unidirectional.
Multiple Working: Within class and with all Classes 8xx.

PDTS. Hitachi Kasado/Newton Aycliffe 2020–21. –/52(+2) 1TD 2W. 47.7 t.
MS. Hitachi Kasado/Newton Aycliffe 2020–21. –/94 1T. 45.0 t.
MS. Hitachi Kasado/Newton Aycliffe 2020–21. –/94. 44.2 t.
MS. Hitachi Kasado/Newton Aycliffe 2020–21. –/94 1T 45.0 t.
PDTS. Hitachi Kasado/Newton Aycliffe 2020–21. –/60(+2) 1TD. 47.8 t.

803001	**LU**	BN *LU*	EC	841001	842001	843001	844001	845001
803002	**LU**	BN *LU*	EC	841002	842002	843002	844002	845002
803003	**LU**	BN *LU*	EC	841003	842003	843003	844003	845003
803004	**LU**	BN *LU*	EC	841004	842004	843004	844004	845004
803005	**LU**	BN *LU*	EC	841005	842005	843005	844005	845005

Name (carried on driving cars):

803005   PROUDLY FROM NEWCASTLE – THE HOME OF STEPHENSON'S
           WORKS BICENTENARY 1823–2023

CLASS 805   HITACHI

13 5-car bi-mode units currently being delivered to Avanti West Coast to replace the Class 221 Voyagers from 2024 and operate services such as Euston–Chester–Holyhead, allowing the elimination of long-distance diesel passenger operation on the West Coast Main Line. Full details awaited.

Formation: PDTS–MS–MS–MS–PDTF.
Systems: Diesel/25 kV AC overhead electric.
Construction: Aluminium.
Engines:
Construction: Aluminium.
Traction Motors:
Wheel Arrangement: 2-2 + Bo-Bo + Bo-Bo + Bo-Bo + 2-2.
Braking: Disc & regenerative.   **Dimensions:**
Bogies: Hitachi.   **Couplers:** Dellner 10.
Gangways: Within unit.   **Control System:** IGBT Inverter.

Doors: Single-leaf sliding.   **Maximum Speed:** 125 mph.
Heating & ventilation: Air conditioning.
Seating Layout:
Multiple Working: Within class and with all Classes 8xx.

PDTS. Hitachi Kasado/Newton Aycliffe 2020–23.
MS. Hitachi Kasado/Newton Aycliffe 2020–23.
MS. Hitachi Kasado/Newton Aycliffe 2020–23.
MS. Hitachi Kasado/Newton Aycliffe 2020–23.
PDTF. Hitachi Kasado/Newton Aycliffe 2020–23.

805 001	**AT**	RR	861001	862001	863001	864001	865001
805 002	**AT**	RR	861002	862002	863002	864002	865002
805 003	**AT**	RR	861003	862003	863003	864003	865003
805 004	**AT**	RR	861004	862004	863004	864004	865004
805 005	**AT**	RR	861005	862005	863005	864005	865005
805 006	**AT**	RR	861006	862006	863006	864006	865006
805 007	**AT**	RR	861007	862007	863007	864007	865007
805 008	**AT**	RR	861008	862008	863008	864008	865008
805 009	**AT**	RR	861009	862009	863009	864009	865009
805 010	**AT**	RR	861010	862010	863010	864010	865010
805 011	**AT**	RR	861011	862011	863011	864011	865011
805 012	**AT**	RR	861012	862012	863012	864012	865012
805 013	**AT**	RR	861013	862013	863013	864013	865013

CLASS 807   HITACHI

7-car electric units for Avanti West Coast which will be similar to Class 801s, in that they will have one diesel engine. They are planned to be used on services between Euston, the Midlands and Liverpool from 2024. Full details awaited.

Formation: PDTS–MS–MS–TS–MS–MC–PDTF.
Systems: 25 kV AC overhead electric, plus one diesel engine per set.
Construction: Aluminium.
Engines:
Construction: Aluminium.
Traction Motors:
Wheel Arrangement:
Braking: Disc & regenerative.   **Dimensions:**
Bogies: Hitachi.   **Couplers:** Dellner 10.
Gangways: Within unit.   **Control System:** IGBT Inverter.
Doors: Single-leaf sliding.   **Maximum Speed:** 125 mph.
Heating & ventilation: Air conditioning.
Seating Layout:
Multiple Working: Within class and with all Classes 8xx.

PDTS. Hitachi Kasado/Newton Aycliffe 2021–23.
MS. Hitachi Kasado/Newton Aycliffe 22021–23.
MS. Hitachi Kasado/Newton Aycliffe 22021–23.
TS. Hitachi Kasado/Newton Aycliffe 22021–23.
MS. Hitachi Kasado/Newton Aycliffe 2021–23.
MC. Hitachi Kasado/Newton Aycliffe 2021–23.
PDTF. Hitachi Kasado/Newton Aycliffe 2021–23.

807 001	**AT**	RR	871001 876001	872001 877001	873001	874001	875001
807 002	**AT**	RR	871002 876002	872002 877002	873002	874002	875002
807 003	**AT**	RR	871003 876003	872003 877003	873003	874003	875003
807 004	**AT**	RR	871004 876004	872004 877004	873004	874004	875004
807 005	**AT**	RR	871005 876005	872005 877005	873005	874005	875005
807 006	**AT**	RR	871006 876006	872006 877006	873006	874006	875006
807 007	**AT**	RR	871007 876007	872007 877007	873007	874007	875007
807 008	**AT**	RR	871008 876008	872008 877008	873008	874008	875008
807 009	**AT**	RR	871009 876009	872009 877009	873009	874009	875009
807 010	**AT**	RR	871010 876010	872010 877010	873010	874010	875010

CLASS 810   AT300 SXR   HITACHI

East Midlands Railway has ordered this fleet of 33 5-car bi-mode units for use on the Midland Main Line, principally between St Pancras and Sheffield/Nottingham, from 2024. They have shorter 24 m bodies to better match platforms on the route. Full details awaited.

Formation: PDTRBF–MC–TS–MS–DPTS.
Systems: Diesel/25 kV AC overhead electric.
Construction: Aluminium.
Diesel engines: Diesel engines are located in cars 1, 2, 4 and 5.
Engines: MTU of 735 kW (985 hp).
Construction: Aluminium.
Traction Motors: Four Hitachi asynchronous of 250 kW.
Wheel Arrangement:
Braking: Disc & regenerative.
Bogies: Hitachi.
Gangways: Within unit.
Doors: Single-leaf sliding.
Dimensions:
Couplers: Dellner 10.
Control System: IGBT Inverter.
Maximum Speed: 125 mph.
Heating & ventilation: Air conditioning.
Seating Layout: 1: 2+1 facing/unidirectional; 2+2 facing/unidirectional.
Multiple Working: Within class and with all Classes 8xx.

PDTRBF. Hitachi Newton Aycliffe 2021–23.
MS. Hitachi Newton Aycliffe 2021–23.
TS. Hitachi Newton Aycliffe 2021–23.
MS. Hitachi Newton Aycliffe 2021–23.
DPTS. Hitachi Newton Aycliffe 2021–23.

810001	**ER**	RR	851001	852001	853001	854001	855001
810002	**ER**	RR	851002	852002	853002	854002	855002
810003	**ER**	RR	851003	852003	853003	854003	855003
810004	**ER**	RR	851004	852004	853004	854004	855004
810005	**ER**	RR	851005	852005	853005	854005	855005
810006	**ER**	RR	851006	852006	853006	854006	855006
810007	**ER**	RR	851007	852007	853007	854007	855007
810008	**ER**	RR	851008	852008	853008	854008	855008
810009	**ER**	RR	851009	852009	853009	854009	855009
810010	**ER**	RR	851010	852010	853010	854010	855010
810011	**ER**	RR	851011	852011	853011	854011	855011
810012	**ER**	RR	851012	852012	853012	854012	855012
810013	**ER**	RR	851013	852013	853013	854013	855013
810014	**ER**	RR	851014	852014	853014	854014	855014
810015	**ER**	RR	851015	852015	853015	854015	855015
810016	**ER**	RR	851016	852016	853016	854016	855016
810017	**ER**	RR	851017	852017	853017	854017	855017
810018	**ER**	RR	851018	852018	853018	854018	855018
810019	**ER**	RR	851019	852019	853019	854019	855019
810020	**ER**	RR	851020	852020	853020	854020	855020
810021	**ER**	RR	851021	852021	853021	854021	855021
810022	**ER**	RR	851022	852022	853022	854022	855022
810023	**ER**	RR	851023	852023	853023	854023	855023
810024	**ER**	RR	851024	852024	853024	854024	855024
810025	**ER**	RR	851025	852025	853025	854025	855025
810026	**ER**	RR	851026	852026	853026	854026	855026
810027	**ER**	RR	851027	852027	853027	854027	855027
810028	**ER**	RR	851028	852028	853028	854028	855028
810029	**ER**	RR	851029	852029	853029	854029	855029
810030	**ER**	RR	851030	852030	853030	854030	855030
810031	**ER**	RR	851031	852031	853031	854031	855031
810032	**ER**	RR	851032	852032	853032	854032	855032
810033	**ER**	RR	851033	852033	853033	854033	855033

6. EUROSTAR UNITS

The original Eurostar Class 373 units were built for and are normally used on services between Britain and continental Europe via the Channel Tunnel.

The trailers from SNCF set 3203/04 were refurbished and renumbered to run with power cars 3211/12 (original power cars 3203/04 have been scrapped, as have the trailers from 3211/12).

Each Class 373 train consists of two 10-car units coupled, with a motor car at each driving end. All units are articulated with an extra motor bogie on the coach adjacent to the motor car.

All Class 373 sets can be used between London St Pancras and Paris, Brussels and Disneyland Paris. Certain sets (shown *) were equipped for 1500 V DC operation for the winter service to Bourg Saint Maurice and the summer service to Avignon. All eight refurbished units are fitted for operation on 1500 V DC.

Seven 8-car Class 373 sets were built for Regional Eurostar services, but apart from power cars 3304 and 3308 which have been preserved, the rest have been scrapped.

The second generation Eurostar trains, the Siemens Class 374s, have replaced most of the Class 373s. Eight Class 373s have been fully refurbished and will be retained as part of Eurostar's long-term fleet – 3007/08, 3015/16, 3205/06, 3209/10, 3211/12, 3219/20, 3221/22 and 3229/30.

CLASS 373   "THREE CAPITALS" EUROSTARS

10-car half-sets. Built for services starting from or terminating in London Waterloo (now St Pancras). Individual vehicles in each set are allocated numbers 373xxx0 + 373xxx1 + 373xxx2 + 373xxx3 + 373xxx4 + 373xxx5 + 373xxx6 + 373xxx7 + 373xxx8 + 373xxx9, where 3xxx denotes the set number.

Formation: DM–MS–4TS–RB–2TF–TBF. Gangwayed within pair of units. Air conditioned.
Construction: Steel.
Supply Systems: 25 kV AC 50 Hz overhead or 3000 V DC overhead (* also equipped for 1500 V DC overhead operation).
Control System: GTO–GTO Inverter on UK 750V DC and 25kVAC, GTO Chopper on SNCB 3000VDC.
Continuous rating: 12 x 240 kW (25 kV AC); 5700 kW (1500 and 3000 V DC).
Wheel Arrangement: Bo-Bo + Bo–2–2–2–2–2–2–2–2.
Lengths: 22.15 m (DM), 21.85 m (MS & TBF), 18.70 m (other cars).
Couplers: Schaku 10S at outer ends, Schaku 10L at inner end of each DM and outer ends of each sub set.
Maximum Speed: 186 mph (300 km/h).
Built: 1992–93 by GEC-Alsthom/Brush/ANF/De Dietrich/BN Construction/ACEC.

DM vehicles carry the set numbers indicated below.

Non-standard livery: 3213 and 3224 – Izy (green, white & purple).

† Refurbished.

At the time of writing the following sets were misformed: 3213 with 3224 and 3214 with 3223.

373xxx0 series. DM. Lot No. 31118 1992–95. 68.5 t.
373xxx1 series. MS. Lot No. 31119 1992–95. –/48 2T. 44.6 t.
373xxx2 series. TS. Lot No. 31120 1992–95. –/56 1T. 28.1 t.
373xxx3 series. TS. Lot No. 31121 1992–95. –/56 2T. 29.7 t.
373xxx4 series. TS. Lot No. 31122 1992–95. –/56 1T. 28.3 t.
373xxx5 series. TS. Lot No. 31123 1992–95. –/56 2T. 29.2 t.
373xxx6 series. RB. Lot No. 31124 1992–95. 31.1 t.
373xxx7 series. TF. Lot No. 31125 1992–95. 39/– 1T. 29.6 t.
373xxx8 series. TF. Lot No. 31126 1992–95. 39/– 1T. 32.2 t.
373xxx9 series. TBF. Lot No. 31127 1992–95. 25/– 1TD. 39.4 t.

3007	†*	**ES**	EU	*EU*	LY	3215	*	**EU**	SF	TI
3008	†*	**ES**	EU	*EU*	LY	3216	*	**EU**	SF	TI
3015	†*	**ES**	EU	*EU*	LY	3217		**EU**	SF	TI
3016	†*	**ES**	EU	*EU*	LY	3218		**EU**	SF	TI
3205	†*	**ES**	SF	*EU*	LY	3219	†*	**ES**	SF	*EU* LY
3206	†*	**ES**	SF	*EU*	LY	3220	†*	**ES**	SF	*EU* LY
3209	†*	**ES**	SF	*EU*	LY	3221	†*	**ES**	SF	*EU* LY
3210	†*	**ES**	SF	*EU*	LY	3222	†*	**ES**	SF	*EU* LY
3211	†*	**ES**	SF	*EU*	LY	3223	*	**EU**	SF	Le Havre
3212	†*	**ES**	SF	*EU*	LY	3224	*	**0**	SF	Le Havre
3213	*	**0**	SF		Le Havre	3229	†*	**ES**	SF	*EU* LY
3214	*	**EU**	SF		Le Havre	3230	†*	**ES**	SF	*EU* LY

Spare DM:

3999	**ES**	EU	*EU*	TI

CLASS 374   SIEMENS VELARO e320

8-car half-sets. These units are similar to the DB Class 407 ICE sets, with distributed power rather than a power car at either end like the Class 373s. The first sets entered service in November 2015, operating initially on the St Pancras–Paris route. They have also been used on the new St Pancras–Amsterdam service from 2018.

The initial order was for ten units (4001–20) and this was then increased by another seven (4021–34) in 2014.

Formation: DMF–TBF–MS–TS–TS–MS–TS–MSRB.
Gangwayed within pair of units. Air conditioned.
Construction: Aluminium.   **Control System:** IGBT Inverter.
Supply Systems: 25 kV AC 50 Hz overhead, 1500 V DC overhead and 3000 V DC overhead.
Continuous rating: 8000 kW (25 kV AC), 4200 kW (1500 and 3000 V DC).
Wheel Arrangement: Bo-Bo + 2-2 + Bo-Bo + 2-2 + 2-2 + Bo-Bo + 2-2 + Bo-Bo.
Lengths: 26.035 m (DMF), 24.775 m (other cars).
Couplers: Dellner 12.   **Maximum Speed:** 200 mph (320 km/h).
Built: 2012–17 by Siemens, Krefeld, Germany.

DM vehicles carry the full 12-digit EVNs as indicated below. For example, set 4001/02 carries the numbers 93 70 3740 011-9 + 93 70 3740 012-7 + 93 70 3740 013-5 + 93 70 3740 014-3 + 93 70 3740 015-0 + 93 70 3740 016-8 + 93 70 3740 017-6 + 93 70 3740 018-4 + 93 70 3740 028-3 + 93 70 3740 027-5 + 93 70 3740 026-7 + 93 70 3740 025-9 + 93 70 3740 024-2 + 93 70 3740 023-4 + 93 70 3740 022-6 + 93 70 3740 021-8.

93 70 3740 xx1-c series. DMF. Siemens Krefeld 2012–17. 40/–. 58.0 t.
93 70 3740 xx2-c series. TBF. Siemens Krefeld 2012–17. 36/– 2T. 59.0 t.
93 70 3740 xx3-c series. MF. Siemens Krefeld 2012–17. 34/–(+2) 1TD 2W. 59.0 t.
93 70 3740 xx4-c series. TS. Siemens Krefeld 2012–17. –/76 2T. 53.0 t.
93 70 3740 xx5-c series. TS. Siemens Krefeld 2012–17. –/76 2T. 53.0 t.
93 70 3740 xx6-c series. MS. Siemens Krefeld 2012–17. –/76 2T. 58.0 t.
93 70 3740 xx7-c series. TS. Siemens Krefeld 2012–17. –/76 2T. 57.0 t.
93 70 3740 xx8-c series. MSRB. Siemens Krefeld 2012–17. –/32 2T. 58.0 t.

4001	**ES**	EU	*EU*	TI		4018	**ES**	EU	*EU*	TI
4002	**ES**	EU	*EU*	TI		4019	**ES**	EU	*EU*	TI
4003	**ES**	EU	*EU*	TI		4020	**ES**	EU	*EU*	TI
4004	**ES**	EU	*EU*	TI		4021	**ES**	EU	*EU*	TI
4005	**ES**	EU	*EU*	TI		4022	**ES**	EU	*EU*	TI
4006	**ES**	EU	*EU*	TI		4023	**ES**	EU	*EU*	TI
4007	**ES**	EU	*EU*	TI		4024	**ES**	EU	*EU*	TI
4008	**ES**	EU	*EU*	TI		4025	**ES**	EU	*EU*	TI
4009	**ES**	EU	*EU*	TI		4026	**ES**	EU	*EU*	TI
4010	**ES**	EU	*EU*	TI		4027	**ES**	EU	*EU*	TI
4011	**ES**	EU	*EU*	TI		4028	**ES**	EU	*EU*	TI
4012	**ES**	EU	*EU*	TI		4029	**ES**	EU	*EU*	TI
4013	**ES**	EU	*EU*	TI		4030	**ES**	EU	*EU*	TI
4014	**ES**	EU	*EU*	TI		4031	**ES**	EU	*EU*	TI
4015	**ES**	EU	*EU*	TI		4032	**ES**	EU	*EU*	TI
4016	**ES**	EU	*EU*	TI		4033	**ES**	EU	*EU*	TI
4017	**ES**	EU	*EU*	TI		4034	**ES**	EU	*EU*	TI

7. EMU VEHICLES IN INDUSTRIAL SERVICE

This list comprises EMU vehicles that have been withdrawn from active service but continue to be used in industrial service or for emergency training.

Cl. 317	71621			Oracle UK, Thames Valley Park, Reading (ex-unit 317 345)
Cl. 332	63400	72412	78400	Siemens, Goole (ex-unit 332 001)
Cl. 390	69133	69833		Avanti West Coast Training Centre, Westmere Drive, Crewe, Cheshire (ex-unit 390 033)
Cl. 390	69933			Safety & Accident Investigation Centre, Cranfield University, Cranfield, Bedfordshire (ex-unit 390 033)
Cl. 508	64649	64712		Emergency Services Training Centre, Seacombe, Merseyside (ex-units 508 201/209)
Cl. 508	64681	71511	64724	The Fire Service College, Moreton-in-Marsh, Gloucestershire (unit 508 212)

8. EMUS AWAITING DISPOSAL

This list comprises EMU vehicles which are awaiting disposal.

The majority of the Class 442s were disposed of during 2021 and only 13 vehicles are left awaiting disposal at either Eastleigh Works or Wolverton Works.

Cl. 309	**RR**	WC	CS	71758				(ex-309 623)
Cl. 313	**BG**	BN	ZG	62529	71213	62593		(unit 313 201)
Cl. 317	**GA**	A	EP	77024	62661	71577	77048	(unit 317 501)
Cl. 317	**GA**	A	EP	77005	62666	71582	77053	(unit 317 506)
Cl. 365	**N**	X	ZN	65919				(ex-365 526)
Cl. 442	**GV**	SW	ZG	71822	71846			(ex-442 405)
Cl. 442	**GV**	SW	ZG	71824	71848	77388		(ex-442 407)
Cl. 442	**GV**	SW	ZG	77393	71829	71853	77417	(ex-442 412)
Cl. 442	**GV**	SW	ZN	62954				(ex-442 418)
Cl. 442	**GV**	SW	ZN	77400				(ex-442 419)
Cl. 442	**GV**	SW	ZG	71841	71865			(ex-442 424)

9. CODES

9.1. LIVERY CODES

AL Advertising/promotional livery (see class heading for details).
AT Avanti West Coast (dark green, dark grey white, cream & orange).
BG BR blue & grey lined out in white.
C2 c2c (white with dark blue doors).
C2C New c2c Class 720 (white with pink doors and end flashes).
CN Connex/Southeastern (white with black window surrounds & grey lower band).
CO Centro (grey & light green with light blue, white & yellow stripes).
ER East Midlands Railway (purple with white or grey lower bodyside lining and doors).
ES Revised Eurostar (deep blue & two-tone grey).
EU Eurostar (white with dark blue & yellow stripes).
FB First Group dark blue.
GA Greater Anglia (white with red doors & black window surrounds).
GR New Greater Anglia (white/grey with black window surrounds & red & dark grey on the lower bodyside).
GV Gatwick Express Class 442 (red, white & indigo blue with mauve & blue doors).
GW Great Western Railway (TOC) dark green.
GX Gatwick Express Class 387 (red with white lining and grey doors).
HC Heathrow Connect (grey with a broad deep blue bodyside band & orange doors).
HT Hull Trains (First Group dark blue with a multi-coloured band on lower bodyside depicting images from the route).
HX Heathrow Express (silver, grey & purple).
LD New London Overground (black upper bodyside with white, orange & blue lower bodyside stripes & orange doors).
LI London Northwestern Railway {interim} (dark green at unit ends and doors applied on **LM** light grey/black livery).
LM London Midland (grey & green with black stripe around the windows).
LN London Northwestern Railway (light grey, dark green & light green).
LO London Overground (all over white with a blue solebar, black window surrounds & orange doors).
LU Lumo (blue).
LZ LNER Azuma (white with red window surrounds).
ME New Merseyrail (grey and yellow with black window surrounds).
MY Merseyrail (all over yellow or all over grey (alternate sides)).
N BR Network SouthEast (white & blue with red lower bodyside stripe, grey solebar & cab ends).
NC National Express white (white with blue doors).
NR New Northern (white & purple).
NX National Express (white with grey ends).
O Non-standard (see class heading for details).
ON Orion (dark blue with light blue doors).
RM Royal Mail (all over red).

RR	Regional Railways (dark blue/grey with light blue & white stripes, three narrow dark blue stripes at cab ends).
SB	Southeastern blue (all over blue with black window surrounds).
SD	Stagecoach/South West Trains outer suburban livery {Class 450 style} (deep blue with red doors & orange & red cab sides).
SE	Southeastern suburban (all over white with black window surrounds, light blue doors and (on some units) dark blue lower bodyside stripe).
SN	Southern (white & dark green with light green semi-circles at one end of each vehicle. Light grey band at solebar level).
SR	ScotRail – Scotland's Railways (dark blue with Scottish Saltire flag & white/light blue flashes).
SS	South West Trains inner suburban {Class 455 style} (red with blue & orange flashes at unit ends).
ST	Stagecoach {long-distance stock} (white & dark blue with dark blue window surrounds and red & orange swishes at unit ends).
SW	South Western Railway (two tone grey with a yellow lower bodyside stripe).
TG	Govia Thameslink interim {Class 387} (white with dark green doors).
TL	Govia Thameslink Railway (light grey & white with light blue doors).
TP	TransPennine Express (silver, grey, blue & purple).
TW	Transport for Wales (white with a broad red stripe at cantrail level & red doors).
TY	Tyne & Wear Metro (light grey, black & yellow).
U	Plain white or grey undercoat.
WI	West Midlands Railway {interim} (gold at unit ends & gold doors applied on **LM** white/grey livery).
WM	West Midlands Railway (gold & metallic purple).
XR	Elizabeth Line (white with black window surrounds & a purple lower bodyside).
Y	Network Rail yellow.

9.2. OWNER CODES

A	Angel Trains
AK	Akiem
AT	Agility Trains
BN	Beacon Rail
CL	Caledonian Rail Leasing
CO	Corelink Rail Infrastructure
CT	Cross London Trains
E	Eversholt Rail (UK)
ER	Eastern Rail Services
EU	Eurostar International
GR	Global Centre of Rail Excellence
LF	Lombard North Central
MT	Merseytravel
P	Porterbrook Leasing Company
QW	QW Rail Leasing
RF	Rail for London (Transport for London)
RM	Royal Mail
RO	Rail Operations Group
RR	Rock Rail

SF   SNCF (Société Nationale des Chemins de fer Français)
SM SMBC Leasing/Equitix
SR   ScotRail
SW South Western Railway
SY   South Yorkshire Passenger Transport Executive
WC West Coast Railway Company
X   Sold for scrap/further use and awaiting collection

9.3. OPERATOR CODES

AW Avanti West Coast
C2   c2c
DB DB Cargo (UK)
EL   Elizabeth Line
EM East Midlands Railway
EU   Eurostar (UK)
GA Greater Anglia
GN Great Northern (part of Govia Thameslink Railway)
GW Great Western Railway
HE   Heathrow Express
HT   Hull Trains
LN   London North Eastern Railway
LO   London Overground
LU   Lumo
ME Merseyrail
NO Northern
SE   Southeastern
SN   Southern (part of Govia Thameslink Railway)
SR   ScotRail
SW South Western Railway
SY   Stagecoach Supertram
TL   Thameslink (part of Govia Thameslink Railway)
TP   TransPennine Express
TW Transport for Wales
VA Varamis Rail
WM West Midlands Trains

9.4. ALLOCATION & LOCATION CODES

Code	Location	Depot Operator
AD	Ashford (Kent)	Hitachi
AK	Ardwick (Manchester)	Siemens
AN	Allerton (Liverpool)	Northern
BD	Birkenhead North	Stadler Rail Service UK
BF	Bedford Cauldwell Walk	Siemens
BI	Brighton Lovers Walk	Govia Thameslink Railway
BM	Bournemouth	South Western Railway
BN	Bounds Green (London)	Hitachi
BO	Bo'ness (West Lothian)	The Bo'ness & Kinneil Railway
BR	MoD Bicester	*Storage location only*

CE	Crewe International	DB Cargo (UK)
CF	Cardiff Canton	Transport for Wales
CN	Castle Donington RFT	*Storage location only*
CS	Carnforth	West Coast Railway Company
CY	Crewe South Yard/Gresty Green	*Storage location only*
DN	Doncaster Carr	Hitachi
EC	Edinburgh Craigentinny	Hitachi
EM	East Ham (London)	c2c
EP	Ely Papworth Sidings	*Storage location only*
GA	Gascoigne Wood Sidings (South Milford)	*Storage location only*
GW	Glasgow Shields Road	ScotRail
HE	Hornsey (London)	Govia Thameslink Railway
IL	Ilford (London)	Greater Anglia/Elizabeth Line
KK	Kirkdale (Liverpool)	Stadler Rail Service UK
LM	Long Marston Rail Innovation Centre	Porterbrook Leasing
LY	Le Landy (Paris)	SNCF
MA	Longsight (Manchester)	Alstom UK
NC	Norwich Crown Point	Greater Anglia
NG	New Cross Gate (London)	London Overground
NL	Neville Hill (Leeds)	Northern
NN	Northampton King's Heath	Siemens
NP	North Pole (London)	Hitachi
NT	Northam (Southampton)	Siemens
NU	Sheffield Nunnery	Stagecoach Supertram
OC	Old Oak Common (London)	Elizabeth Line
RG	Reading	Great Western Railway
RM	Ramsgate	Southeastern
RY	Ryde (Isle of Wight)	South Western Railway
SG	Slade Green (London)	Southeastern
SL	Stewarts Lane (London)	Govia Thameslink Railway/Belmond
SO	Soho (Birmingham)	West Midlands Trains
SU	Selhurst (Croydon)	Govia Thameslink Railway
TB	Three Bridges (Crawley)	Siemens
TI	Temple Mills (London)	Eurostar
WA	Warrington Walton Old Jn Sidings	*Storage location only*
WB	Wembley (London)	Alstom UK
WD	Wimbledon (London)	South Western Railway
WI	Widnes (Cheshire)	Alstom UK
WN	Willesden (London)	Alstom UK
WS	Worksop (Nottinghamshire)	Harry Needle Railroad Company
YA	Great Yarmouth	Eastern Rail Services
ZA	RTC Business Park (Derby)	LORAM (UK)
ZB	Doncaster Works	Wabtec Rail
ZD	Derby Works	Alstom UK
ZG	Eastleigh Works	Arlington Fleet Services
ZI	Ilford Works	Alstom UK
ZJ	Stoke-on-Trent Works	Axiom Rail (Stoke)
ZK	Kilmarnock Works	Brodie Engineering
ZN	Wolverton Works	Gemini Rail Group
ZR	Holgate Works (York)	Network Rail